MINDY N. LEVINE, who grew up just outside of New York City, has been going to Off Off Broadway theatre since she was a teenager.

Involved in theatre and dance at Yale, she has kept active in dance as student, performer and choreographer. She is the author of *AMERICAN DANCE DIRECTORY 1979-1980*. Working with the New York Tourist Bureau, Mindy Levine helped promote Off Off Broadway theatre. Today she is a mem- of OOBA—Off Off Broadway Alliance—which cooperated in the production of this authoritative guide, *NEW YORK'S OTHER THEATRE: A Guide to Off Off Broadway*.

NEW YORK'S OTHER THEATRE

A GUIDE TO OFF OFF BROADWAY

MINDY N. LEVINE

**in cooperation with OOBA—
the Off Off Broadway Alliance**

Introduction by
JOSEPH PAPP

A DISCUS BOOK/PUBLISHED BY AVON BOOKS

NEW YORK'S OTHER THEATRE–A GUIDE TO OFF OFF BROADWAY is an original publication of Avon Books. This work has never before appeared in book form.

AVON BOOKS
A division of
The Hearst Corporation
959 Eighth Avenue
New York, New York 10019

Published by arrangement with Mindy N. Levine
in cooperation with OOBA
Library of Congress Catalog Card Number: 80-69918
ISBN: 0-380-77909-9

First Discus Printing, July, 1981

Printed in the U.S.A.

10 9 8 7 6 5 4 3 2 1

ACKNOWLEDGMENTS

Research and writing of this book was made possible through the generous support of the New York Community Trust Corporate Special Projects Fund, whose membership, at the time of publication, was composed of Equitable Life Assurance Society, Exxon Corporation, Gulf & Western, International Paper, RCA, Sperry Rand, Freeport Minerals, Inc. and The Grace Foundation, Inc.

Special thanks to all those who gave of their time and intelligence to this project: the OOBA staff—particularly former Executive Director Ellen Rudolph for her guidance and good humor; Tom Shelton and Melinda Gros (editorial assistants); Robert Fitzpatrick (map design); Carole Pipolo (typist); and above all, the artists and administrators whose commitment to the theatre makes Off Off Broadway possible.

TABLE OF CONTENTS

INTRODUCTION

The Off Off Broadway Alternative
by Joseph Papp

Off Off Broadway is an alternative theatre. It takes the playgoer off the beaten track—not just geographically, but also artistically. At its best, it is an idea about theatre, a commitment to theatre as an art form and to theatre as a vehicle for responding to that which is contemporary. People who work Off Off Broadway don't sit around waiting for a job. Driven by a clear design and sense of purpose, playwrights, actors, and directors perform and produce, working not for monetary compensation, but because there is something they feel compelled to communicate.

The alternatives Off Off Broadway offers to an audience are many. Economically, it provides an inexpensive way to be entertained. Geographically, it offers a chance to venture to some of the highways and byways of New York City. Just as one wants to see more than the Champs Elysées when one visits Paris, more than the West End when one visits London, one should not restrict a visit to New York to the midtown area. By venturing into Soho, Chelsea, Queens, Bedford Stuyvesant, the Upper West Side, Harlem, or any of the many neighborhoods where Off Off Broadway theatres are tucked away, one begins to see the strivings of people who have a serious interest in theatre beyond glitter, glamour and tinsel. There's something inherently dramatic about visiting Off Off Broadway theatre. A life force, a sense of vitality often infuses these theatres where artists frequently must struggle to stay afloat. Theatregoing becomes a more personalized experience. There's a sense of community, a homegrown spirit that you will not find in more formal Broadway theatres. You generally know who is running the store in these small nonprofit operations, and may even be greeted by the artistic or managing director as you enter the theatre.

However, the most important alternative Off Off Broadway offers concerns the style and content of the work presented. Most people associate theatre with Broadway's glittering lights and elaborately produced musical comedies. There is no question that Broadway is a place where careers can be made, where some of our most skilled professionals work, and where one can see some very interesting theatre. But because it is a place where millions of dollars are involved, where every seat in a house of 2,000–3,000 is worth a fortune, the primary purpose of putting on plays must be to make money, even when artistic goals are involved. If the house isn't filled, the play can't survive. So, questions concerning what will appeal to the most people take precedence over factors relating to artistic quality.

The alternative theatre movement began with the recognition that many serious plays failed on Broadway, not because they were not good plays, but because they did not appeal to a sufficiently broad audience. But it is not inconsistent to have a good time at something that is serious and complex and challenging—both to the mind and to the imagination. It was with this recognition that approximately twenty-five years ago theatres like the Circle in the Square began reviving plays such as Tennessee Williams' *Summer and Smoke* and Eugene O'Neill's *The Iceman Cometh*, both of which received mixed notices when they opened on Broadway. Other theatres, mine included, did Shakespeare. But what became truly exciting about the early days of the arena were not revivals, but new plays that were emerging from groups that had particular ideas about how to present theatre. I'm referring to groups such as the Open Theatre, La Mama E.T.C., the Living Theatre, the Bread and Puppet Theatre, and many others, as well as to the emergence of important black playwrights like Ed Bullins, Richard Wesley, and Leroi Jones. Since their work was more left wing than that of Off Broadway, it became known as Off Off Broadway. I use the word "left wing" not just in the political sense, but to define anything that is not part of the center, the established structure—those works that reach beyond mainstream, ordinary Broadway fare.

Today, Off Off Broadway is any place that is not the commercial Broadway theatre. Even productions that call themselves Off Broadway (because of the number of seats in their theatre and the type of contract that they sign with the actors' union) I consider Off Off Broadway, for all of them share a commitment to a certain idea about the function of theatre.

Since their inception, Off and Off Off Broadway theatres have been characterized by a spirit of radicalism. Not in an active way, but by their very existence as an alternative to Broadway, these theatres went against the establishment. During the sixties, theatre became increasingly more radicalized as artists felt impelled to respond to the times in which they were living. As the civil rights movement, the feminist movement, and the Vietnam War raged, very little was changing on Broadway—she remained the same lady that she is. The commercial theatre has a capacity to remain untouched by events. That's part of its attraction: you don't have to juxtapose what's happening in your own life and the world with what you see; for a few moments you can suspend your anxieties and your fears. But when you come out of the theatre your personal and political problems remain, and you have to face them. It's like coming out of the movies in the middle of the afternoon—the sun is blazing and suddenly you are blinded by what is real. All theatre is escapist, as is all art, but it's a question of how you escape and whether that escape strengthens you or gives you more fantasies about life.

There's a marvelous triple metaphor in *Hamlet* which explains what I believe the relationship between the individual, the theatre, and the world should be. Just after Hamlet sees the ghost he says:

> "Remember thee! Ay poor ghost, while memory holds a seat in this distracted globe. Remember thee!"

On the literal level he is saying "I will remember you as long as I have my own mind." But actually, "globe" refers to three things: it is the world, it is the Globe Theatre, and it is his mind. A performance can't just be in an individual head; it can't just be in one's head and the theatre—that's like placing your head in the sand; it has to encompass all three—one's head, the theatre, the world. In our own time people are finding it increasingly difficult to make these interconnections because the world outside seems so unfathomable. Yet, I believe the theatre is the arena where this effort must be made—and that these links can be achieved through good comedy as well as serious drama; original musicals as well as reinterpretations of old classics.

Off Off Broadway productions range from the very raw to the highly polished. There is so much to choose from—and it's interesting to explore and take chances. One may stumble unknowingly upon an extraordinary artistic experience or uncover an exceptionally talented artist. It's nice to be able to rely on your own resources rather than the reviews of a handful of critics, to be able to say, "I was at this little place on East 4th Street and had an absolutely unique evening in the theatre."

Off Off Broadway is a place where people can work with dignity and purpose. It is not the bush leagues, but an arena with an identity all its own. At its best, Off Off Broadway is a true alternative theatre—with a distinctive style and content and a reason for being all its own.

EXPLANATORY NOTES: EXPLORING OFF OFF BROADWAY

New York is the theatre capital of the world and increasingly it is acknowledged that Off Off Broadway is the lifeblood of the theatre. It is here that a playgoer can experience truly exciting, creative theatre—from an innovative interpretation of an old classic, to a new experimental play, to next season's Broadway hit—at a fraction of the cost. Beyond the footlights of Broadway, past its glittering marquees, New York's other theatre provides an equally exciting, very different type of entertainment. For the adventurous playgoer who wants to be stimulated and entertained and wishes to participate in the vanguard of theatrical activity, there is nothing comparable to Off Off Broadway theatre—in the United States or in the world.

More and more playgoers are discovering that for less than half the price of a rear balcony Broadway ticket they can sit a few feet from the scene of the action and experience the excitement of being a participant in, as well as an observer of, a theatrical event and perhaps even have the chance to meet with the cast after the show. Off Off Broadway is the place where people who love the theatre spend their evenings. In addition to providing for the development of new talent, it is the location where our most famous actors, actresses and directors repeatedly return to explore and extend their range.

This guidebook was developed to make this vast, diverse network of theatres understandable and accessible for tourists, New Yorkers who appreciate the theatre but are uninformed about Off Off Broadway, and for the theatrical community that spans the country.

Off Off Broadway theatres populate all of New York's neighborhoods, so visiting Off Off Broadway provides a perfect way to explore the ethnic and cultural diversity that is the heartbeat of New York City. Each Off Off Broadway theatre is unique, but it also influences and is influenced by its neighborhood. More importantly, Off Off Broadway has been a primary stimulus to neighborhood revitalization. These theatres frequently move to less than desirable neighborhoods in their search for low rental facilities. They discover and convert every and any kind of building—factories, warehouses, stores—and before long, restaurants, shops, and exciting night-life begin to proliferate. It happened on the Bowery, it happened in Soho, and it happened on West 42nd Street. Decaying tenements, industrial warehouses and defunct porno houses quickly gave way to thriving cultural activities as the theatres moved in. To assist the reader in exploring New York and its other theatre at one and the same time, this guidebook begins with an introductory section of theatres by neighborhood, including easy reference maps and brief neighborhood descriptions.

Profiles of eighty-four theatres (the members of the Off Off Broadway Alliance at the time this book was researched) will be found here. While not a comprehensive listing (there are over two-hundred Off Off Broadway theatres), the theatres profiled provide an excellent representative sampling of what's available Off Off Broadway.

In addition, a description of not-for-profit theatres that have been in existence for five years or more (non–OOBA members at the time this book was written) is included at the end of the book. These theatres (many of them technically considered Off Broadway because of the number of seats in the house), along with the OOBA members, belong to a large network of New York theatres that provide an important alternative to the commercial Broadway theatre. Of course, new theatres are founded all the time and one shouldn't hesitate to explore them simply because they are not described in these pages.

Every effort has been made to keep information in this guidebook as up-to-date as possible. However, because Off Off Broadway is an arena of creativity and flux, not all theatres will last a lifetime, nor will they necessarily remain in the same location. Also, because theatre, like everything else, is affected by inflation, ticket prices are subject to change. Use them as a guideline, but call the theatre to verify current ticket price.

The phrase "TDF voucher accepted" refers to a voucher program sponsored by the Theatre Development Fund (the same people who run the TKTS booth at Times Square where you can purchase half-price tickets to Broadway shows on the day of performance). This program affords the theatregoer significant savings on already low-priced Off Off Broadway theatre tickets. Vouchers are made available to people on TDF's mailing list and are sold in sets of five at $10.00 per set. Each voucher may be used for one admission to those performances that accept vouchers. Some theatres charge a small surcharge in addition to the voucher. Students, teachers, union members, clergy, performing arts professionals, members of youth, community and church groups, and retired persons are eligible for TDF's mailing list and to purchase vouchers. Send a self-addressed stamped envelope to Applications, Theatre Development Fund, 1501 Broadway, New York, New York 10036.

New York's Other Theatre should be used in conjunction with current newspaper listings. So, read through this guidebook, find a theatre whose work sounds interesting, consult the newspaper for the theatre's current productions, and plan an exciting afternoon or evening in the theatre. Alternately, scan the newspaper, choose a play, then turn to this book to find more detailed information about the group who is producing it. The following resources provide up-to-date production information:

The Village Voice: The Village Voice reviews many Off Off Broadway shows and provides a weekly listing of productions. Many Off Off Broadway theatres advertise here. Published each Wednesday.

The *Soho Weekly News:* Like *The Village Voice*, the *Soho Weekly News* reviews many Off Off Broadway shows, provides weekly listings, and frequently runs feature articles on OOB experimental theatre artists. Published each Wednesday.

Other Stages: Other Stages was founded to give more critical attention to Off Off Broadway theatre. Published biweekly, it is distributed free of charge at Off Off Broadway theatres and is available at newsstands for fifty cents. In addition to reviews, listings, and advertisements, the publication runs numerous features on OOB theatres, theatre artists, and issues related to this arena.

The New York Times: A listing of Off Off Broadway productions appears in the Sunday "The Guide" Section of *The New York Times.*

New York On Stage: Published each month by the Theatre Development Fund, *New York On Stage* provides a day-by-day listing of Off Off Broadway productions. (Dance, music, Broadway, and Off Broadway productions are also listed.) Available free of charge to TDF voucher-holders, this publication may also be ordered by subscription. Write *New York On Stage,* Theatre Development Fund, 1501 Broadway, New York, New York 10036.

Another valuable source of information is the Off Off Broadway Alliance (OOBA), a coalition of New York's major not-for-profit professional Off Off Broadway theatres. For up-to-date information or referrals, call or write:

OOBA
162 West 56th Street, Room 206
New York, New York 10019
(212) 757-4473

From Soho to the Upper West Side, from Chelsea to the Bowery, Off Off Broadway represents some of the most exciting activity in the city. So be informed, be entertained, be adventurous. Explore—New York and its other theatre.

THEATRES BY NEIGHBORHOOD

LOWER EAST SIDE

BUS ROUTES

LINE NUMBER —(M5)→ DIRECTION

SUBWAY STATIONS

EXPRESS LOCAL

BMT

IND

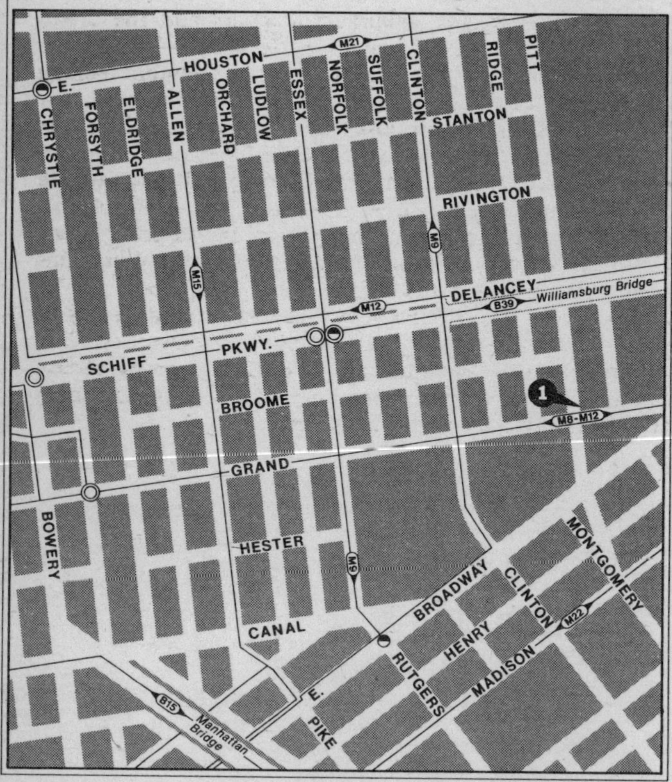

LOWER EAST SIDE

THE THEATRES

1. New Federal Theatre at Henry Street Settlement (p. 121)

Blintzes and bargains, suburban shoppers and the urban poor, religious Jews and young Puerto Ricans—the Lower East Side continues to celebrate America's mythic melting pot. If most of the European Jews who came to start new lives at the turn of the century have moved elsewhere, the synagogues and shops they established remain, as does a colorful theatre of the streets as dazzling as Broadway. On Sunday, when Orchard Street is closed to traffic, an eclectic, international assortment of shoppers, rich and poor, elbow their way through its open-air market in search of bargains —discount designer clothes, cut-rate appliances, pickles and pastrami. There is no better way to conclude a day of sightseeing and shopping than to visit a Lower East Side theatre. Here the hymn to survival that plays on the streets is echoed in the voices of minority playwrights explaining and exploring their vision of America.

SOHO

BUS ROUTES

LINE NUMBER —(M6)→ DIRECTION

SUBWAY STATIONS

EXPRESS LOCAL

IRT - West Side

BMT

IND

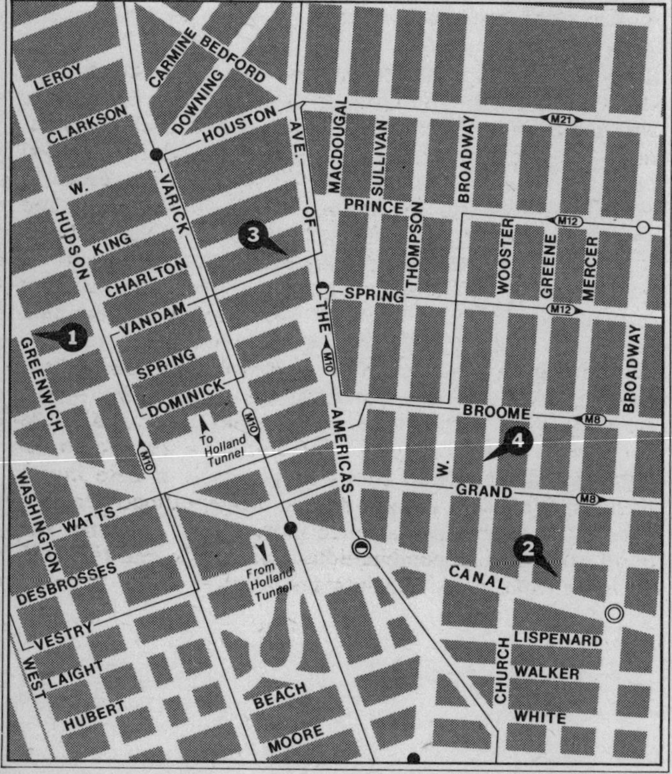

SOHO

THE THEATRES

Soho—the name stands for south of Houston Street—is a study in dramatic contrasts. Here industrious artists mix with industrial workers; white-walled, sun-drenched restaurants fill dingy commercial loft buildings; finely detailed canvases decorate imposing warehouses. Artists came to Soho in the sixties, converting lofts to work spaces and dance studios. And where the artists went, the galleries followed. Soon there were restaurants, boutiques, and an international crowd of tourists and residents spilling through the neighborhood's streets. Nowhere is the link between a neighborhood and its theatres more clearly evidenced than in Soho. So, to conclude a day of Soho gallery viewing with a theatre visit is to see a panorama of the art world—on and off the stage. From photo-realism to conceptual sculpture, from confrontational theatre to revivals of classics, Soho pulses with a spirit of bold inventiveness. With each passing day the neighborhood becomes a bit more established, a touch more stylish and chic. But Soho's paradoxical combination of pure style and rich substance is what gives it its unique character.

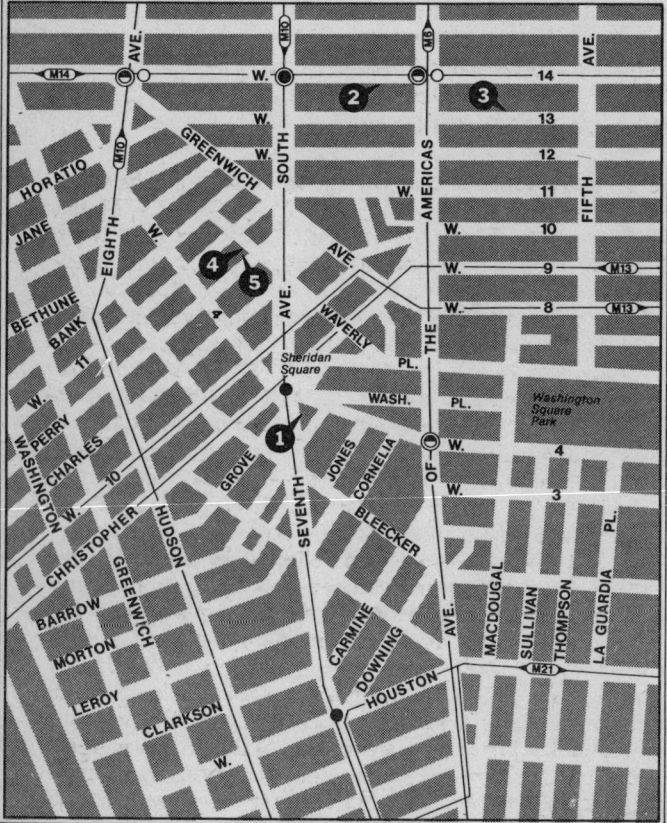

WEST VILLAGE

BUS ROUTES

LINE NUMBER — M5 — DIRECTION

SUBWAY STATIONS

EXPRESS	LOCAL	
◉	●	IRT-West Side
◎	○	BMT
◉	◓	IND

M14
W. 14
M10
M6
2
3
W. 13
W. 12
W. 11
W. 10
W. 9
M13
W. 8
M13
AVE.
SOUTH AVE.
AMERICAS
THE
OF
AVE.
FIFTH AVE.
GREENWICH AVE.
HORATIO
JANE
EIGHTH AVE.
M10
W.
4
5
4
BETHUNE
BANK
11
W.
PERRY
CHARLES
WASHINGTON
10
W.
WAVERLY PL.
Sheridan Square
WASH. PL.
Washington Square Park
1
W. 4
W. 3
GROVE
JONES
CORNELIA
CHRISTOPHER
HUDSON
SEVENTH
BLEECKER
LA GUARDIA PL.
BARROW
GREENWICH
CARMINE
MACDOUGAL
SULLIVAN
THOMPSON
MORTON
DOWNING
M21
HOUSTON
LEROY
CLARKSON
W.

THE WEST VILLAGE

THE THEATRES

The West Village is where Off Off Broadway got its start. Here makeshift theatres like Cafe Cino, Cafe La Mama and Judson Poets' Theater presented experimental work informally long before anyone thought to call this emergent artistic activity Off Off Broadway. The character of the Village has changed—no longer is it an intimate community where sidewalk cafes and small shops overflow with writers, artists, and performers. Yet it remains infused with a special creative energy. As if in a willful assertion of nonconformity, its twisted streets refuse to follow a regular street grid system. As block winds into block, there's a continually shifting mood—elegant townhouses give way to the honky-tonk of 8th Street, to the street musicians of Washington Square Park. This bold eccentricity, and diversity is likewise reflected in the neighborhood's theatres where one can see everything from mime to the classics. There is probably no better place than the West Village to enjoy an evening in the theatre and a night on the town. Its restaurants are an epicurean's delight, its sidewalk cafes provide a panoramic view of the city, its streets overflow with activity at all hours of the day and night, and its jazz clubs showcase some of the nation's finest talents. In addition, many Off Off Broadway productions that received critical acclaim may be viewed in the Village's larger commercial Off Broadway theatres.

NOHO-EAST VILLAGE

BUS ROUTES

LINE NUMBER —(M3)▶ DIRECTION

SUBWAY STATIONS

EXPRESS LOCAL

IRT-East Side

BMT

IND

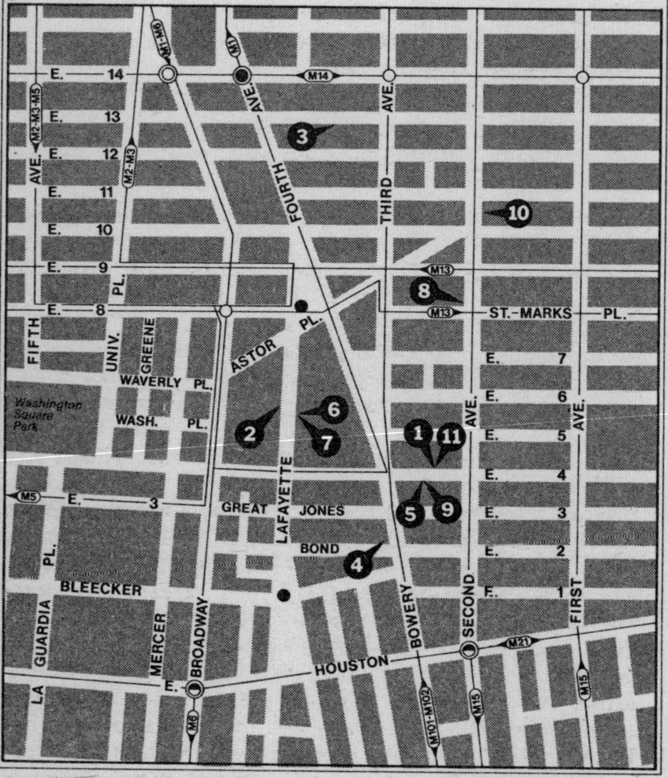

NOHO—EAST VILLAGE

THE THEATRES

Noho—that area north of Houston Street—and the East Village provide a microcosm of the Off Off Broadway theatre movement. One of New York's most ethnically diverse neighborhoods, its theatres offer playgoers every type of theatre experience imaginable. Two of the city's most influential theatrical institutions are located here—the New York Shakespeare Festival and La Mama E.T.C.—as well as ethnic theatres, experimental theatres, theatres that focus on classics, and theatres that present revivals and new American plays. Noho and the East Village also provide a striking example of how Off Off Broadway theatres have promoted neighborhood revitalization. When this area was considered off-bounds to all but bowery bums, theatres moved in because it's abandoned buildings and lofts offered low-cost performing space. Soon stores and restaurants were established to cater to this new residential population. Now Noho and the East Village boast an exciting nightlife—a crazy confusion of punk rockers, artists, and more staid, old-time residents. In this downtown equivalent of Broadway you can dine at a place like Phebe's Place where many actors congregate, or, if your taste tends towards international cuisine, sample some of the city's best Ukrainian, Indian, and Oriental fare. Wherever you go, the streets surge with a spirit of creative energy and high spirits.

CHELSEA

BUS ROUTES

LINE NUMBER —(M6)▶ DIRECTION

SUBWAY STATIONS

EXPRESS LOCAL

IRT - West Side

BMT

IND

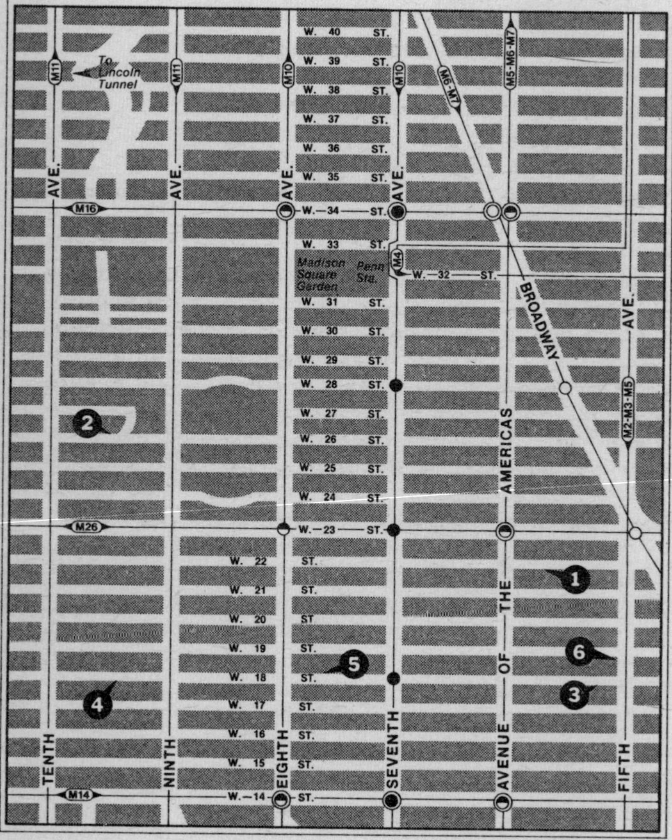

CHELSEA

THE THEATRES

1. **Golden Fleece Limited (p. 78)**
2. **Hudson Guild Theatre (p. 79)**
3. **Medicine Show Theatre Ensemble (p. 116)**
4. **Off Center Theatre (p. 138)**
5. **The Production Company (p. 147)**
6. **WPA Theatre (p. 213)**

Chelsea is a quiet, rambling neighborhood, a crisscross of industrial buildings, row houses, and churches. If its character is less clearly delineated than many of New York's neighborhoods, that's what makes it a particularly exciting place to visit. Chelsea is a place for exploration and discovery, a place to uncover a theatre or restaurant that one can possessively embrace as one's very own. The theatres here are tucked away like jewels. You'll find them in lofts, old storefronts, converted garages, and schoolhouses. Restaurants here frequently must be ferreted out, but many are unique and worth a special visit. There's no glitter in Chelsea, just good theatre. The sparkle is inside on the stage where new works and old classics are brought to life.

GRAMERCY

BUS ROUTES

LINE NUMBER —(M3)→ DIRECTION

SUBWAY STATIONS

EXPRESS LOCAL

IRT-East Side

BMT

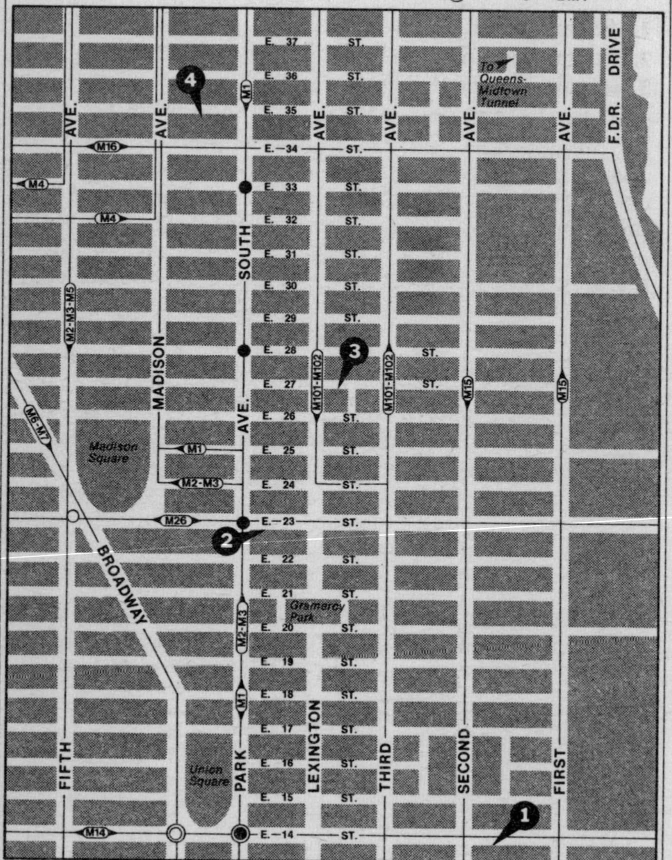

GRAMERCY

THE THEATRES

A visit to the Gramercy neighborhood is incomplete without a stop at Gramercy Park, for it provides a touch of England right in the middle of New York. This small private park—accessible only to tenants who live nearby—is surrounded by some of the city's most elegant nineteenth-century townhouses. Beyond the park, Gramercy is basically a middle-class neighborhood with a mixture of high-rises, townhouses, restaurants, stores, and of course, theatres. In this safe, low-key neighborhood you can choose from Hispanic theatre, classics, new plays, and revivals. All of Gramercy's theatres are comfortable and accessible by public transportation.

CLINTON-THEATRE ROW

BUS ROUTES

LINE NUMBER —(M6)▶ DIRECTION

SUBWAY STATIONS

EXPRESS	LOCAL	
◉	●	IRT-West Side
◎	○	BMT
◉	◓	IND
	⊕	42 St. Shuttle

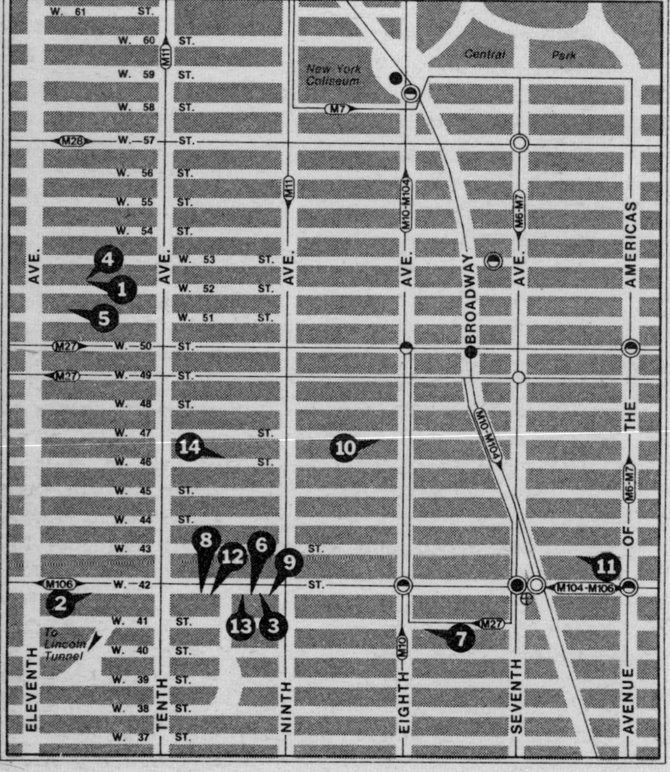

CLINTON—THEATRE ROW

THE THEATRES

1. Ensemble Studio Theatre (p. 64)
2. Fantasy Factory (p. 67)
3. INTAR (p. 84)
4. Interart (p. 86)
5. Irish Rebel Theatre (p. 88)
6. Lion Theatre (p. 103)
7. Manhattan Punch Line (p. 110)
8. Nat Horne Musical Theatre (p. 118)
9. Playwrights Horizons (p. 144)
10. Puerto Rican Traveling Theatre (p. 150)
11. Quaigh Theatre (p. 152)
12. The Raft Theatre (p. 155)
13. South Street Theatre Company (p. 179)
14. Theatre at St. Clement's (p. 189)

Like Chelsea, much of Clinton is a mixture of industrial buildings, brownstones, and churches. But the real Clinton story is on West 42nd Street, now popularly known as Theatre Row. Playwrights Horizons moved to 42nd Street in 1975 when the street was a seedy strip of massage parlors and pornographic movie theatres. Where once hawkers on dimly lit streets cajoled passersby to "check it out," theatregoers now safely check into some of the city's finest theatres, most interesting restaurants, and contemporary shops. From its centralized box office that services all the street's theatres, to the availability of dinner-theatre packages, Theatre Row makes every effort to accommodate the theatregoer. Scattered throughout the Clinton neighborhood are more than a half-dozen other important theatres housed in everything from hotels to firehouses. With the coming of urban renewal projects, and particularly with the building of the New York Convention Center, Clinton is undergoing rapid revitalization, sure to bring added life to the theatre in this neighborhood.

UPPER WEST SIDE

BUS ROUTES

LINE NUMBER — M5 ▶ DIRECTION

SUBWAY STATIONS

EXPRESS LOCAL

IRT-West Side

IND

RIVERSIDE DR.
CLAREMONT AVE.
BROADWAY
W. 123 ST.
W. 122 ST.
W. 121 ST.
W. 120 ST.
M5
M104
6

W. 87 ST.
W. 86 ST.
W. 85 ST.
W. 84 ST.
W. 83 ST.
W. 82 ST.
W. 81 ST.
W. 80 ST.
W. 79 ST.
W. 78 ST.
W. 77 ST.
W. 76 ST.
W. 75 ST.
W. 74 ST.
W. 73 ST.
W. 72 ST.
W. 71 ST.
W. 70 ST.
W. 69 ST.
W. 68 ST.
W. 67 ST.
W. 66 ST.
W. 65 ST.
W. 64 ST.
W. 62 ST.
W. 61 ST.
W. 60 ST.

HENRY HUDSON PKWY.
RIVERSIDE DR.
WEST END AVE.
AMSTERDAM AVE.
BROADWAY
COLUMBUS AVE.
CENTRAL PARK WEST

Museum of Natural History
Central Park
Lincoln Center

M18
M17
M10
M104
M7-M11
M7-M11
M5
M30
M29
M29
M5-M30-M104
M103

1
2
3
4
5
7

UPPER WEST SIDE

THE THEATRES

As Broadway stretches northward past the theatre district, its glittering marquees vanish, but not its vitality. On the Broadway of the Upper West Side the only names in lights are those of fruitstands, supermarkets, and Chinese restaurants. But theatre is alive in this friendly neighborhood where busy thoroughfares are intersected by treelined streets, where the rich and poor mingle freely together. The theatres on the Upper West Side all have a special commitment to serving their immediate neighborhood and since many actors and dancers live here, don't be surprised if performers take their seats by your side as well as their places on the stage.

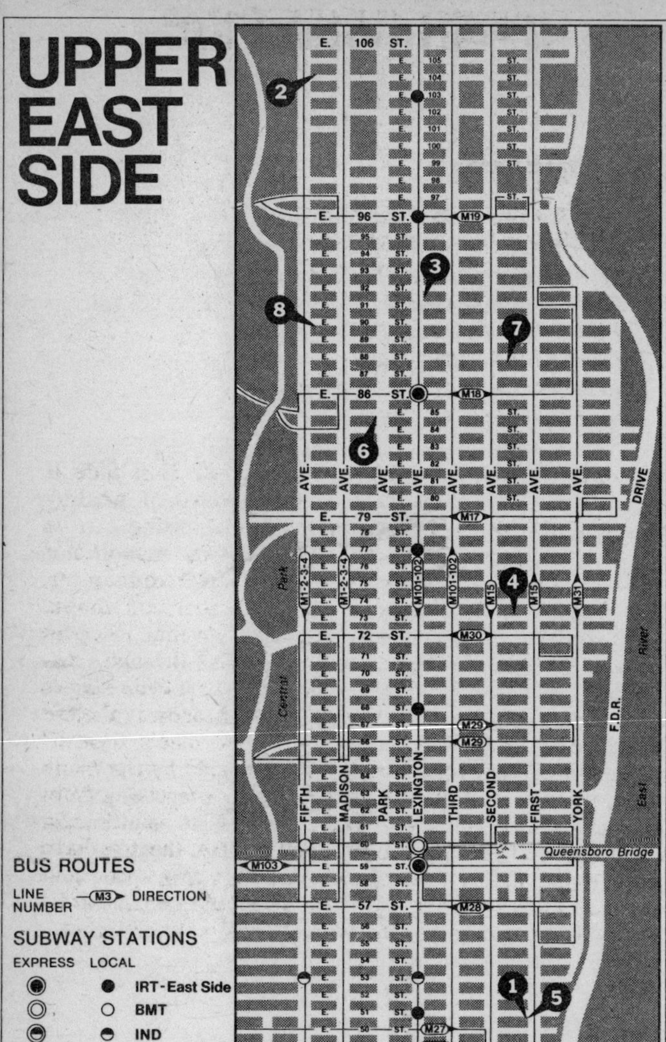
UPPER EAST SIDE
E. 106 ST.
E. 96 ST.
E. 86 ST.
E. 79 ST.
E. 72 ST.
E. 57 ST.
FIFTH AVE.
MADISON AVE.
PARK AVE.
LEXINGTON AVE.
THIRD AVE.
SECOND AVE.
FIRST AVE.
YORK AVE.
F.D.R. DRIVE
Central Park
East River
Queensboro Bridge
M19
M18
M17
M30
M29
M28
M27
M103
M1-2-3-4
M101-102
M15
M31
BUS ROUTES
LINE NUMBER
M3
DIRECTION
SUBWAY STATIONS
EXPRESS
LOCAL
IRT-East Side
BMT
IND

UPPER EAST SIDE

THE THEATRES

Depending on who you talk to, the Upper East Side is either condemned or extolled as the enclave of wealthy Manhattanites. While living, shopping, and eating can be expensive here, the neighborhood is hardly monolithic: there are coffee shops as well as fine French restaurants, thrift shops as well as haute couture. Whether you choose to visit the fine museums that line Fifth Avenue, shop in Madison Avenue's designer boutiques, stroll through Central Park, or enjoy a drink at an Upper East Side singles bar, a visit to an Upper East Side Off Off Broadway theatre should be on your itinerary. That "poor man's theatre" can exist in a "rich man's world" is evidenced by the many OOBA theatres that work here, presenting everything from interracially cast musicals, to new plays, to multimedia presentations. The Upper East Side's OOBA theatres have shown remarkable resourcefulness in acquiring space and can be found in everything from an old Armenian social hall, to an orphanage, to community centers, to churches.

QUEENS

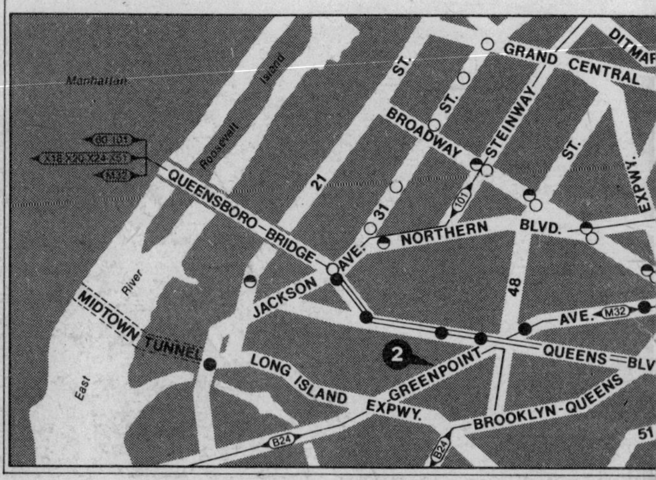

Manhattan
Roosevelt
Island
East
River
QUEENSBORO-BRIDGE
MIDTOWN
TUNNEL
21
31
ST.
ST.
GRAND
CENTRAL
BROADWAY
STEINWAY
ST.
EXPWY.
NORTHERN
BLVD.
JACKSON
AVE.
48
AVE.
M32
101
QUEENS
LONG ISLAND
EXPWY.
GREENPOINT
BROOKLYN-QUEENS
B24
51
2

QUEENS

THE THEATRES

1. Playwrights Horizons—Queens **(p. 144)**
2. Thalia Spanish Theatre **(p. 187)**

There's more to New York City than Manhattan and New York's other theatre extends beyond the inner city. Boroughs like Queens are far more than bedroom commuter communities. They are beginning to develop an independent cultural life. In addition to theatre, sites of interest in Queens include the Jamaica Bay Wildlife Preserve, Shea Stadium, Flushing Meadow Park—the home of the 1964 World's Fair—and the famed Astoria Movie Studio.

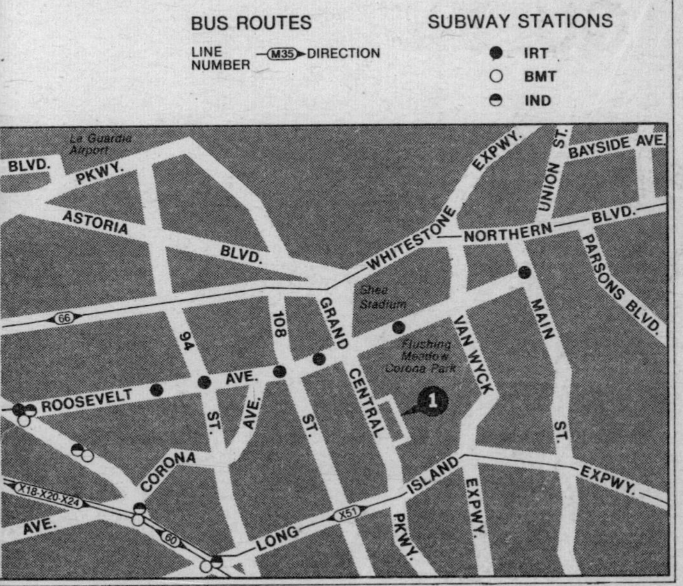

THEATRES THAT PERFORM IN VARIOUS LOCATIONS

THE THEATRES

Many theatres perform throughout the city, rather than restricting themselves to a single theatre. Sometimes this is out of choice—maintaining a permanent theatre becomes an unnecessary burden if you tour extensively or if you devote extended time to developing new works through workshops. Sometimes it is out of necessity—adequate permanent performing spaces are not always easy to locate in the city. The best way to keep in touch with the artistic activities of these theatres is to follow the weekly listings in such papers as the *Village Voice* and the *Soho Weekly News* or contact the theatre directly at its office address.

THE OOBA THEATRES

WHO: ACADEMY ARTS THEATRE COMPANY

Artistic Director: Robert Cusack
Managing Directors: Bridget Cusack, David McNitt
Founders: Robert Cusack, Bridget Cusack, Karen Hoffman, Michael Bright, David McNitt, Peter Garvey, Linda Cool, Richard Press, Marsha Dembecki, Jill Yager, Joseph Quarinale, Linda Gibbony; 1974

WHERE:

Neighborhood: Upper East Side
Theatre Address:
Eastside International Community Center
931 First Avenue (at 51st Street)
New York, New York 10022
Office Address:
424 East 57th Street, #3C
New York, New York 10019
(212) 486-1431
The Space: Located in the Eastside International Community Center—on the spot where Nathan Hale uttered his famous words, "I regret I have only one life to give for my country"—Academy Arts Theatre Company has converted a large, first-floor, open hallway into a 100-seat performing space. Functional, simple sets are employed, as the space is used for community activities during the day. Shirtsleeve Theatre (see p. 172) also uses the space.

WHAT:

Artistic Profile: Founded by a core of actors who studied together at the American Academy of Dramatic Arts, the Academy Arts Theatre Company presents a diversified season of over twenty new and classic plays chosen principally for the challenge and experience they can provide for the actor. In addition, the company has been instrumental in exploring theatre for the deaf, translating productions into sign language simultaneously with performance. Recently, the company's children's programs—which stress active participation by the audience —have likewise been interpreted for the deaf. Future plans include the development of a video library for the deaf.

Productions 1978/79:

Welded, Eugene O'Neill
The Great Nebula in Orion, Lanford Wilson
What the Butler Saw, Joe Orton (translated for the deaf)
The Giant Jack and the Beanstalk Show, adapted by Bridget Cusack (translated for the deaf, children's show)
The Gingham Dog, Lanford Wilson
Synchrony, Steven Braustein
Dial M for Murder, Frederick Knott
Baba Yaga, adapted by Patricia Kellis from a Russian folktale
Towards Zero, Agatha Christie
Charlie and Belle, David Libman
The Catbox, David Libman
Ex-Miss Copper Queen on a Set of Pills, Megan Terry

Productions 1979/80:

The Rats, Agatha Christie
The Patient, Agatha Christie
The Mad Dog Blues, Sam Shepard
Cinderella, music by Richard Palucci; lyrics by James F. Kinney; adaptation by Robert Goldberg
The Owl and the Pussycat, Bill Manhoff
Snow White and the Seven Dwarfs, adaptation by Bridget Cusack (translated for the deaf, children's show)
Private Lives, Noel Coward
Can't Imagine Tomorrow, Tennessee Williams
Bring on the Night, John Tulsee (in association with Rennicke Steele Productions)
In Celebration, David Storey (in association with June Rovinger Productions)
BB, adapted from Bertolt Brecht's writings by Helene Cara and Bridget Cusack
A Murder Has Been Arranged, Emlyn Williams (translated for the deaf)

Special Programs: Pre-performance workshops for deaf audiences; children's theatre programs; in-schools program; local touring.

GETTING THERE:

Subway: Lexington Avenue IRT 6 to 51st Street; IND E, F to 53rd Street.

Bus: Uptown: First Avenue (M15); Downtown: Second Avenue (M15); Crosstown West: 49th Street (M27); Crosstown East: 50th Street (M27).

Parking: Street parking after 7:00 P.M.; nearest lot on 56th Street and First Avenue.

RESERVING SEATS:

Box Office Telephone: 486-1431

Ticket Price: $3.00–$3.50 or TDF voucher. Students and senior citizens, $2.50.

Reservations: Call theatre, tickets held until ten minutes before curtain.

Subscriptions: Playpass for six evening productions or four evening productions and two children's shows. May be shared with another theatregoer.

Group Rates: Available, contact the theatre.

Performing Schedule: Performances most weekends from September through June. Evenings: Friday through Sunday; Matinees (children's shows): Saturday, Sunday.

ACADEMY ARTS THEATRE COMPANY RECOMMENDS:

Beekman Place Cookshop: 936 First Avenue, between 51st and 52nd Streets, 752-7989. Reservations recommended. French–Middle European. Noon till 11:00 P.M., seven days. Closed Saturday lunch. Lunch: $4.00–$8.00; Dinner: $6:25–$12.00, a la carte. All credit cards except Carte Blanche accepted.

Joe Burns: 903 First Avenue, between 50th and 51st Streets, 759-6696. Reservations required Saturday, Sunday, and evenings. American. Monday through Friday: noon till 3:30 P.M., 6:30 P.M. till 11:00 P.M.; Saturday and Sunday: noon till 4:00 P.M., 6:30 P.M. till 11:00 P.M.; Bar: till 1:00 A.M. Lunch: $3.50–$6.00, a la carte; Dinner: $7.50–$12.75, a la carte; Sunday brunch: $6.50, complete; Amex, Visa and MC. Jazz: Friday, 9:00 P.M. till 1:00 A.M.; Classical music: Sunday, noon till 4:00 P.M.

The Castillian Room: 303 East 56th Street. between First and Second Avenues, 688-6435. Reservations accepted. Spanish-American. Noon till midnight, seven days. All items $6.95, a la carte. All credit cards accepted.

WHO: AMAS REPERTORY THEATRE

Artistic Director: Rosetta LeNoire
Co-Administrative Directors: Jerry Lapidus, Elizabeth Omilami
Founder: Rosetta LeNoire; 1969

WHERE:

Neighborhood: Upper East Side
Theatre Address:
1 East 104th Street
New York, New York 10029
(212) 369-8000

The Space: At the upper reaches of Fifth Avenue—past the Metropolitan Museum of Art, the Guggenheim Museum, and just around the block from the Museum of the City of New York—AMAS Repertory Theatre makes its home. Housed in a third-floor room of an enormous, multi-use, city-owned building (formerly an orphanage) the stage space is a 99-seat thrust. With just three rows of seats, this long, rectangularly shaped theatre generates a special feeling of intimacy.

WHAT:

Artistic Profile: AMAS—the word means "you love." Created as a response to the racial polarization that swept the country during the 1960s, AMAS was one of the first performing arts organizations to actively embrace multiracial integration, bringing people of all ages, races, and creeds together to work and learn in a common effort. Devoted to the development of original musical talents, the company places a particular emphasis on creating a library of musical biographies based on the lives of important black artists such as Bill "Bojangles" Robinson, Langston Hughes, Scott Joplin, Eubie Blake, and Ethel Waters. Recent productions include the Broadway success *Bubbling Brown Sugar*, the Mitgang-Strouse-Cahn *Bojangles*, Micki Grant's *It's So Nice to Be Civilized*, and *Come Laugh and Cry with Langston Hughes*. Additional programs of the theatre—all guided by Rosetta LeNoire's unflagging humanistic spirit—include a summer Street-Theatre Touring Program; the Eubie Blake Children's Theatre (offering comprehensive music, dance, and dramatic training to children between the ages of nine and sixteen); and an adult workshop program.

Productions 1978/79:

Sparrow in Flight, conceived by Rosetta LeNoire; book by Charles Fuller; music from the repertoire of Ethel Waters

Helen, book by Lucia Victor; music and lyrics by Johnny Brandon

It's So Nice to Be Civilized, book, music, and lyrics by Micki Grant

Suddenly the Music Starts, book, music, and lyrics by Johnny Brandon

Productions 1979/80:

And Still I Rise, book and lyrics by Maya Angelou; music by Lalo Schifrin

Before the Flood, book by Rudy Gray; music by Paul Piteo; lyrics by David Blake

Dunbar, concept and original adaptation by Ayanna; adaptation for AMAS by Ron Stackler Thompson in consultation with Ayanna; lyrics by Paul Laurence Dunbar; music by Quitman Fludd, III, Connie Hewitt, Paul E. Smith; additional lyrics by Quitman Fludd

Jam, John Gerstad

Special Programs: Professional acting and voice training, classes for nonprofessionals and children, internships, statewide touring, children's theatre for children.

GETTING THERE:

Subway: Lexington Avenue IRT 6 to 103rd Street (not recommended in the evening).

Bus: Uptown: Madison Avenue (M1, M2, M3, M4) to 104th Street; Downtown: Fifth Avenue (M1, M2, M3, M4); Crosstown West and East: 96th Street (M19).

Parking: Street parking after 6:00 P.M.; nearest lot on Madison Avenue between 105th and 106th Streets.

RESERVING SEATS:

Box Office Telephone: (212) 369-8000

Ticket Price: $5.00 or TDF voucher.

Reservations: Call theatre, tickets held until a half hour prior to curtain.

Group Rates: $4.00 for groups of ten or more. A prepayment is required.

Performance Schedule: Four productions presented October through May. Evenings: Thursday through Saturday; Matinees: Sunday. Street theatre productions during the summer.

AMAS REPERTORY THEATRE RECOMMENDS:

Nodelini's Park East: 1311 Madison Avenue at 93rd Street, 369-5677. Reservations accepted. Seafood, steaks. 11:00 A.M. till 12:30 A.M., seven days. Lunch: $2.95–$4.95, a la carte; Dinner: $3.95–$8.95, a la carte. No credit cards accepted.

Summerhouse: 1269 Madison Avenue, at 91st Street, 289-8062. Reservations accepted. Quiche, omelettes, soups. Noon till 10:00 P.M., seven days. Sunday Brunch: noon till 3:00 P.M. $3.00–$12.00, a la carte. No credit cards accepted. Bring your own liquor.

WHO: THE AMERICAN ENSEMBLE COMPANY

Artistic Director: Robert Petito

Founder: Robert Petito; 1969

WHERE:

Theatre Address: Performs in various locations.
Office Address:
P.O. Box 5478
Grand Central Station
New York, New York 10017
(212) 571-7594

WHAT:

Artistic Profile: In existence for over a decade, The American Ensemble Company is a group of actors who have worked together for many years, refining their craft and focusing on the presentation of revivals. The company has a firm commitment to understanding the stylistic requirements of various scripts—Molière, Shakespeare, Greek tragedy—and each year focuses on mastering a particular acting style by studying the history and culture of the period as well as its dramatic texts. The American Ensemble Company prides itself on having "the greatest roster of mature actors working Off Off Broadway." Increasingly, the company is also incorporating small musicals, revues, and new plays into its repertory.

Productions 1978/79:
The Immoralist, Ruth and Augustus Goetz, based on André Gide's novel

Productions 1979/80:
These Little Pigs, book and lyrics by Stuart Summerville; music by Joseph D'Elia and Len Phillips
Friends and Lovers, book by Patricia Ryan; music by Robert Mitchell
O'Neill, Timothy Dugan

Special Programs: Advanced professional class focusing on a different acting style each year (Molière, Greek tragedy, Shakespeare); acting classes for nonprofessionals; touring to local hospitals.

GETTING THERE:

Contact the office for current performing location and directions.

RESERVING SEATS:

Box Office Telephone: (212) 571-7594
Ticket Price: Variable, TDF vouchers accepted. Discounts for students and senior citizens.
Reservations: Call the theatre, tickets held until fifteen minutes before curtain.
Group Rates: Available for groups of ten or more.
Performance Schedule: Variable performance schedule. Contact the theatre for current productions.

WHO: AMERICAN JEWISH THEATRE AT THE Y

Artistic Director: Stanley Brechner
Founder: Stanley Brechner; 1974

WHERE:

Neighborhood: Upper East Side
Theatre Address:
92nd Street YM/YWHA
1395 Lexington Avenue
New York, New York 10028
(212) 427-6000, Extension 220
The Space: The American Jewish Theatre at the Y makes its home in an intimate studio theatre at the 92nd Street YM-YWHA, a renowned cultural institution with a fifty-year tradition of presenting well-known artists in music, dance, opera, poetry, and theatre. Located in a safe, residential neighborhood, the theatre is fully accessible to the handicapped.

WHAT:

Artistic Profile: The broad range of work presented by the American Jewish Theatre at the Y has included Yiddish classics in English, well-known plays with Jewish themes, an experimental play exploring aspects of concentration camp behavior through direct audience participation, and a play based on Russian dissident Anatole Sharansky's trial. Unifying this diverse repertory is a deep commitment to the exploration and illumination—through the comic and the serious—of the dynamics of Jewish life. During the 1980/81 season, American Jewish Theatre shifted its home base from the Henry Street Settlement, a Lower East Side community service organization, to the 92nd Street YM/YWHA.

Productions 1978/79:

Green Fields, Peretz Hirshbein
The God of Vengeance, Sholem Asch
The Treasure, David Pinski
The Cup of Fury, based on the Sharansky trial
Molly's Daughters, Shellen Lubin

Productions 1979/80:

At the YM/YWHA:
Three One-Acts:
In Search of Justice, Bertolt Brecht
The Irish Hebrew Lesson, Wolf Mankowitz
Arthur and the Acetone, George Bernard Shaw
King David and His Wives, David Pinski
The Tenth Man, Paddy Chayefsky
At the Henry Street Settlement:
I Never Saw Another Butterfly, music by Peter Schlosser; choreography by Wendy Osserman
Warsaw Opera, Nancy Heikin
Variations on The Merchant of Venice, Charles Marowitz

Special Programs: Jewish theatre workshops, internships, touring.

GETTING THERE:

Subway: Lexington Avenue IRT 4, 5, 6 to 86th Street; Lexington Avenue IRT 6 to 96th Street.

Bus: Uptown: Third Avenue (M101); Downtown: Lexington Avenue (M101); Crosstown West and East: 96th Street (M19) and 86th Street (M18).

Parking: Street parking after 7:00 P.M.; nearest garage on 92nd Street between Second and Third Avenues.

RESERVING SEATS:

Box Office Telephone: (212) 427-4410
Ticket Price: $5.00, TDF vouchers accepted.
Reservations: Tickets must be picked up at the box office. No phone reservations accepted. Box office hours are Monday through Thursday, 11:00 A.M. to 9:00 P.M.; Friday, 11:00 A.M. to 4:00 P.M.; Saturday, 6:00 P.M. to 9:00 P.M.; Sunday, noon to 5:00 P.M.
Group Rates: Available, contact the theatre.
Subscriptions: Available, may be ordered by phone with Master Charge or Visa.
Performance Schedule: Five or six productions presented October through May. Evenings: Thursday, Saturday, Sunday; Matinees: Sunday.

AMERICAN JEWISH THEATRE RECOMMENDS:

Rupert's: 1662 Third Avenue, on the corner of 93rd Street, 831-1900. Reservations required for parties of six or more. Continental. Sunday through Thursday: noon till 12:30 A.M.; Friday and Saturday: till 3:00 A.M. Lunch: $2.00–$4.50, a la carte; Dinner: $5.50–$10.00, a la carte; Saturday and Sunday Brunch: $3.25–$5.00, a la carte. Amex, MC, Visa, and Diner's Club accepted. Piano Bar: Tuesday through Saturday, from 5:00 P.M. Classical music at brunch.
Cockeyed Clams: 1678 Third Avenue, on the corner of 94th Street, 831-4121. Reservations suggested. Burgers, seafood. 11:30 A.M. till 12:30 A.M., seven days. Brunch: Saturday, Sunday. Lunch: $2.95–$4.95, a la carte; Dinner: $4.95–$8.95, complete. No credit cards accepted.

WHO: AMERICAN RENAISSANCE THEATRE

Artistic Director: Robert Elston
Associate Artistic Director: Elizabeth Perry
Assistant Director: Susan Reed
Founders: Robert Elston, Elizabeth Perry; 1975

WHERE:

Neighborhood: West Village
Theatre Address:
112 Charlton Street (enter on Greenwich Street)
New York, New York 10014
(212) 929-4718
The Space: American Renaissance Theatre's pristine white exterior provides a welcome contrast to the surrounding loft buildings. Its ground floor, air-conditioned, flexible, 70-seat space has a mixture of traditional theatre seats, dark-wood, fold-up chairs, and platforms. Comfortable and homey, the theatre's walls are decorated with flyers, photos, and works of art by company members.

WHAT:

Artistic Profile: The American Renaissance Theatre provides an environment where mature artists can develop and extend their craft. Company members (approximately 130) are free from the type of pigeonholing that restricts theatre artists to specific roles: composers have the opportunity to direct, directors to sing, actors to write. Members meet weekly—on Monday theatrical works in progress are presented and discussed while Tuesday is devoted to songs and cabaret acts. A work is given a formal, public performance when the group agrees that it is sufficiently developed. A.R.T. strives to make audiences as well as member artists feel that the theatre is home and spectators are invited to remain after the program and interact with the performers.
Productions 1978/79:
An Act of Kindness, Joseph Julian
Molly Bloom and the Woman of Ireland, adaptation: Donna Wilshire
Two One-Acts by Stan Edelman:
Storytime
Magic Time
Notes from Underground, based on Thoreau's *Walden*, Kafka's *Report to an Academy* and Dostoevsky's *Notes from Underground*

Women in Concert: Phyllis Rice, Marcia Brushingham
Radical Solutions, David Libman

Productions 1979/80:

Ruby Ruby Sam Sam, Stan Edelman
Three One-Acts by Patricia Ryan:
Equal
Silences
Curses
Women in Ireland, Susan Reed and Bambi Linn
Jered Holmes in Concert
Archy and Mehitabel, based on stories of Don Marquis; book by Joe Darion and Mel Brooks; music by George Kleinsinger; lyrics by Joe Darion
Chared Paper, Walter Layden Brown
Did You See the Elephant?, Elizabeth Perry

Productions 1980/81:

After Many a Summer, Robert Elston
Did You Hear the Rumor, Jeffrey Knox
Judith Leslie in Concert
Portrait of a Man, Robert Elston

Special Programs: Classes in acting, musical comedy, and opera; local touring; pre- and post-performance lectures; theatre rentals.

GETTING THERE:

Subway: Seventh Avenue IRT 1 to Houston Street, walk two blocks south and two blocks west.

Bus: Uptown: Hudson Street (M10); Downtown: Seventh Avenue (M10); Crosstown West and East: Houston Street (M21).

Parking: Street parking after 6:00 P.M. and on weekends; nearest lot on the corner of King and Hudson Streets, one block north.

RESERVING SEATS:

Box Office Telephone: (212) 929-4718

Ticket Price: $4.00 or TDF voucher, $3.00 on Thursday evening, $1.00 discount for students and senior citizens.

Reservations: Call theatre, tickets held until ten minutes before curtain.

Group Rates: $1.00 discount for groups larger than fifteen.

Performance Schedule: Six full public productions plus cabarets and concerts presented September through June. Evenings: Thursday through Saturday; Matinees: Saturday, Sunday.

AMERICAN RENAISSANCE THEATRE RECOMMENDS:

Ear Inn: 326 Spring Street, between Greenwich and Washington Streets, 226-9060. Reservations required for parties over six. American-International. Sunday through Friday: noon till 1:00 A.M.; Saturday: 6:00 P.M. till midnight. $2.50–$6.50, a la carte. No credit cards accepted. Entertainment: folk, new wave music, Thursday through Sunday nights and Sunday brunch; poetry reading Saturday at 2:00 P.M.

Elephant & Castle: 68 Greenwich Avenue, between Seventh Avenue and 11th Street, 243-1400. Omelettes, salads, burgers. Monday through Thursday: 9:00 A.M. till midnight; Friday: 9:00 A.M. till 1:00 A.M.; Saturday: 11:00 A.M. till 1:00 A.M.; Sunday: 10:00 A.M. till 12:00 A.M. $3.00–$7.00, a la carte. All major credit cards except MC accepted.

WHO: AMERICAN STANISLAVSKI THEATRE

Artistic Director: Sonia Moore
Executive Assistant: Dorothy Hesselman
Founder: Sonia Moore; 1970

WHERE:

Theatre Address: Performs in various locations.
Office Address:
485 Park Avenue, #6A
New York, New York 10022
(212) 755-5120

WHAT:

Artistic Profile: American Stanislavski Theatre is a repertory ensemble of the American Center for Stanislavski Theatre Art, a teaching and performing organization dedicated to the perpetuation of Stanislavski's final conclusions on Theatre Art. Artistic Director and Founder Sonia Moore, who studied at the Moscow Art Theatre, has dedicated herself to the study and perpetuation of Stanislavski's theories. In her teaching and directing she emphasizes Stanislavski's final conclusions on acting—the Method of Physical Action, striving to link internal and external behavior. In the future the company hopes to establish an accredited national school for acting training.

Productions 1978/79:

A Streetcar Named Desire, Tennessee Williams
Baby Face, Joseph Caruso
A Long Day's Journey into Night, Eugene O'Neill

Productions 1979/80:

The Stronger, August Strindberg
This Property Is Condemned, Tennessee Williams

Special Programs: Classes in acting, Alexander Technique, Shakespeare, directing, speech, script interpretation, mime; college residency touring program.

RESERVING SEATS:

Box Office Telephone: Company performs in various locations. Contact office at (212) 755-5120 for ticket information.

Ticket Price: $6.00 or TDF voucher, $3.50 for students and senior citizens.

Group Rates: $3.00 for groups of ten to fifteen; $2.75 for groups of fifteen to twenty; $2.50 for groups larger than twenty.

Subscription: Two admissions for the price of one pass.

Performance Schedule: Variable schedule. Each production runs in repertory for five weeks. Evenings: Thursday through Saturday; Matinees: Sunday.

WHO: BOND STREET THEATRE COALITION

Artistic Director: Patrick Sciarratta
Managing Director: Joanna Sherman
Founder: Patrick Sciarratta, Joanna Sherman; 1976

WHERE:

Neighborhood: Performs in various locations
Office Address:
2 Bond Street
New York, New York 10012
(212) 254-4614

WHAT:

Artistic Profile: The Bond Street Theatre Coalition is an ensemble of actors, mimes, acrobats, jugglers, musicians, magicians, and puppeteers who use their skills within a theatrical framework, revitalizing classic theatrical structures (commedia dell'arte, myth, cabaret, and folklore) and creating a theatrical form that is immediately accessible, spontaneous, and highly improvisatory. Through its theatre of dexterity and perception, the company seeks to make theatre socially relevant and environmentally conscious. For example, *Powerplay*, an anti-nuclear play, which included everything from God as a twenty-foot puppet to a melt-down tap number, was performed for the workers at Con Edison. Deeply committed to generating theatre that is accessible to *all* people, Bond Street Theatre Coalition tours to parks, festivals, camps, and fairs throughout the summer, and to schools, shopping malls, and community centers throughout the year. In addition, the ensemble brings their productions to the Off Off Broadway stage during the winter months.

Productions 1978/79:
Capidome, or the Malling of America, collaboratively developed
A Tale of Vision, collaboratively developed
Bond Street Funnies, collaboratively developed
Bits and Pieces, collaboratively developed
The Flying Doctor, Molière

Productions 1979/80:

Powerplay (outdoor version and indoor version), collaboratively developed

Bond Street Funnies

Body Works, Lisa Löving, Joanna Sherman

The Strongbox Was Locked, collaboratively developed

Special Programs: Two-week intensive workshop retreat at Shelter Island; Apprentice Program (college credit available through NYU and Adelphi University); workshops and lecture demonstrations; spring and fall open public classes at NYU in Commedia, the Mask and Circus Arts for the Actor; national and international touring; two-week, intensive workshop retreat at Camp Brookwood; children's programs.

GETTING THERE:

Subway: IND B, D, F to Broadway/Lafayette Street; Lexinton Avenue IRT 6 to Bleecker Street.

Bus: Uptown: Third Avenue (M101, M102); Downtown: Broadway (M1, M 6).

Parking: Street parking; garage at corner of Great Jones and Lafayette Streets.

RESERVING SEATS:

Box Office Telephone: (212) 254-4614

Ticket Price: Free outdoor performances; indoor performances range from $3.00–$6.00, TDF voucher accepted. Discounts for students and senior citizens; special discounts on Wednesday, Thursday, and Sunday. $1.00 off ticket price with newspaper ad or flyer.

Reservations: Call theatre, tickets held until fifteen minutes before curtain.

Performing Schedule: Variable schedule of indoor and outdoor performances throughout the year. Contact the theatre for times, dates, and locations.

WHO: CHERUBS GUILD

Artistic Directors: Carol Avila, Hillary Wyler, Lesley Starbuck, Robert Avila
Resident Playwrights: Daniel Judah Sklar, Matt Williams, Toni Press
Founders: Carol Avila, Hillary Wyler, Lesley Starbuck, Robert Avila; 1977

WHERE:

Neighborhood: Noho–East Village
Theatre Address:
83 East 4th Street (between Second Avenue and the Bowery)
New York, New York 10003
(212) 533-5893
The Space: Bustling with theatres, punk-rockers, and bowery bums, East 4th Street is to downtown what Broadway is to uptown. Unlike many functional, simple spaces which are the norm in this area, Cherubs Guild makes its home in an exceedingly handsome, well-furbished, 99-seat proscenium theatre on the second floor of a converted brownstone. The space has a long history of being used as a professional theatre and belonged, during the 1960s, to Edward Albee and Richard Barr.

WHAT:

Artistic Profile: Under the collaborative artistic direction of its four officers—whose expertise ranges from acting, to directing, to management—Cherubs Guild is dedicated to the production of new plays and to developing the skills of American playwrights. The theatre has a particular interest in plays which explore themes related to human dignity and interpersonal relationships.
Productions 1978/79:
The Legendary Stardust Boys, D. B. Gilles
Pandamonium, Harold Callen

Productions 1979/80:
The Crunch, Marcus Campbell
The Queen and the Rebels, Ugo Betti
Free Ride, Daniel Judah Sklar
Peach and Powder, Judy Engels

Special Programs: Playreadings; theatre rentals.

GETTING THERE:

Subway: BMT LL (Canarsie 14th Street Line) to Third Avenue/14th Street; BMT RR to 8th Street; IND F to Second Avenue/Houston Street; Lexington Avenue IRT 6 to Astor Place.

Bus: Uptown: Third Avenue (M101, M102); Downtown: Broadway (M1, M6) and Second Avenue (M15).

Parking: Street parking; lot in filling station on corner of East 4th Street and the Bowery.

RESERVING SEATS:

Box Office Telephone: (212) 533-5888

Ticket Price: $4.00 or TDF voucher. Student and senior citizen discounts available.

Reservations: Call theatre, tickets held until fifteen minutes before curtain.

Group Rates: Available, contact the theatre.

Performance Schedule: Four productions presented September through June. Evenings: Wednesday through Sunday; Matinees: Sunday. Informal playreadings presented twice per month.

CHERUBS GUILD RECOMMENDS:

Phebe's Place: 361 Bowery, at 4th Street, 473-9008. American-Continental. Noon till 4:00 A.M., seven days. $1.65–$9.00, a la carte. All credit cards accepted.

Hisae's Place: 35 Cooper Square, between 5th and 6th Streets, 228-6886. Reservations required for parties of four or more. Oriental. Monday through Thursday: 5:00 P.M. till midnight; Friday and Saturday: 5:00 P.M. till 1:00 A.M.; Sunday: 5:00 P.M. till 11:00 P.M. $5.95–$10.95, a la carte. No credit cards.

Second Avenue Deli: 156 Second Avenue, on the corner of 10th Street, 677-0606. Kosher. 7:00 A.M. till midnight, seven days. $3.50–$8.00, a la carte. No credit cards. Personal checks accepted.

Shagorika Bangladesh Restaurant: 100 Second Avenue, between 6th and 7th Streets, 982-0533. Reservations required. Indian. Lunch: 11:30 A.M. till 3:00 P.M., Monday through Friday; Dinner: 5:00 P.M. till 11:00 P.M., seven days. $3.00–$5.25, a la carte. All credit cards accepted.

WHO: CIRCLE REPERTORY COMPANY

Artistic Director: Marshall W. Mason
Producing Director: Porter W. Van Zandt, Jr.
Founders: Marshall W. Mason, Robert Thirkield, Lanford Wilson, Tanya Berezin; 1969

WHERE:

Neighborhood: West Village
Theatre Address:
99 Seventh Avenue South
New York, New York 10011
Office Address:
161 Sixth Avenue
New York, New York 10012
(212) 691-3210

The Space: On a busy Greenwich Village thoroughfare, one of New York's most active not-for-profit theatres makes its home. A colorful banner and production photos mark the building's exterior. Inside, a comfortable, flexible theatre seats 160.

WHAT:

Artistic Profile: Circle Repertory Company, part of the nation's network of not-for-profit theatres, has been instrumental in developing important new works for the theatre. It is unique in that major playwrights-in-residence create roles for specific members of its resident ensemble of actors. The Rep is an important national as well as New York resource, for plays given birth through its developmental programs have been presented in fifty-six professional productions, at thirty-four regional theatres, and in some seven hundred forty-three amateur productions in all fifty states and eight foreign countries. Its distinguished productions include the Pulitzer Prize–winning *Talley's Folly, The Hot L Baltimore, When You Comin' Back Red Ryder?, The Sea Horse, 5th of July, Gertrude Stein Gertrude Stein Gertrude Stein,* and *Gemini.* In addition to its annual season of new plays, classics, revivals, and Projects-in-Progress series, the company sponsors a developmental workshop—the Circle Lab. Here theatre artists develop projects free from critical and commercial pressures.

Productions 1978/79:

Glorious Morning, Patrick Meyers
In the Recovery Lounge, James Farrell
The Runner Stumbles, Milan Stitt
Winter Signs, John Bishop
Talley's Folly, Lanford Wilson
Gertrude Stein Gertrude Stein Gertrude Stein, Marty Martin
Buried Child, Sam Shepard

Productions 1979/80:

Reunion, David Mamet
Hamlet, William Shakespeare
Mary Stuart, Friedrich Schiller
Innocent Thoughts, Harmless Intentions, John Hever
Back in the Race, Milan Stitt
The Wool Gatherer, William Mastrosimone

Special Programs: Internships; post-performance lectures; Projects-in-Progress series; Circle Lab—an exploratory developmental workshop; theatre rentals (summer only); cooperative programs with other not-for-profit regional theatres.

GETTING THERE:

Subway: Seventh Avenue IRT 1 to Christopher Street; IND A, AA, B, CC, D, E, F to West 4th Street, Washington Square.

Bus: Uptown: Sixth Avenue (M6, M10); Downtown: Seventh Avenue (M10); Crosstown West: 9th and Christopher Streets (M13); Crosstown East: 8th and Christopher Streets (M13).

Parking: Street parking difficult; nearest garage three blocks south at corner of Morton Street and Seventh Avenue South.

RESERVING SEATS:

Box Office Telephone: (212) 924-7100

Ticket Price: $10.00–$12.00; TDF vouchers not accepted. Student and senior citizen rush discount.

Reservations: Call theatre—reservations made the day of performance held until a half hour before curtain; reservations made during the week of performance held until two hours before curtain; reservations made more than a week in advance must be picked up at least one day before performance. Box office opens at 1:00 P.M., Tuesday through Sunday.

Group Rates: Available, contact the theatre.

Subscription: Six major productions at reduced rates, free admission to Projects-in-Progress, discounts to special musical events and commercial transfers of Rep productions.

Performance Schedule: Six major productions presented October through June. Evenings: Tuesday through Sunday; Matinees: Sunday. Five or six Projects-in-Progress presented for four performances each. Staged readings presented each Friday.

CIRCLE REPERTORY COMPANY RECOMMENDS:

Le Jules Verne: 189 West 10th Street, between West 4th and Bleecker Streets, 929-9400. Reservations accepted. French. 6:00 P.M. till 10:30 P.M., seven days. Sunday Brunch: noon till 4:30 P.M. $9.50–$18.00, a la carte. MC, Visa, Diner's, and Amex accepted.

Claudio's: 289 Bleecker Street, on the corner of Seventh Avenue, 242-4889. Reservations recommended. Italian. Sunday through Thursday: 5:30 P.M. till 11:30 P.M.; Friday and Saturday: 5:30 P.M. till 12:30 A.M.; Saturday and Sunday Brunch: noon till 3:30 P.M. $10.00–

$15.00, a la carte; Brunch: $5.00. Visa, Diner's, Amex accepted. Chamber music at brunch.

Blue Mill Tavern: 50 Commerce Street, between Seventh Avenue and Hudson Street, 243-7114. American-Portuguese. Lunch: Monday through Friday, noon till 2:00 P.M.; dinner: 5:00 P.M. till 9:30 P.M.; Saturday Dinner: 5:00 P.M. till 10:30 P.M. Closed Sunday. $4.95–$6.95, a la carte. All credit cards accepted.

The Lion's Head: 59 Christopher Street, between Sixth and Seventh Avenues, 929-0670. Reservations accepted. Continental. Noon till 4:00 A.M., seven days. Kitchen closes at 2:30 A.M. $3.00–$11.00, a la carte. Visa, MC, Diner's, Amex accepted.

Blazing Salads: 228 West 4th Street, just off Seventh Avenue, 929-3432. Reservations accepted. American, salads. Monday through Thursday: noon till Midnight; Friday through Sunday: noon till 1:00 A.M. $2.25–$6.95, a la carte. No credit cards accepted.

Each of the above restaurants provides a discount to CRC subscribers.

WHO: CITHAERON

Artistic Director: Steven Brant
Managing Director: Jorie MacKinnon
Founders: Mara Beckerman, Steven Brant, Marietta Pucillo; 1974

WHERE:

Theatre Address: Performs in various locations.
Office Address:
154 26th Street
Brooklyn, New York
(212) 768-3761

The Space: Cithaeron performs in various locations, always constructing a totally-new, environmental setting for each production. For example, in *Macbeth*, twenty-nine spectators sat around a single ring only twenty-feet across and looked down upon the sloping sides of a pit in which the action took place. *Waiting for Godot* was played on a long narrow strip of "road," with the spectators looking down from balconies. In *The Caucasian Chalk Circle*, spatial division between performer and audience territories was eradicated as the audience followed the performers from scene to scene through a multi-level environment.

WHAT:

Artistic Profile: Cithaeron takes its name from the holy mountain outside Athens where the rituals of Dionysus were celebrated and finally reached such a degree of complexity that a division between spectator and performer was introduced. The exploration of this separation between spectator and performer, and of the mythic aspects of drama, is integral to Cithaeron's aesthetic. Their work involves both the reexamination of classics through intimate environmental stagings as well as multimedia, non-narrative theatre pieces based on important cultural texts. A core group of designers, directors, musicians, filmmakers and video artists collaboratively develop each production through long-term exploratory workshops.

Productions 1978/79:

Workshops—no formal performances

Productions 1979/80:

The Three Christs of Ypsilanti, script by Steven Brant and Jorie MacKinnon; group-developed

Lilith, script by Jorie MacKinnon; group-developed

Vachel Lindsay, conceived by Dennis Thread

The Life and Death of King Richard II, Steven Brant's adaptation of William Shakespeare's play

Special Programs: Company workshop—open to the public one night per week; local touring.

GETTING THERE:

Contact the office for current performing location and directions.

RESERVING SEATS:

Box Office Telephone: (212) 768-3761
Ticket Price: $3.50–$5.00 or TDF voucher.
Reservations: Call theatre, phone reservations accepted.
Group Rates: Available for groups of fifteen or more.
Performance Schedule: Variable.

WHO: THE CLASSIC THEATRE

Executive Producer: Nicholas John Stathis
Artistic Director: Maurice Edwards
Founder: Sala Staw; 1961

WHERE:

Neighborhood: West Village
Theatre Address:
114 West 14th Street (between Sixth and Seventh Avenues)
New York, New York 10011
(212) 929-8033

The Space: The Classic Theatre is a welcome new tenant on 14th Street—a block that can only be described as baroque, with its ever-active merchants hustling wares, fast-food stands, and ethnic restaurants. The company has just completed an impressive renovation of a second-floor space, turning it into an intimate 75-seat proscenium theatre with a comfortable lobby space.

WHAT:

Artistic Profile: The Classic Theatre presents outstanding but neglected works from the world repertory of classics as well as worthy new plays. Founded in 1961 by the late Sala Staw as a "theatre for the poor," the company began by presenting Shakespeare in modern dress at New York City libraries. Over the years productions have included plays by Strindberg, Turgenev, Euripides,

Jonson, and Büchner. In the future the company also plans to produce poetry readings, dance concerts, musical recitals, and chamber operas.

Productions 1977/78:

Charles II, or The Merry Monarch, John Howard Payne and Washington Irving
Bremen Coffee, Rainer Werner Fassbinder
The Country Gentleman, Sir Robert Howard Villiers
The Malcontent, John Marston
Saturday Adoption, Ron Cowen

Productions 1978/79:

Pygmalion, George Bernard Shaw

Productions 1979/80:

Notes from Underground, Part I, Fyodor Dostoyevsky
Journey's End, R. C. Sherriff
The Bachelor, Ivan Turgenev
More Stately Mansions, Eugene O'Neill
Beckett, Alfred Lord Tennyson
Love Affairs and Wedding Bells, Johann Nestroy

GETTING THERE:

Subway: BMT LL (Canarsie 14th Street Line) to Sixth Avenue; IND B, F to 14th Street; PATH train to 14th Street.
Bus: Uptown: Sixth Avenue (M6); Downtown: Seventh Avenue (M10); Crosstown West and East: 14th Street (M14).
Parking: Lots available on 13th Street.

RESERVING SEATS:

Box Office Telephone: (212) 242-3900
Ticket Price: $3.00 or TDF voucher. Student discount, $2.00.
Reservations: Call theatre, held until ten minutes prior to curtain.
Group Rates: Available, contact the theatre.
Performance Schedule: Five or six productions presented September through June. Evenings: Thursday through Sunday.

THE CLASSIC THEATRE RECOMMENDS:

Spain Restaurant: 113 West 13th Street, between Sixth and Seventh Avenues, 929-9580. Reservations accepted. Noon till 1:00 A.M., seven days. Lunch: $3.75–$7.00, a la carte; Dinner: $4.85–$10.00, a la carte. No credit cards accepted.

San Francisco Plum: 544 Sixth Avenue on the corner of 15th Street, 924-9125. Reservations recommended for large parties. American-Continental. 11:00 A.M. till 3:00 A.M., seven days. Kitchen closes at 2:00 A.M. Brunch: Saturday and Sunday, noon till 5:00 P.M.; Lunch: $3.50–$6.50, a la carte; Dinner: $3.50–$7.50, a la carte. All credit cards accepted.

WHO: COLONNADES THEATRE LAB

Artistic Director: Michael Lessac
Managing Director: Mary T. Nealon
Founder: Michael Lessac; 1974

WHERE:

Neighborhood: Noho–East Village
Theatre Address:
428 Lafayette Street
New York, New York 10003
(212) 598-4620

The Space: Colonnades Theatre Lab's space is located in a landmark building that once housed the Jacob Astor Mansion. Later converted to a warehouse, the space was claimed by CTL and literally went up on the company's back, as company members—in between rehearsals—cleared out the rubble and replaced interior pillars with steel girders. A large, handsome foyer (also used as a rehearsal space) retains the building's former elegance and adjoins a 75-seat flexible space.

WHAT:

Artistic Profile: To provide a permanent home for a resident acting company and to be able to pay these actors a living wage—essentially a regional theatre in the middle of New York City—was the founding purpose of Colonnades Theatre Lab. While currently working with a more flexible, larger company of regular actors, CTL continues to work towards this financially taxing but artistically important goal. Critical successes in recent years range from *Molière in Spite of Himself*, an intensely dramatic study of power, seduction, and corruption, to *Guests of the Nation* and *The Irish Hebrew Lesson*, two one-acts that emphasize the conflicts one confronts in a revolutionary struggle. The company is expanding its activities to include First Draft Theatre (a developmental series for new plays), a chamber music theatre ensemble, and hopefully a larger space.

Productions 1978/79:

Molière in Spite of Himself, adaptation by Michael Lessac from Mikhail Bulgakov's *A Cabal of Hypocrites*.

The Ballroom in St. Patrick's Cathedral, Lou Phillips

Productions 1979/80:

Shakespeare's Cabaret, lyrics by William Shakespeare; music by Lance Mulcahy; conceived by Michael Lessac

Guests of the Nation, adapted by Neil McKenzie from a short story by Frank O'Connor

The Irish Hebrew Lesson, Wolf Mankowitz

Molière in Spite of Himself, adaptation by Michael Lessac from Mikhail Bulgakov's *A Cabal of Hypocrites*

Keystone, group-developed

Special Programs: Professional training in acting, production and administration; internships; teaching residencies; national touring; workshop productions and staged readings; theatre rentals.

GETTING THERE:

Subway: Lexington Avenue IRT 6 to Astor Place; BMT RR to 8th Street; BMT B, D, F to Broadway/Lafayette Street.

Bus: Uptown: Third Avenue (M101, M102); Downtown: Broadway (M6, M7) and Fifth Avenue (M5); Crosstown East: 8th Street (M13); Crosstown West: 9th Street (M13).

Parking: Street parking after 6:00 P.M.; nearest lot next door.

RESERVING SEATS:

Box Office Telephone: (212) 673-2222

Ticket Price: $5.00–$11.00, TDF voucher accepted. Discounts for students and senior citizens.

Reservations: Tickets must be paid for twenty-four hours in advance. Phone reservations accepted the day of performance and held until one hour before curtain.

Group Rates: Available, contact theatre.

Performance Schedule: Approximately two or three productions presented September through June. Each production runs at least one month. Evenings: Wednesday through Saturday; Matinees: Saturday, Sunday.

COLONNADES THEATRE LAB RECOMMENDS:

Pirandello's: 7 Washington Place, on the corner of Mercer Street, 260-3066. Reservations accepted. Northern Italian. 5:30 P.M. till 11:30 P.M. Closed Sunday. $6.00–$12.00, a la carte. Amex accepted.

WHO: CSC REPERTORY

Artistic Director: Christopher Martin

Executive Director: Dennis Turner

General Manager: Alberto Tore

Founder: Christopher Martin; 1967

WHERE:

Neighborhood: Noho–East Village

Theatre Address:

136 East 13th Street (between Third and Fourth Avenues)

New York, New York 10003

(212) 477-5808

The Space: CSC Repertory is one of the most beautifully designed theatres in all of the city, a jewel tucked away on an East Village street of warehouses and small stores. There's nothing makeshift or improvisational about its stylishly decorated lobby where there's ample seating, a long wooden bar, hanging plants, and streamlined graphics decorating deep brown and white brick walls. A spacious 200-seat theatre offers all the comforts of an uptown theatre, while its large thrust stage insures that an atmosphere of intimacy remains.

WHAT:

Artistic Profile: Classics in the present tense is the artistic imperative that governs the work of CSC Repertory. The Company focuses on rarely performed classics and new plays by foreign authors. Productions are intended to recreate the play's original impact for contemporary American audiences. With its ensemble company performing five plays in rotating repertory, CSC provides playgoers with the opportunity to see several compelling classics within the same week. The maintenance of a dialogue with major European theatres has also been an important concern of CSC since its inception.

Productions 1978/79:
Richard II, William Shakespeare
Henry IV, Part I, William Shakespeare
Henry IV, Part II, William Shakespeare
Wild Oats, John O'Keeffe
The Marquis of Keith, Frank Wedekind; translated by Christopher Martin

Productions 1979/80:
Cuchulain, the Warrior King, William Butler Yeats
The Cavern, Jean Anouilh
Dr. Faustus, Christopher Marlowe
Don Juan, Molière
The Merchant of Venice, William Shakespeare
Leonce and Lena, Georg Büchner
A Baloon Will Rise, Karen Sunde

Special Programs: Workshop productions; staged readings; internships; post-performance lectures.

GETTING THERE:

Subway: Lexington Avenue IRT 4, 5, 6 to Union Square/ 14th Street; BMT N, QB, RR, LL (Canarsie) to Union Square/14th Street.

Bus: Uptown: Third Avenue (M101, M102); Downtown: Fifth Avenue (M1) via Park Avenue South and Fourth Avenue; Crosstown West and East: 14th Street (M14).

Parking: Street parking after 6:00 P.M.; two lots on the block.

RESERVING SEATS:

Box Office Telephone: (212) 677-4210

Ticket Price: $7.95–$9.95, TDF vouchers not accepted. Half-price, student-rush tickets available.

Reservations: Accepted, tickets held until fifteen minutes before curtain.

Group Rates: Available, contact the theatre.

Subscription: Series of five plays at a discount.

Performance Schedule: Five major productions plus workshop productions presented October through May. Evenings: Tuesday through Sunday; Matinees: Saturday, Sunday. Free public playreadings presented the first Monday of each month.

CSC REPERTORY RECOMMENDS:

The Cedar Tavern: 82 University Place, between 11th and 12th Streets, 929-9089. Reservations accepted. American. Noon till 1:30 A.M., seven days. $2.50–$9.75, a la carte. No credit cards accepted.

Dumpling House: 207 Second Avenue, on the corner of 13th Street, 473-8557. Reservations accepted. Szechuan-Mandarin. Lunch: 11:00 A.M. till 3:00 P.M.; Dinner: 5:00 P.M. till 10:30 P.M., seven days. Lunch: $3.50–$8.00; Dinner: $6.00–$8.00, a la carte. All major credit cards accepted.

Dardanelles Armenian Restaurant: 86 University Place, between 11th and 12th Streets, 242-8990. Reservations recommended. Armenian, seafood. Lunch: noon till 2:30 P.M.; Dinner: 4:30 P.M. till midnight, Monday through Friday. $5.95–$8.95, a la carte. All credit cards accepted.

WHO: DIRECT THEATRE

Artistic Director: Allen R. Belknap
Founder: Allen R. Belknap; 1974

WHERE:

Neighborhood: Performs in various locations
Office Address:
115 West 77th Street, #4R
New York, New York 10024
(212) 362-0657

WHAT:

Artistic Profile: Direct Theatre quickly developed from a laboratory workshop, founded in 1971 when Artistic Director Allen Belknap was a professor at Hunter College, into a company that has been instrumental in developing and producing new American playwrights. Christopher Durang, Albert Innaurato, Dennis McIntyre, and Tom Thomas have all participated in the theatre's playwrights-in-residence program, producing works such as Durang's *Titanic* and *Das Lusitania Songspiel*, written with Sigourney Weaver; Innaurato's Obie Award winning *The Transfiguration of Benno Blimpie*; and McIntyre's *Modigliani*, all of which later moved to Off Broadway. *Modigliani* is slated to become a major feature film directed by Herbert Ross and starring Al Pacino. Direct Theatre is also committed to bridging the gap between university training and the professional theatre and is forming an intern company which will perform the classics. In addition, the company produces an annual International Directors' Festival which hosts more than fifty productions from all over the world.
Productions 1978/79:
Approaching Zero, adapted from Georg Kaiser's *The GAS Trilogy* by Thom Thomas
The Nature and Purpose of the Universe, Christopher Durang
Jaywalkin', lyrics by Fran Landesman; music by Jason McAuliffe

Productions 1979/80:
International Directors' Festival
The Interview, Thom Thomas
The Golden Fleece, A. R. Gurney, Jr. (New York Deaf Theatre Production)

RESERVING SEATS:

Box Office Telephone: (212) 580-1514
Ticket Price: $8.00, TDF voucher accepted.
Reservations: Call theatre, tickets held until fifteen minutes prior to curtain.
Group Rates: $5.00 for groups of twenty or more.
Performance Schedule: Four productions, including Directors' Festival presented September through June. Evenings: Wednesday through Sunday; Matinees: Saturday, Sunday.

WHO: FREDERICK DOUGLASS CREATIVE ARTS CENTER

President and Artistic Director: Fred Hudson
Administrator and Associate Producer: Hector Lino
Founders: Budd Schulberg, Fred Hudson; 1971

WHERE:

Theatre Address: Performs in various locations
Office Address:
276 West 43rd Street
New York, New York 10036
(212) 944-9870

WHAT:

Artistic Profile: The Frederick Douglass Creative Arts Center (FDCAC) developed as an outgrowth of the acclaimed Watts Writers' Workshop, begun in Los Angeles in 1965 by author Budd Schulberg. Under the direction of playwright and screenwriter Fred Hudson, the Center offers professional training in all forms of creative writing—playwriting, screenwriting, poetry. In addition, a performing ensemble, a Black Actors' Lab, and film workshops are integral to the Center's program. FDCAC aims to bring professional theatre to the community *from* the community, develop black writers, and place artists in positions of economic viability. Through its showcase productions, FDCAC works to gain greater exposure for black writers. Works developed at the Center subsequently have been produced by the New York Shakespeare Festival, KCET-TV, La Mama E.T.C., the Negro Ensemble Company, the American Place Theatre, Theatre Genesis, New Heritage Theatre, and the Manhattan Theatre Club.

Productions 1978/79:

Crucificado, Edgar White
Emily-T, Dan Owens
Transcendental Blues, Aisha Rahman
Sandra Lane, Dan Owens

Productions 1979/80:

Trio, Rudy Gray
Fraudulent Claims, Joseph Barnes
Mary Goldstein and the Author, Oyano
Miss Ann Don't Cry No More, Pat Gibson
The More You Get the More You Want, book by Dan Owens; music and lyrics by Johnny Brandon

Special Programs: Actors' workshop; playwright workshop; media workshops; poetry workshops; quarterly magazine—*American Rag*; staged readings; internships.

GETTING THERE:

Call theatre for current performing location and directions.

RESERVING SEATS:

Box Office Telephone: (212) 944-9870

Ticket Price: \$5.00–\$6.00, TDF voucher accepted. Special discounts for student groups.

Reservations: Call the office; tickets are held until a half hour before curtain. Advance sale tickets are available through the office.

Group Rates: $1.00 off the ticket price for groups of ten or more.

Performance Schedule: Approximately four-to-six full productions plus staged readings presented October through June. Evenings: Tuesday through Sunday; Matinees: Sunday.

WHO: DRAMA COMMITTEE REPERTORY THEATRE

Artistic Director: Arthur Reel
Founders: Arthur Reel, Zachery Silver, Laura Darius; 1975

WHERE:

Neighborhood: Performs in various locations
Theatre Address:
c/o Arthur Reel
118 West 79th Street
New York, New York 10024
(212) 595-1733

WHAT:

Artistic Profile: Operating year-round in rotating repertory, the Drama Committee Repertory Theatre produces as many as twenty-five plays per year, mounting seldom seen classics and creating and producing dramatizations from world literature. Conrad's *Heart of Darkness*, Voltaire's *Candide*, and Gogol's *Dead Souls* are just a few of the literary classics dramatized by Artistic Director Arthur Reel, a recipient of the 1980 National Endowment for the Arts Award to Playwrights. With its marathon of theatre activity, the theatre provides opportunities for over 300 theatre artists each year. Committed to educating and entertaining, the company presented a series of never or rarely seen early American plays during the 1980 season.

Productions 1979:

Heart of Darkness, Joseph Conrad; adapted by Arthur Reel
An Ideal Husband, Oscar Wilde
The League of Youth, Henrik Ibsen
A Body in Every Bed, Frieda Horowitz
Candide, Voltaire; adapted by Arthur Reel
The Birds, Aristophanes
Bartleby the Scrivener, Herman Melville; adapted by Syms Wyeth and Sharon Dennis
Dead Souls, Nikolai Gogol; adapted by Arthur Reel
The Terrorist, Arthur Reel
Miss Stanwyck Is Still in Hiding, Larry Puchall and Reigh Hagen
Lady Windemere's Fan, Oscar Wilde
Major Barbara, George Bernard Shaw
She Stoops to Conquer, Oliver Goldsmith
The Doctor in Spite of Himself, Molière
Overruled, George Bernard Shaw
Two One-Acts:
Tinker's Wedding, John Millington Synge
The Anniversary, Anton Chekov
The Doctor's Dilemma, George Bernard Shaw
The Jew and the Lion, Maxim Gorky; adapted by Arthur Reel
Whorehouse, Anton Chekov; adapted by Arthur Reel
You Never Can Tell, George Bernard Shaw
Uncle Vanya, Anton Chekov
Variable Lengths, William E. Hunt
Ward 6, Anton Chekov; adapted by Arthur Reel

Productions 1980:

A Woman of No Importance, Oscar Wilde
The Doctor's Dilemma, George Bernard Shaw
The Philanderer, George Bernard Shaw
The Great Divide, William Vaughan Moody
The Mulligan Guard Ball, Edward Harrigan
Heartbreak House, George Bernard Shaw
Candide, Voltaire; adapted by Arthur Reel
William Dean Howells One Acts, William Dean Howells
Captain Brassbound's Conversion, George Bernard Shaw
An Ideal Husband, Oscar Wilde
A Glance at New York, Benjamin Baker

The Bitter Enemies, Anton Chekov; adapted by Arthur Reel
Mrs. Warren's Profession, George Bernard Shaw
Masque of the Red Death, Edgar Allan Poe; adapted by Arthur Reel
Getting Married, George Bernard Shaw
The Climbers, Clyde Fitch
Wall Street, Richard Mead
Great Diamond Robbery, Alfriend & Wheeler
The Secret Sharer, Joseph Conrad; adapted by Arthur Reel
The American, Henry James
Sherlock Holmes, William Gillette
Heart of Darkness, Joseph Conrad
10 Nights in a Barroom, W. H. Pratt

Special Programs: Acting workshops; internships.

GETTING THERE:

Contact the office for current performing location and directions.

RESERVING SEATS:

Box Office Telephone: (212) 595-1733
Ticket Price: $4.00 weekdays; $5.00 weekends; TDF voucher accepted. Senior citizens and students, $3.00 weekdays; $4.00 Friday and Sunday.
Reservations: Call theatre, tickets held until fifteen minutes prior to curtain.
Group Rates: Available for groups of twenty or more.
Performance Schedule: Performances presented year-round in rotating repertory.

WHO: ENCOMPASS THEATRE

Artistic Director: Nancy Rhodes
Producing Director: Roger Cunningham
Founders: Nancy Rhodes, Roger Cunningham; 1975

WHERE:

Theatre Address: Performs in various locations.
Office Address:
2 Times Square
New York, New York 10036
(212) 575-1558
Mailing Address:
P.O. Box 229
New York, New York 10036

WHAT:

Artistic Profile: You don't have to go to Lincoln Center for opera—there's another, often overlooked, distinctive American operatic tradition that Encompass Theatre is exploring through its presentation of adventurous, vital productions. The company focuses on small-scale, intimate American operas and contemporary music-theatre. To demystify opera and give new music-theatre a striking presentation is the company's aim, and its productions have included Virgil Thompson's and Gertrude Stein's *The Mother of Us All*—the first American opera; Aaron Copland's *The Tender Land*, Marc Blitzstein's *Regina*, as well as contemporary, avant-garde productions.

Productions 1978/79:
Regina, Marc Blitzstein
Porch, Jeffrey Sweet
A Threat of Scarlett, Ella Gerber and Harold Richardson
Fantasies Take Flight (six short operas)
A Hand of Bridge, book by Gian-Carlo Menotti; music by Samuel Barber
Frustration, Sheldon Harnick
Satisfaction, Charles Strouse
Introductions and Goodbyes, book by Gian-Carlo Menotti; music by Samuel Barber
Mr. and Mrs. Diskobobolous, music by Peter Westergaard, from a poem by Edward Lear
The Four Note Opera, Tom Johnson
The Wise Woman, Carl Orff

Productions 1979/80:

A Postcard from Morocco, Domenick Argento

Elizabeth and Essex, book by Michael Stewart and Mark Bramble; music by Douglas Katsaros; lyrics by Richard Enquist

Der Vampyr, Heinrich Marshner; new translation by Michael Feingold; new orchestration by Jack Gaughan

Special Programs: Composer and librettist workshop; internships; touring.

RESERVING SEATS:

Box Office Telephone: (212) 575-1558

Ticket Price: $10.00 or TDF voucher plus surcharge. Students and senior citizens, $6.00.

Reservations: Call office for reservation policy.

Group Rates: $6.00 for groups of at least twenty.

Subscription: Pass to three music-theatre events at a discount.

Performance Schedule: Variable.

WHO: ENSEMBLE STUDIO THEATRE (E.S.T.)

Artistic Director: Curt Dempster

Founder: Curt Dempster; 1971

WHERE:

Neighborhood: Clinton

Theatre Address:

549 West 52nd Street (between Tenth and Eleventh Avenues)
New York, New York 10019
(212) 247-4982

The Space: Large warehouses, open parking lots, old houses—at first glance West 52nd Street gives little promise of cultural activity. But on the second and sixth floors of a large city-owned warehouse building, Ensemble Studio Theatre has not only created two performing spaces—a 90-seat theatre and a small workshop space—but also has established an environment of vital creative activity that theatre artists can call home.

WHAT:

Artistic Profile: The Ensemble Studio Theatre is a membership organization consisting of over 200 playwrights, actors, directors, designers, and technicians. Dedicated to developing new works for the stage and providing artistic and financial support to the individual theatre artist, E.S.T.'s principal programs include a Major Production Series of five new American plays; ten to fifteen workshop productions and forty to fifty playreadings; a Playwrights Unit in which twenty-five participating writers meet regularly to present works in progress and discuss craft problems; a Theatre Bank, providing financial support in the form of production-related expenses, commissions, emergency grants, and loans; a Summer Theatre Colony at the Barlow School in upstate New York; and the Ensemble Studio Institute for Professional Training. Since 1978 the revitalization of the one-act, through an annual spring Marathon, has been an important artistic concern of the theatre.

Productions 1978/79:

End of the War, Vincent Canby
"Three":
Bicycle Boys, Peter Maloney
Playing Dolls, Susan Nanus
Buddy Pals, Neil Cuthbert
"A Special Evening":
The Man with the Flower in His Mouth, Luigi Pirandello
The Old Tune, Robert Pinget; adapted by Samuel Beckett
Welfare, Marcia Haufrecht
Marathon 1979, thirteen one-act plays

Productions 1979/80:

The Invitational: A celebration of the one-act play.
Tennessee, Romulus Linney

The Pushcart Peddlers, Murray Schisgal
Sister Mary Ignatius Explains It All For You, Christopher Durang
Shoeshine, David Mamet
The Laundromat, Marsha Norman
Life Boat Drill, Tennessee Williams
The Perfect Stranger, Neil Cuthbert
What's So Beautiful about a Sunset over Prairie Avenue?, Edward Allan Baker
Marathon 1980, a series of one-act plays.

Special Programs: Ensemble Studio Theatre Institute—professional classes in acting, directing, playwriting; playwrights unit; actors unit; cold Shakespeare readings; post-performance discussions; music series; script library.

GETTING THERE:

Subway: IND AA, CC, E to 50th Street.

Bus: Uptown: Tenth Avenue (M11); Downtown: Ninth Avenue (M11); Crosstown West: 49th Street (M27); Crosstown East: 50th Street (M27).

Parking: Street parking; nearest lot on 52nd Street, directly across the street.

RESERVING SEATS:

Box Office Telephone: (212) 247-4982

Ticket Price: $4.00–$6.00, TDF voucher accepted. Discounts for students and senior citizens. Half-price tickets for previews.

Reservations: Call the theatre, tickets held until a half hour before curtain.

Group Rates: Available for groups larger than ten. Contact the theatre.

Subscription: Available, contact the theatre.

Performance Schedule: Five major productions, fifteen workshops, readings, and special events presented October through June. Evenings: Wednesday through Sunday; Matinees: Saturday.

ENSEMBLE STUDIO THEATRE RECOMMENDS:

Landmark Tavern: Corner of Eleventh Avenue and 46th Street, 757-8595. Reservations suggested. American-Irish. Weekdays: noon till midnight; Weekends: noon till 1:00 A.M.; Lunch: $3.00–$8.00, a la carte; Dinner: $5.00–$14.00, a la carte. No credit cards accepted.

B.J.'s Saloon: 736 Tenth Avenue, at 50th Street, 581-4244. Reservations required for large parties only. Burgers, soups. 11:30 A.M. till midnight, seven days. Saturday and Sunday brunch. $1.75–$4.25, a la carte. No credit cards accepted.

Tyson's: 755 Ninth Avenue, at the corner of 51st Street, 397-9027. Reservations accepted. American. 11:00 A.M. till 4:00 A.M., seven days. Kitchen closes at 1:00 A.M. Sunday brunch. $2.25–$10.00, a la carte. MC, Visa, Amex accepted. Piano: 6:30 P.M.; Jazz: 11:00 P.M.; Talent Showcase: 9:00 P.M., Thursdays.

WHO: FANTASY FACTORY

Artistic Director: Bill Vitale
Playwright-in-Residence: Ed Kuczewski
Founder: Bill Vitale; 1975

WHERE:

Neighborhood: Clinton–Theatre Row
Theatre Address:

524 West 42nd Street (between Tenth and Eleventh Avenues)
New York, New York 10036
(212) 575-9654

The Space: Fantasy Factory is located on 42nd Street, just west of the string of newly renovated theatres known as Theatre Row. The company uses the first floor auditorium space of the neighborhood's day-care center as its performing space.

WHAT:

Artistic Profile: Fantasy Factory was founded by a group of actors who decided to write and produce their own material rather than spend their time at endless audition line-ups. With $10,000 Artistic Director Bill Vitale had won on a TV quiz show, the company produced its first original musical, *A Mass Murder in the Balcony of the Old Ritz Rialto.* In addition to winning the NEA Musical Theatre Competition, the work moved to Off Broadway and was presented by the Santa Fe Theatre and Opera Festivals. Producing Brechtian-style, original musicals, new plays, and children's shows, the company's work has ranged from *My Child,* a musical based on slave child Phyllis Wheatley's life, to a musical version of *King Kong.* The company prides itself on being the champion of the underdog, employing people of all ages, ethnic groups, and social backgrounds—animals too, in productions that celebrate this diversity.

Productions 1978/79:

Hot Voodoo Massage, music and lyrics by Bill Vitale and Ed Kuczewski

Like the Song Says, Ed Kuczewski

Indulgences, Ed Kuczewski, Bill Vitale, and Richard Foltz

My Child, book, music, and lyrics by Ben Finn

Attachments, Ed Kuczewski

Productions 1979/80:

Animals Are People Too, book by Mary Bloom; music and lyrics by Bill Vitale

B.V.D.'s, Bill Vitale, Donna Lee Betz, Gary Deaton

Ape over Broadway, book by Andrew Herz; music by Steve Ross; lyrics by Bill Vitale

Special Programs: Children's shows; internships; classes for children and adults; theatre rentals; touring.

GETTING THERE:

Subway: IND A, AA, CC, E to 42nd Street.

Bus: Uptown: Tenth Avenue (M11, M16); Downtown: Ninth Avenue (M11); Crosstown West and East: 42nd Street (M106).

Parking: Street parking after 7:00 P.M.; nearest garage at Manhattan Plaza.

RESERVING SEATS:

Box Office Telephone: (212) 575-9654
Ticket Price: $3.50–$5.00, TDF voucher not accepted.
Reservations: Call theatre, tickets held until fifteen minutes prior to curtain.
Group Rates: Available for groups of ten or more. Contact the theatre for rates.
Performance Schedule: Variable schedule of performances throughout the year.

FANTASY FACTORY RECOMMENDS:

West Bank Cafe: 407 West 42nd Street in Manhattan Plaza, 695-6909. Reservations required 6:00 P.M.–8:00 P.M. American-Continental-Oriental. Monday through Saturday: noon till 1:00 A.M.; Sunday: noon till 11:00 P.M.; Lunch: $2.50–$4.25, a la carte; Dinner: $4.25–$8.75, a la carte. MC, Visa, Amex accepted. Jazz, Big Bands, Comedy, Singers, Broadway Personalities: Tuesday through Saturday at 8:30 P.M. and 10:30 P.M.
Hell's Kitchen: 598 Ninth Avenue, on the corner of 43rd Street, 757-5329. Reservations accepted. American. Noon till Midnight, seven days. Brunch: Saturday and Sunday, 12:30 P.M. till 4:30 P.M. $3.00–$9.00, a la carte. Diner's, Carte Blanche, Amex accepted.

WHO: FIRST ALL CHILDREN'S THEATRE

Artistic Director: Meridee Stein
Business Manager: Thomas Fordham
Founder: Meridee Stein; 1969

WHERE:

Neighborhood: Upper West Side
Theatre Address:
37 West 65th Street (between Columbus Avenue and Central Park West)
New York, New York 10023
(212) 873-6400

The Space: On a smaller scale, First All Children's Theatre is every bit as much a performing arts center as its neighbor, Lincoln Center. The theatre's entrance is marked only by a small, colorful shingle that hangs outside an office building, but a quick elevator ride to the second floor reveals an impressive theatre complex. A spacious, comfortable lobby, decorated with production photos and energized by the constant presence of children, adjoins a 180-seat theatre with a thrust stage.

WHAT:

Artistic Profile: First All Children's Theatre (First ACT) presents shows for young audiences by casts of children belonging to its two interracial companies, the Meri-Mini Players (ages six to thirteen) and the Teen Company (ages fourteen to seventeen). Dedicated to the highest standards of professional theatre, First ACT also serves as a training center for young performers and a catalyst for writers, composers, and lyricists. Each season five original musicals are produced, ranging from renowned playwright-composer Elizabeth Swados' *The Incredible Feeling Show*, to *Clever Jack and the Magic Beanstalk*—a fast, funny version of a well-known children's tale, to a forthcoming work by Charles Strouse (composer of the Broadway musical *Annie*). The company has appeared at the New York Shakespeare Festival's Public Theatre; at the O'Neill Center and the Annenberg Center for Communications; on all three major television networks; on the international telecast that inaugurated the International Year of the Child in 1979; and with the Belgian Company of Young Performers at Lincoln Center and in Washington, D.C. The theatre also actively engages in community outreach programs.

Productions 1978/79:

Three Tales at a Time, C. Crisman, S. Dias, M. Kaplowitz, M. Stein, J. Thomas, D. Kalvert, and D. Nelson

Alice Through the Looking Glass, book by Susan Dias and Meridee Stein; music by Phillip Namanworth; lyrics by Susan Dias

The Pushcart Fables, book by Betsy Shevey; music and lyrics by Judie Thomas

Clever Jack and the Magic Beanstalk, book by Ian Elliot and Meridee Stein; music and lyrics by Judie Thomas and John Forster

The Incredible Feeling Show, book, music, and lyrics by Elizabeth Swados

Productions 1979/80:

Clever Jack and the Magic Beanstalk

Alice Through the Looking Glass

The Incredible Feeling Show

Grown-Ups, Vickey Blumenthal and John Forster; book consultant: M. Stein

Special Programs: Professional training in acting, production, and administration—children admitted to the company by interview-audition devote up to thirty hours a week to after-school and weekend rehearsals and performances; summer workshops open to the public; internships; teacher training seminars; anthology of original plays and musical scores (Bantam Books).

GETTING THERE:

Subway: Seventh Avenue IRT 1 to 66th Street.

Bus: Uptown: Eighth Avenue (Central Park West) (M10); Downtown: Columbus Avenue (M7, M11) and Broadway (M104).

Parking: Street parking on weekends; nearest lot at Lincoln Center.

RESERVING SEATS:

Box Office Telephone: (212) 873-6400

Ticket Price: $4.00 or TDF voucher.

Reservations: Call theatre, tickets held until fifteen minutes before curtain.

Group Rates: $3.75 for groups of ten or more.

Performance Schedule: Approximately five original musicals presented October through May, Saturday and Sunday, at 2:00 P.M. and 4:00 P.M.

FIRST ALL CHILDREN'S THEATRE RECOMMENDS:

The Saloon: 1920 Broadway, at the corner of 64th Street, 874-1500. Reservations recommended. American. 11:30 A.M.–4:00 A.M., seven days. Kitchen closes at 2:00 A.M. $3.00–$11.00, a la carte. All credit cards except Carte Blanche accepted.

WHO: FORCE 13 THEATRE COMPANY

Artistic Director: Bill Patton
Managing Director: Margery Dignan
Founders: Bill Patton, Margery Dignan, Morrie Piersol; 1978

WHERE:

Neighborhood: West Village
Theatre Address:
43 West 13th Street (between Fifth and Sixth Avenues)
New York, New York 10011
(212) 924-7277
The Space: For anyone interested in architectural renovation, a visit to Force 13 Theatre is a must. In the heart of Greenwich Village the company has converted the first floor of a loft building—now housing luxury apartments—into a flexible, open loft space which creatively exploits the eccentric angles and configurations of the space.

WHAT:

Artistic Profile: Cartwheels, splits, rolls, and balances—Force 13 Theatre Company fuses acrobatic movement with the disciplines of acting, mime, and music. In an effort to revive the spirit of collaboration between the physical and performing arts, this unique approach is used to 1) reinterpret well-known plays (for example, in Jean-Claude van Itallie's *Interview* the ordinary language of the interview situation is translated into stylized acrobatic movement); and 2) to develop original works which incorporate music, mime, acrobatic movement, and dance. Of special interest is the theatre's wine and cheese cabaret evenings.

Productions 1979/80:

Acrobats, Israel Horowitz

Interview, Jean-Claude van Itallie; music by Margery Dignan

The Ballad of Bernie Babcock, book by Bill Patton; music by Margery Dignan

Special Programs: Wine and cheese cabaret evenings; classes in acting, acrobatics, music, and body-conditioning; touring; theatre rentals.

GETTING THERE:

Subway: BMT RR, N, QB, to 14th Street; BMT LL (Canarsie) to Sixth Avenue; IND B, F to 14th Street.

Bus: Uptown: Sixth Avenue (M6, M10); Downtown: Fifth Avenue (M2, M3, M5); Crosstown West and East: 14th Street (M14).

Parking: Street parking after 6:00 P.M.; three garages on the block.

RESERVING SEATS:

Box Office Telephone: (212) 924-7277

Ticket Price: $3.00–$5.00 or TDF voucher; discounts for students and senior citizens.

Reservations: Call theatre, held until fifteen minutes before curtain.

Group Rates: Available, contact theatre.

Performance Schedule: Variable.

FORCE 13 THEATRE COMPANY RECOMMENDS:

Whole Wheat 'N Wild Berrys: 57 West 10th Street, between Fifth and Sixth Avenues, 677-3410. 11:30 A.M. till 10:45 P.M. Closed Monday. $2.50–$7.00, a la carte. No credit cards accepted.

La Gauloise: 502 Sixth Avenue, between 12th and 13th Streets, 691-1363. Reservations accepted. French Bistro. Lunch: Sunday through Friday, noon till 3:00 P.M.;

Dinner: 5:45 P.M. till 11:30 P.M.; Saturday Dinner: 5:45 P.M. till midnight. Saturday and Sunday Brunch: noon till 4:30 P.M. Lunch: $4.50–$7.50, a la carte; Dinner: $7.75–$12.00, a la carte. MC, Visa, Diner's, Amex accepted.

Taste of Tokyo: 54 West 13th Street, 691-8666. Japanese. Monday through Thursday: 6:00 P.M. till 11:30 P.M.; Friday and Saturday: 6:00 P.M. till 12:30 A.M.; Sunday: 5:30 P.M. till 11:00 P.M. $6.50–$6.95. Amex accepted.

WHO: GENE FRANKEL THEATRE WORKSHOP

Artistic Director: Gene Frankel
Founder: Gene Frankel; 1972

WHERE:

Neighborhood: Upper West Side
Theatre Address:
36 West 62nd Street (between Broadway and Columbus Avenue)
New York, New York 10023
(212) 581-2775

The Space: Just off Broadway in a building housing numerous rehearsal studios (and also the Richard Allen Center for Culture and Art, see p. 160), the Gene Frankel Theater Workshop performs in a second floor, small 99-seat proscenium theatre.

WHAT:

Artistic Profile: Presenting both revivals and new plays, the Gene Frankel Theatre Workshop provides a forum where actors, directors, and writers can explore their craft. The company was founded by Gene Frankel, a noted acting teacher who directed landmark productions of Jean Genet's *The Blacks* off Broadway and Arthur Kopit's *Indians* on Broadway. Plagued with an unfortunate series of space problems—which began with the physical collapse of its first home, the Mercer Arts

Center—the Workshop has continued to produce plays and train theatre artists for close to a decade.

Productions 1978/79:

Delicious Madness, John Guare, Terrence McNally, and Charles Dizenzo
Chamber Piece, John O'Keefe
Dylan, Sidney Michael
Jardie's Roommate, John Cromwell

Productions 1979/80:

Warplay and *The Marriage*, William Packard
Kohlhass, Heinrich von Kleist; adaptation by Stan Kurta

Special Programs: Writers' and Directors' Workshop; professional training school; special ten-hour documentary film, *In Quest of the Actor*; theatre rentals.

GETTING THERE:

Subway: Seventh Avenue IRT 1 to 66th Street.

Bus: Uptown: Eighth Avenue (M10); Downtown: Broadway (M104); Crosstown West and East: 59th Street (M103).

Parking: Street parking after 7:00 P.M.; nearest lot at Lincoln Center.

RESERVING SEATS:

Box Office Telephone: (212) 581-2775

Ticket Price: $3.50–$5.00, TDF voucher accepted.

Reservations: Call theatre, tickets held until twenty minutes before curtain.

Group Rates: Available, contact the theatre for rates.

Subscription: Available.

Performance Schedule: Three to five productions presented year-round. Evenings: Friday through Sunday; Matinees: Sunday.

GENE FRANKEL THEATRE WORKSHOP RECOMMENDS:

Loki Restaurant: 38 West 62nd Street, between Broadway and Columbus Avenue, 582-7484. Reservations accepted. American-Continental. Noon till 1:00 A.M. Closed Sunday. Lunch: $3.95–$6.95, a la carte; Dinner: $6.50–$11.95, a la carte. MC, Visa, Diner's, Amex accepted.

O'Neals' Baloon: 48 West 63rd Street, between Ninth Avenue and Broadway, 399-2353. Reservations recommended for parties of three or more. American-Continental. 11:30 A.M. till 2:00 A.M., seven days. $3.25–$10.50, a la carte. All credit cards accepted.

WHO: THE GLINES

Artistic Director and Executive Producer: John Glines
Managing Directors: Barry Laine and Lawrence Lane
Founders: John Glines, Barry Laine, and Jerry Tobin; 1976

WHERE:

Theatre Address: Performs in various locations.
Office Address:
c/o John Glines
28 Willow Street
Brooklyn, New York 11201
(212) 522-5567
Manuscript Review:
James Saslow
75 East 55th Street
Room 306
New York, New York 10022

WHAT:

Artistic Profile: The Glines is a multi-arts organization which produces plays that explore the gay experience. For the gay world The Glines has sought to develop self-acceptance and positive self-images; for the non-gay world, to foster understanding and dispel stereotyping. Plays produced in showcase by The Glines frequently go on to commercial production in New York as well as nationally. In 1980 The Glines sponsored a six-week Gay American Arts Festival, presenting other theatre groups, films, poetry, dance, music, and seminars by well-known gay artists, culminating in a gala benefit at Avery Fisher Hall.

Productions 1979:

A Perfect Relationship, Doric Wilson
The Haunted Host, Robert Patrick
The West Street Gang, Doric Wilson
Prisoner of Love, Richard Hall
T-Shirts, Robert Patrick
Mischief Mime, Barbara Anger, Anne Rhodes
The Bearded Lady's Reflection, James McSwain
Kitchen Duty, Victor Bumbalo
Marriage a la Mode, Graham Jackson
Ethyl Eichelberger (a one-man show)
News Boy, Arch Brown

Productions 1980:

The Rights, George Whitmore
Last Summer at Bluefish Cove, Jane Chambers
Forever After, Doric Wilson
T-Shirts, Robert Patrick
Lying in State, Laine Bateman (co-produced with Out and About Theatre Company)
Richmond Jim, Cal Yeoman (co-produced with Theatre Rhinoceros)

Special Programs: Playwriting workshop; workshop for gay women in theatre; sponsorship of film, poetry, and cabaret evenings.

GETTING THERE:

The Glines performs at various locations. Check for advertisement in the *Village Voice* for current location and directions.

RESERVING SEATS:

Box Office Telephone: (212) 522-5567
Ticket Price: Variable, TDF voucher accepted.
Reservations: Tickets held until fifteen minutes prior to curtain.
Group Rates: Available and variable. Contact the office.
Performance Schedule: Full season of plays and special events.

WHO: GOLDEN FLEECE LTD.

Artistic Director: Lou Rodgers
Musical Director: John Klingberg
Business Administrator: Wallace J. Norman
Founders: Lou Rodgers, Stuart Michaels; 1976

WHERE:

Neighborhood: Chelsea
Theatre Address:
Theatre 22
54 West 22nd Street (off Fifth Avenue)
New York, New York 10011
(212) 691-6105

The Space: Housed in a second-floor Chelsea loft, Golden Fleece Ltd. performs in a flexible space. Folding chair seating accommodates fifty to seventy-two.

WHAT:

Artistic Profile: Golden Fleece Ltd. provides for the opera composer what playwright workshops provide for the writer—a supportive environment where the theatrical viability of new work can be explored. The company specializes in chamber and small scale musical productions. Golden Fleece Ltd. also presents music concerts.

Productions 1978/79:
Canticle II Abraham and Isaac, Benjamin Britten
Three Sisters Who Are Not Sisters, Ned Rorem, based on a play by Gertrude Stein
The Specialist, music by Lou Rodgers; libretto by Stuart Michaels
Nathan the Wise, Sam Raphling
Opera Why?, Lou Rodgers, based on Hansel and Gretel

Productions 1979/80:
Hansel and Gretel, Engelbert Humperdink
The Examination, Robert Mitchell
I Rise in Flame Cried the Phoenix, Thomas J. Flanagan
The Specialist, music by Lou Rodgers; libretto by Stuart Michaels

Special Programs: Classes in singing, opera technique, theatre technique for children; community service presentations; touring; children's programs.

GETTING THERE:

Subway: Seventh Avenue IRT 1 to 23rd Street; IND F to 23rd Street.

Bus: Uptown: Sixth Avenue (M6, M7); Downtown: Fifth Avenue (M2, M3, M5, M32); Crosstown West and East: 23rd Street (M26).

Parking: Street parking after 6:00 P.M.; nearest lot on 23rd Street between Fifth and Sixth Avenues.

RESERVING SEATS:

Box Office Telephone: (212) 691-6105

Ticket Price: $4.00 or TDF voucher plus $1.00. Students and senior citizens, $3.00.

Reservations: Call theatre, tickets held until ten minutes before curtain.

Performance Schedule: Variable schedule of productions presented October through June.

GOLDEN FLEECE LTD. RECOMMENDS:

The Angry Squire: 216 Seventh Avenue, at 23rd Street, 242-9066. Reservations accepted. English-Continental. Lunch: noon till 3:00 P.M.; Dinner: 5:00 P.M. till midnight; Bar: till 4:00 A.M., seven days. $3.00–$9.00, a la carte. No credit cards accepted. Jazz: Friday and Saturday nights.

WHO: HUDSON GUILD THEATRE

Producing Director: David Kerry Heefner
Managing Director: Judson Barteaux
Founder: John Lovejoy Elliot; 1922

WHERE:

Neighborhood: Chelsea
Theatre Address:
441 West 26th Street (between Ninth and Tenth Avenues)
New York, New York 10001
(212) 760-9836

The Space: Hudson Guild Theatre's performing space is a traditional, comfortable 138-seat theatre located within the facilities of the Hudson Guild, a social-service agency that has been serving the Chelsea-Clinton neighborhood since 1896. The playground outside the Guild's entrance, the colorful arts and crafts exhibits in the building's entrance display cases, and the constant presence of neighborhood children participating in the Guild's activities all correctly suggest that the theatre is closely linked to its community as well as being an important artistic resource for the entire city.

WHAT:

Artistic Profile: Hudson Guild Theatre produces five new plays each year. Some have been first plays by previously unknown writers such as Ernest Thompson's *On Golden Pond*. Others have been new pieces by established authors, such as Tennessee Williams' *A Lovely Sunday for Creve Coeur*. HGT strives to provide an environment where new works can develop free from the hit-or-miss pressure of the commercial theatre and insists on the right to fail. Nevertheless, the theatre has had notable success in producing plays that later moved to Broadway, including *On Golden Pond*, the Tony Award winning *Da*, and Phyllis Newman and Arthur Laurents' *My Mother Was a Fortune Teller* (retitled *The Madwoman of Central Park West* for its Broadway run). Productions at HGT feature both new talent and such veterans as Tammy Grimes, Barnard Hughes, Shirley Knight, and Frances Sternhagen.

Productions 1978/79:

On Golden Pond, Ernest Thompson
Winning Isn't Everything, Lee Kalcheim
A Lovely Sunday for Creve Coeur, Tennessee Williams
Ride a Cock Horse, David Mercer
Devour the Snow, Abe Polsky

Productions 1979/80:

Banana Box, Eric Chappell
My Sister's Keeper, Ted Allan
Snapshots, Mitchell Bernard and Herbert Kaplan
Come Back to the Five and Dime, Jimmy Dean, Jimmy Dean, Ed Graczyk

The Penultimate Problem of Sherlock Holmes, John Nassivera

Special Programs: Classes for nonprofessionals and children; administrative and technical-production internships; workshop performances.

GETTING THERE:

Subway: IND AA, CC, E to 23rd Street; Seventh Avenue IRT 1 to 28th Street.

Bus: Uptown: Tenth Avenue (M11); Downtown: Ninth Avenue (M11); Crosstown West and East: 23rd Street (M26).

Parking: Street parking available; nearest lot on 26th Street between Eighth and Ninth Avenues.

RESERVING SEATS:

Box Office Telephone: (212) 760-9847

Ticket Price: $7.00–$8.00, TDF voucher accepted. Discounts for senior citizens.

Reservations: Accepted by telephone with credit cards, or by mail order. Advance sale tickets may be picked up at the box office, 11:00 A.M.–6:00 P.M.

Subscription: Available for five-play series. Rates vary for weekday and weekend series.

Performance Schedule: Five plays produced September through June. Each play runs five weeks. Evenings: Wednesday through Sunday; Matinees: Saturday and Sunday. Also five workshop productions presented for eight performances each. Evenings: Monday, Tuesday.

HUDSON GUILD THEATRE RECOMMENDS:

R.J. Scotty's: 202 Ninth Avenue, between 22nd and 23rd Streets, 741-2148. Reservations required Thursday through Sunday. Italian, seafood. Noon till 1:00 A.M., seven days. $4.50–$9.00, a la carte. MC, Visa accepted.

Chelsea Commons: 242 Tenth Avenue, on the corner of 24th Street, 929-9424. Burgers, omelettes. Noon till 2:00 A.M., seven days. Kitchen closes at midnight. $2.50–$7.00, a la carte. No credit cards accepted.

McFeely's: 565 West 23rd Street, on the corner of Eleventh Avenue, 929-4432. Reservations recommended on weekends. Continental-American. Monday through Saturday: 4:00 P.M. till 2:00 A.M.; Sunday Brunch: noon till 4:00 P.M. Kitchen closes at midnight. $6.95–$12.50, a la carte. MC, Visa, Amex accepted. Piano: Tuesday through Sunday.

WHO: IMPOSSIBLE RAGTIME THEATRE

Artistic Directors and Co-producers: Ted Story, Cynthia Crane

Founders: Ted Story, George Ferencz, Pam Mitchell, Cynthia Crane; 1974

WHERE:

Neighborhood: Performs in various locations

Office Address:

142 West 11th Street
New York, New York 10011
(212) 243-7494

WHAT:

Artistic Profile: IRT is a director's theatre—a unique focus in a theatre community where playwright's theatres and actor's theatres predominate. The company believes that since the life of a play ultimately is determined by the director's decisions—how the actors will move on stage, how they will speak their lines, how the stage will look—it is essential that there exist a forum where directors can analyze, discuss, and share ideas about directing. IRT's joint mission is to advance the art and craft of directing while providing high-quality theatre for its audience. The theatre embraces an eclecticism in both its choice of scripts and in directional style employed. A typical season may range from an Agatha Christie murder mystery to a work of Bertolt Brècht, with an emphasis on new scripts.

Productions 1978/79:

Peril at End House, Arnold Ridley, from Agatha Christie's novel
The Unicorn in Captivity, Mel Arrighi
Windfall Apples, Roma Greth
Brand, Henrik Ibsen; translated by Michael Meyer
Suicide in B Flat, Sam Shepard
Three Men on a Horse, John Cecil Holm and George Abbott
Wed-Lock:
Trifles, Susan Glaspell
The Color of Heat, Saul Zachary
Illegal Use of Hands, Michael Zettler
Victoria's Closet, Laurence Carr
The Glass of Water, Eugene Scribe; translated by De-Witt Bodeen
Take Death to Lunch, book and lyrics by Thomas L. Faitos and Amielle Zemach; music by T. L. Faitos

Productions 1979/80:

The Cat and the Canary, John Willard
The Shem Plays, Samuel Shem
Napoleon's Dinner
Room for One Woman
Dark Ages, Kevin O'Morrison
Jesse and the Bandit Queen, David Freeman
When the War Was Over, Max Frisch
The Seagull, Anton Chekov

Special Programs: TNT—Tuesday night playreading series focusing on director-playwright collaboration; internships; post-performance lectures on the first Monday of each run.

GETTING THERE:

Contact the theatre for current performing location and directions.

RESERVING SEATS:

Box Office Telephone: (212) 243-7494
Ticket Price: Weekdays: $4.00; weekends: $5.00. TDF voucher plus surcharge accepted. Student and senior citizen discount of $3.00 on Monday, Thursday, and Sunday.

Reservations: Call theatre, tickets held until a half hour before curtain. Front row seats are reserved for subscribers.
Group Rates: $3.00 for groups of fifteen or more.
Subscription: Six plays for the price of five. Variable rates for weekday, weekend, and opening night series.
Performance Schedule: Theatre was reevaluating their performing schedule during 1980/81. Contact the office for current schedule.

WHO: INTAR (International Arts Relations)

Artistic Director: Max Ferra
Founders: Max Ferra, Elsa Robles, and Frank Robles; 1968

WHERE:

Neighborhood: Clinton–Theatre Row
Theatre Address:
420 West 42nd Street (between Ninth and Tenth Avenues)
New York, New York 10036
(212) 695-6134
The Space: INTAR is housed in a new 107-seat proscenium theatre on Theatre Row—a once bleak, porno-infested neighborhood that now boasts eight Off Off Broadway playhouses, an artist's housing complex and innumerable thriving businesses and restaurants. Upstairs is an art gallery which presents six yearly exhibits of Hispanic artists. Gallery Hours: Monday through Friday, 10:00 A.M. to 5:00 P.M.

WHAT:

Artistic Profile: INTAR (International Arts Relations) is an arena for the exposure of the best Latin talent within the United States and abroad. Many well-known Hispanic artists consider the theatre their home base, for it provides an environment where they can freely explore the Hispanic experience, breaking away from stereotypical roles. The oldest permanent Spanish theatre company in New York, INTAR has recently shifted its focus from the production of mostly Spanish-language plays to the development and presentation of English-language plays and musicals by contemporary Hispanic writers—thus bringing the company's talent not only to the Hispanic audience, but also to the larger American theatre-community. The company also produces three yearly concerts and exhibits local visual artists in its gallery space above the theatre.

Productions 1978/79:
Carmencita, Manuel Martin
La Gran Decision, Miguel Mihura (in Spanish)
Eyes on the Harem, Maria Irene Fornes
Columbus, Columbus, Osvaldo Pradere (children's theatre)

Productions 1979/80:
Rice and Beans, Hector Quintero
Swallows, Manuel Martin
Blood Wedding, Federico García Lorca

Special Programs: Master workshops in acting, singing, production, and administration; playwright's unit; internships; concerts; art exhibitions; theatre rentals.

GETTING THERE:

Subway: IND A, AA, CC, E to 42nd Street.
Bus: Uptown: Tenth Avenue (M11, M16); Downtown: Ninth Avenue (M11); Crosstown West and East: 42nd Street (M106).
Parking: Manhattan Plaza garage across the street.

RESERVING SEATS:

Box Office Telephone: (212) 279-4200 (Ticket Central)
Ticket Price: $5.00 or TDF voucher plus surcharge, reserved seats. Students and senior citizens, $3.00.
Reservations: Call Ticket Central. Reservations held until a half hour before curtain. Credit card phone orders accepted.
Group Rates: Available, contact theatre.
Performance Schedule: Three or four productions presented September through June. Evenings: Thursday through Saturday; Matinee: Sunday.

INTAR RECOMMENDS:

Hell's Kitchen: 598 Ninth Avenue, on the corner of 43rd Street, 757-5329. Reservations accepted. American. Noon till midnight; Saturday and Sunday Brunch: 12:30 A.M. till 4:30 P.M. $3.00–$9.00, a la carte. Diner's, Carte Blanche, Amex accepted.

La Rousse: 414 West 42nd Street, on Theatre Row, 736-4913. Reservations recommended. French Peasant. 11:30 A.M. till midnight, seven days. Lunch: $3.95–$8.95, a la carte; Dinner: $5.95–$9.95, a la carte. All credit cards except Carte Blanche accepted. Note: La Rousse occasionally features a complete Dinner-Theatre Ticket Package for productions playing on Theatre Row. Call Peter Howard at the restaurant for information.

Angelo's: 859 Ninth Avenue, at 56th Street, 586-0159. Reservations accepted. Italian. 11:00 A.M. till midnight, seven days. $4.00–$7.50, a la carte. No credit cards accepted.

WHO: INTERART THEATRE

Artistic Director: Margot Lewitin
Managing Director: Abigail Franklin
Founders: Marjorie De Fazio, Margot Lewitin, Alice Rubinstein, and Jane Chambers; 1970

WHERE:

Neighborhood: Clinton
Theatre Address:

549 West 52nd Street (between Tenth and Eleventh Avenues)
New York, New York 10019
(212) 246-1050

The Annex
552 West 53rd Street
New York, New York 10019

The Space: Located in a city-owned warehouse between Tenth and Eleventh Avenues, the Interart Theatre is just ten minutes from the nearest subway and well worth the walk. Not only does it have a flexible 40-to-90-seat performing space, but also, an art gallery that features the work of contemporary artists and sculptors. Around the corner the Annex provides an additional, flexible loft-space for performances.

WHAT:

Artistic Profile: Interart Theatre is one component part of the Women's Interart Center, Inc., a multi-arts organization that presents work by women artists, explores the interactive process that occurs when artists of various disciplines share ideas and responses, and provides training programs and workshops. The Interart Theatre does not identify itself as a feminist theatre. Rather, it provides women artists with the opportunity to draw on their own life-experiences in an effort to discover a sensibility that historically has not achieved expression in the theatre.

Productions 1978/79:

The Price of Genius, Betty Neustat
Sister/Sister, company-developed
Daughters, company-developed
Olympic Park, Myrna Lamb
Sunday, Michael Deutsch; translation by Françoise Kourilsky and Lynne Greenblatt
Antony and Cleopatra, William Shakespeare

Productions 1979/80:

The Daughters Cycle, Clare Coss, Sondra Segal, Roberta Sklar
Part I: Daughters
Part II: Sister/Sister
Part III: Electra Speaks
Yesterday Is Over, Mady Christian
In the Summer House, Jane Bowles

Special Programs: Integrated Media Studies—a nine-month program in film, video, writing, and acting (thirty college credits available); internship programs; workshops; post-performance discussions; film series; poetry readings;

seminars; darkroom, ceramic studio, and silkscreening facilities; film and video training and access.

GETTING THERE:

Subway: IND AA, E, CC, to 50th Street.
Bus: Uptown: Tenth Avenue (M11); Downtown: Ninth Avenue (M11); Crosstown West: 49th Street (M27); Crosstown East: 50th Street (M27).
Parking: Street parking easily available after 7:00 P.M.; lot directly across the street.

RESERVING SEATS:

Box Office Telephone: (212) 279-4200 (Ticket Central)
Ticket Price: $4.00, TDF voucher accepted.
Reservations: Call Ticket Central, tickets held until a half hour before curtain. MC, Visa, and Amex accepted.
Performance Schedule: Five productions presented October through June. Evenings: Thursday through Sunday; Matinees: Sunday.

INTERART THEATRE RECOMMENDS:

Landmark Tavern: Corner of Eleventh Avenue and 46th Street, 757-8595. Reservations recommended. American-Irish. Weekdays: noon till midnight; Weekends: noon till 1:00 A.M. Lunch: $3.00–$8.00, a la carte; Dinner: $5.00–$14.00, a la carte. No credit cards accepted.
B.J.'s Saloon: 736 Tenth Avenue, at 50th Street, 581-4244. Reservations required for large parties only. Burgers, soups. 11:30 A.M. till midnight, seven days. Kitchen closes at midnight. Saturday and Sunday brunch. $1.75–$4.25, a la carte.

WHO: IRISH REBEL THEATRE

Director of Dramatic Committee: Patrick King
Managing Director: Nye Heron
Founders: Members of the Irish Arts Center; 1972

WHERE:

Neighborhood: Clinton
Theatre Address:
553 West 51st Street (between Tenth and Eleventh Avenues)
New York, New York 10019
(212) 757-3318

The Space: The Irish Rebel Theatre wants people to think of it as a home-away-from-home, and every effort has been made to make the space a comfortable gathering place. In a spacious lobby (also used for classes and informal evenings of song and dance) coffee, tea, cookies, and cakes are served. The intimate proscenium theatre seats sixty-nine.

WHAT:

Artistic Profile: The Irish Rebel Theatre is just one of the many cultural and artistic activities sponsored by the Irish Arts Center, a community organization founded to increase awareness of Irish artistic expression. The theatre derives its name from a century-old tradition of rebellion against that which extinguishes distinctive expressive forms, and considers itself political in the cultural rather than partisan sense. In addition to reviving the works of Yeats, Synge, O'Casey, and O'Neill, the company showcases contemporary playwrights.

Productions 1978/79:
I Know A Spot, Mickey Kelly
Didja See That?, Nye Heron
The Great Hunger, Michael McQuaid, Judy Trupin
The Playboy of the Western World, J. M. Synge

Productions 1979/80:
Houses of Jasper, Streets of Gold, Marla Collins
The Risen People, James Plunkett
Philadelphia, Here I Come!, Brian Friel
The Great Blasket, Mary Kane
The Weaver's Grave, Michael O'hAodha

Special Programs: *Seisiun*—informal evening of traditional Irish music, dancing, and singing; *Ceilis*—Irish dances; *Ais-Eiri*—twice-yearly magazine; free classes in Irish language, traditional Irish instruments, acting, dancing, playwriting.

GETTING THERE:

Subway: IND AA, CC, E to 50th Street.
Bus: Uptown: Tenth Avenue (M11); Downtown: Ninth Avenue (M11); Crosstown West: 49th Street (M27); Crosstown East: 50th Street (M27).
Parking: Street parking after 6:00 P.M.; nearest lot at 62nd Street and Eleventh Avenue.

RESERVING SEATS:

Box Office Telephone: (212) 757-3318
Ticket Price: $3.00 or TDF voucher. $2.00 for senior citizens, free for children.
Reservations: Call theatre, tickets held until fifteen minutes before curtain.
Performance Schedule: Variable performance schedule. Productions presented September through June. Evenings: Friday through Sunday; Matinees: Sunday.

IRISH REBEL THEATRE RECOMMENDS:

Landmark Tavern: On the corner of Eleventh Avenue and 46th Street, 757-8595. Reservations accepted. American-Irish. Sunday through Thursday: noon till midnight; Friday and Saturday: noon till 1:00 A.M. Lunch: $3.00–$8.00, a la carte; Dinner: $5.00–$14.00, a la carte. No credit cards accepted.
La Palma Oriental Restaurant: 765 Ninth Avenue, between 51st and 52nd Streets, 265-6545. Chinese-Spanish. 11:00 A.M. till 11:00 P.M., seven days. $2.00–$12.00, a la carte.

WHO: JEAN COCTEAU REPERTORY

Artistic Director: Eve Adamson
Managing Director: Andy Cohn
Founder: Eve Adamson; 1971

WHERE:

Neighborhood: Noho–East Village
Theatre Address:
Bouwerie Lane Theatre
330 Bowery (at 2nd Street)
New York, New York 10012
(212) 677-0060

The Space: The historic Bouwerie Lane Theatre is an elegantly designed, landmark building that was built in 1874 as a bank and converted to a theatre in the early sixties. With its old oak doors, graceful glass chandeliers and gilded box office window grate (the original bank teller's window) the building continues to evoke an old-world sophistication. Its narrow proscenium theatre seats 140. The large downstairs lounge offers refreshments and also has a wall display of the building's original, intricately carved masonry.

WHAT:

Artistic Profile: At Jean Cocteau Repertory, the playgoer may view innovative productions of enduring classics and rarely performed works that are seen more often in the pages of anthologies than on the stage. All plays are performed by a resident acting company, some of whom have been with the Cocteau since its inception. By presenting plays in a rotating repertory format, Jean Cocteau Repertory provides the audience with the opportunity of seeing familiar actors playing dramatically different roles in a variety of great classics.

Productions 1978/79:
Exit the King, Eugene Ionesco
In the Bar of a Tokyo Hotel, Tennessee Williams
As You Like It, William Shakespeare
The Changeling, Thomas Middelton and William Ronley
A Mad World My Masters, Thomas Middelton
The Scarecrow, Percy MacKaye
Volpone, Ben Jonson
The Cid, Pierre Corneille
Hamlet, William Shakespeare

Productions 1979/80:

Exit the King
Kirche, Kutchen und Kinder, Tennessee Williams
Ruy Blas, Victor Hugo
The Tempest, William Shakespeare
He Who Gets Slapped, Leonid Andreyev
The Roman Actor, Philip Massinger
Hamlet, William Shakespeare
In the Bar of a Tokyo Hotel, Tennessee Williams

Special Programs: Internships; volunteer programs; student matinee-performances; post-performance seminars.

GETTING THERE:

Subway: Lexington Avenue IRT 6 to Bleecker Street; IND B, D, F to Broadway/Lafayette Street; BMT RR to 8th Street.

Bus: Uptown: Park Row/Bowery (M101, M102); Downtown: Second Avenue (M15).

Parking: Ample street parking at all times.

RESERVING SEATS:

Box Office Telephone: (212) 677-0060

Ticket Price: $6.00, TDF voucher accepted. $4.00 for students and senior citizens.

Reservations: Call theatre, tickets held until a half hour before curtain.

Group Rates: Available, contact the Audience Development Director at the office.

Subscription: Four plays at a discount, plus discounts to at least two other annual productions.

Performance Schedule: Eight productions presented in rotating repertory, August through June. Evenings: Thursday through Sunday; Matinees: Sunday. Special matinee series for school groups presented twice yearly for a six-week period.

JEAN COCTEAU REPERTORY RECOMMENDS:

Garvin's: 19 Waverly Place, between Broadway and University Place (Fifth Avenue), 473-5261. Reservations suggested. Continental. 11:30 A.M. till 3:00 A.M., seven days. Kitchen closes at 1:30 A.M. Lunch: $3.50–$9.00, a la carte; Dinner: $6.00–$18.00, a la carte. All credit cards accepted. Piano: Thursday through Saturday.

Spring Street Bar: 401 West Broadway, on the corner of Spring Street, 431-7637. Reservations accepted. American-French-Mexican. Lunch: noon till 4:00 P.M.; Dinner: 6:00 P.M. till 11:00 P.M.; Supper: 11:00 P.M. till 2:00 A.M.; Bar till 4:00 A.M., seven days. $1.50–$12.00, a la carte. MC, Visa, Amex accepted.

Hisae's Place: 35 Cooper Square, between 5th and 6th Streets, 228-6886. Reservations required for parties of four or more. Oriental. Monday through Thursday: 5:00 P.M. till midnight; Friday and Saturday: 5:00 P.M. till 1:00 A.M.; Sunday: 5:00 P.M. till 11:00 P.M. $5.95–$10.95, a la carte. No credit cards accepted.

Phebe's Place: 361 Bowery, at 4th Street, 473-9008. American-Continental. Noon till 4:00 A.M., seven days. $1.65–$9.00, a la carte. All credit cards accepted.

WHO: JEWISH REPERTORY THEATRE

Producer: Ran Avni
Founder: Ran Avni; 1974

WHERE:

Neighborhood: Gramercy
Theatre Address:
Emanu-El Midtown YM-YWHA
344 East 14th Street (between First and Second Avenues)
New York, New York 10003
(212) 674-7200

The Space: Located on the second floor of the Emanu-El Midtown YM-YWHA, the Jewish Repertory Theatre performs in a recently renovated 100-seat air-conditioned, proscenium theatre.

WHAT:

Artistic Profile: The Jewish Repertory Theatre presents plays in English that relate to the Jewish experience.

Productions 1978/79:

Triptych, Ernest A. Joselovitz
The Halloween Bandit, Mark Medoff
Unlikely Heroes, adaptation of Phillip Roth short stories by Larry Arrick
Loyalties, John Galsworthy
The Gentle People, Irwin Shaw
Rocket to the Moon, Clifford Odets

Productions 1979/80:

Liliom, Ferenc Molnar
Benya the King, Richard Schotter
The Matchmaker, Thornton Wilder
Green Fields, Peretz Hirshbein
Come Blow Your Horn, Neil Simon
"36", Norman Lessing

Special Programs: Playwrights Lab.

GETTING THERE:

Subway: Lexington Avenue IRT 4, 5, 6 to 14th Street; BMT N, QB, RR to 14th Street; BMT LL (Canarsie 14th Street Line) to First Avenue.

Bus: Uptown: First Avenue (M15); Downtown: Second Avenue (M15); Crosstown West and East: 14th Street (M14).

Parking: Street parking after 7:00 P.M. Lot parking in Stuyvesant Town across First Avenue.

RESERVING SEATS:

Box Office Telephone: (212) 674-7200

Ticket Price: Saturday evening and Sunday matinee: $6.00 or TDF voucher plus surcharge; Wednesday, Thursday, Sunday evenings: $4.00 or TDF voucher.

Reservations: Phone reservations taken day of performance only; held until half hour before curtain. Box office hours: Monday through Thursday, 1:00 P.M.–9:00 P.M.

Group Rates: Fifty-cent discount for groups larger than twenty, contact the theatre.

Subscription: Available, contact the theatre.

Performance Schedule: Five productions presented October through June. Evenings: Wednesday, Thursday, Saturday, Sunday; Matinees: Sunday.

JEWISH REPERTORY THEATRE RECOMMENDS:

Dumpling House: 207 Second Avenue, on the corner of 13th Street, 473-8557. Reservations accepted. Szechuan-Mandarin. Lunch: 11:00 A.M. till 3:00 P.M.; Dinner: 5:00 P.M. till 10:30 P.M., seven days. Lunch: $3.50–$8.00; Dinner: $6.00–$8.00, a la carte. All major credit cards accepted.

San Stefano: 322 East 14th Street, between First and Second Avenues, 473-5953. Reservations required on weekends. Northern Italian. Monday through Saturday: 5:30 P.M. till 11:00 P.M.; Sunday: 4:00 P.M. till 10:00 P.M. Closed Monday. $6.50–$11.50, a la carte. All credit cards accepted.

Second Avenue Deli: 156 Second Avenue, on the corner of 10th Street, 677-0606. Kosher. 7:00 A.M. till midnight, seven days. $3.50–$8.00. Personal checks accepted.

WHO: LA MAMA E.T.C.

Executive Director: Ellen Stewart
Business Manager: James Moore
Artistic Director: Wesley Jensby
Founder: Ellen Stewart; 1962

WHERE:

Neighborhood: Noho–East Village
Theatre Address:

74-A East 4th Street (between Second Avenue and the Bowery)
New York, New York 10003
(212) 254-6468

The Annex
66 East 4th Street
New York, New York 10003

The Space: When La Mama E.T.C. moved to East 4th Street the neighborhood was considered off-bounds by all but Bowery bums. Now it's a thriving downtown theatre district where artists, theatregoers, and old-time residents mingle freely on the streets, in restaurants, and in the many theatres that now line the block. La Mama E.T.C. maintains two theatre buildings, a main theatre that houses two 99-seat, flexible spaces and a large adjacent Annex. The Annex (which also houses the Millennium, an experimental film center) seats 250 in an air-conditioned, flexible space. Its enormous, high ceiling, rectangular playing area, and its walls lined with stamp metal provide a striking backdrop for the many experimental productions presented here.

WHAT:

Artistic Profile: It's impossible to talk about Off Off Broadway without talking about La Mama E.T.C. and its director, Ellen Stewart, for this theatre was presenting non-commercial, unconventional theatre long before anyone thought to identify an Off Off Broadway theatre movement. Begun in a Greenwich Village basement, the theatre recruited its audiences from passers-by at either end of the street. First known as Cafe La Mama, since for licensing reasons coffee was served, and later incorporated as La Mama E.T.C. (Experimental Theatre Club), the theatre's work falls into three major evolutionary phases. The first period includes the first productions (or nearly first productions) of many writers who have since become well-established, among them Paul Foster, Israel Horovitz, Tom Eyen, Sam Shepard, Megan Terry, and Jean-Claude Van Itallie. The second phase was strongly influenced by Tom O'Horgan (director of *Hair* and *Lenny* on Broadway) who came to La Mama in 1964 and took La Mama's first troupe to Europe. During its most recent period strong emphasis has been placed on resident troupes and the creation, through extended exploratory workshops, of productions that combine acting, singing, story, dance, acrobatics, film, and mime. Resident companies at La Mama include the Repertory Troupe directed by Andrei Serban; the

ETC Company directed by Wilford Leach and John Braswell; bilingual troupes (Spanish-English, Chinese-English); the Jarboro Company (a training and performing company highly physical in approach). In addition, John Vaccaro has based his Play-House of the Ridiculous at La Mama since 1971. La Mama E.T.C. has been instrumental in bringing internationally acclaimed experimental theatre artists to the United States.

Productions 1978/79:

La Mama-Ceta Cabaret, Reynold Scott
There Appeared a Knight, Charsu Theatre Tehran
Yakshagana of India, Children's Troupe
What If?, Akin Babatunde
Siberia & Friends, collaborative work
From A to Z, book by Estrella Artau; music by Jimmy Lopez
Theatre Raun Raun, Folk Lore Drama
Warsaw Mime Theatre
Happy New Year, Flavio Marcio
The Dowager, book by Ernest Abuba; music by Simeon Westbrooke
Some Such Things, book by Rina Yerushalmi; music by Simeon Westbrooke
Ningyo Shimai, Taeko Tomioka (The Doll Sisters; Ritsudosha, Inc.-Japan)
American Babies, book by Ruis Woertendyke, Gaetan Young; music by Ian Michael Ephron
Endgame, Hubert Jappelle Marionettes
Agamos el Amor Sin H, Edmundo Villarroel (La Compañía de Los Cuatro)
El Cepillo de Dientes, Felix Diaz (La Compañía de Los Cuatro)
cummings & goinngs, book and music by Ada Janik
Silence, Grazielle Martinez
Ultraje, book by Estrella Artau; music by Simeon Westbrooke
Appearing in Person: Your Mother, Pedro Juan Pietri
Through This Black Woman's Eyes, Sary Guinier
My Old Friends, book and music by Mel Mandel and Norman Sachs
Approaching Zero, book by Thom Thomas; music by Steven Oirich
Gulliver's Travels, William Hoffman

Missionary Ridge, John Ferdon
360 Degrees of Feeling, directed by Dwight Carson
Medha Yodh, a solo concert
Hearing Solar Winds, directed by David Hykes
Child Year Corps Project
Franky & Ruby, John Morrow
Book of Etiquette, book by William M. Hoffman; music by John Braden
Fugue in a Nursery, book by Harvey Fierstein; music by Ada Janik
Man and Artifact, Pupodrom Puppet Theatre from Austria
The Dead Class, Cricot 2 Theatre Co., Poland
The Servant of Two Masters, book by Carlo Goldoni; music by Simeon Westbrooke
Dark Twist, book by Jeff Weiss; music by James Sanchez Lopez
Re-Arrangements, directed by Joseph Chaikin; music by Peter Golub and Skip La Plante
The Birds, Aristophanes; music by William Schimmel
Bound Feet/Nijinsky, Winston Tong
A Moroccan Evening-Inosis, The Moroccan Berber Ballet
Spiral Complex (Japan)
3rd World Liturgy
Indonesian Dance Theatre
Fragments of a Trilogy, directed by Andréi Serban; music by Elizabeth Swados
Painting on Glass, Francoise Grund Khaznadar
Beouwulf, A Pageant, book by Ingrid Furlong; music by Roger Bourland (Stagespace)
Cesc Gelabert, Spanish dance concert
La Mama Ceta Twitas, Instituto Colombiano de Bienestar Familiar
God's Forgotten, Pieter-Dirk Uys
Dreams of a Mischievous Heart Shipwrecked on Illusion, Ernesto de Albuguerque vieira Santos Filho (Brazilian Dramatic Co.)
Butterfly Love, Zignali I Theatre
The Little Elephant is Dead, Kobo-Abe (An Exhibition of Images)
And That's How the Rent Gets Paid, Jeff Weiss
Point of Origin, The Veterans Ensemble Theatre Co.

God! It's Too Late, book by Yutaka Okada; music by Yukiko Amino
Elizabeth I/The Lost Letter, Paul Foster, Ion Caragiale (Bulandra Theatre of Romania)
Theatre of Latin America
And the Soul Shall Dance, Wakako Yamauchi (Pan Asian Repertory)
Vulgar Lives, book by Rosalyn Drexler; music by Richard Weinstock
Ang Tatay Mong Kalbo, Phillipine Forum of N.Y. Inc. & Ningas Magazine
Love Is Not for Sale, Renaldo Eugenio Ferrada
Cooper Square Festival

Productions 1979/80:

Moroccan Night, an evening of Moroccan theatre
And the Soul Shall Dance, Wakako Yamauchi (Pan Asian Repertory)
Widows and Children First, Harvey Fierstein
Rat "Vanemuise" Naitleja-Lavastaja (Estonian)
Sexy Saint James, book by Robert Sealy; music by Alan Lloyd
Recent Ruins, book and music by Meredith Monk
Drawing Room Tragedy, Joseph Renard
A Piece of Monologue, Samuel Beckett
The Mystic Paper Beasts, Melisande Potter
The Nutcracker in the Land of Nuts, book by Ronald Tavel; music by Simeon Westbrooke
The Glass House, book by Fatima Dike; music by Baba Femi
As You Like It, William Shakespeare; music by Elizabeth Swados
Mami Wata, Rose Marie Guiraud
I Can't Keep Running In Place, book and music by Barbara Schottenfeld
I Can't Hear the Birds Singing, Brenda Faye Collie
A Midsummer Night's Dream, William Shakespeare; music by Steven Margoshes
Made by Two, Gertrude Stein; music by William Turner (The Theatre Express Co.)
Colloquies, Nimbus Dance Theatre Co.
Sunrise, Cao Yu
Portuguese Love Letters, Mariana Alcoforado (The Lisbon Theatre Co.)

Two by Beckett, Samuel Beckett
Chopelia, Farid Chopel (A one-man show)
Nelly Vivas, solo performance
A Circular Play, Gertrude Stein
Dario Dambrosio, solo performance
The Theatre of Ken Togo from Japan
In the Summer House, Jane Bowles (co-produced with The Interart Theatre)
Ruis Woertendyke, solo performance
Tad Truesdale, solo performance
The Spoon Connection, Paul Thompson
Winter Project—Part IV, Joseph Chaikin
Peter Brook's Le Centre International de Creations Theatrales in Repertory:
L'os/Ubu
The Ik
The Conference of the Birds

Special Programs: National and international touring; Third World Institute of Theatre Arts Studio (TWITAS)—an ongoing bilingual children's workshop for Lower East Side residents; internships.

GETTING THERE:

Subway: BMT RR to 8th Street; Lexington Avenue IRT 6 to Astor Place; IND B, D, F to Broadway/Lafayette Street.
Bus: Uptown: Third Avenue (M101, M102); Downtown: Second Avenue (M15).
Parking: Street parking after 6:00 P.M.; nearest lot on corner of East 4th Street and the Bowery.

RESERVING SEATS:

Box Office Telephone: (212) 475-7710 or 475-7908
Ticket Price: Main Theatre: \$3.00–\$5.00; Annex: \$7.00–\$10.00, TDF voucher accepted. Student discount: \$1.00 off ticket price.
Reservations: Main Theatre: call theatre, tickets held until

fifteen minutes before curtain; Annex: policy varies for each production, call the box office.

Group Rates: Available, contact the theatre.

Performance Schedule: Continuous presentation of productions in Main Theatres and Annex, September through July. Main Theatres: Evenings, Thursday through Sunday. Annex: Evenings, Tuesday through Sunday; Matinees: Saturday, Sunday.

LA MAMA E.T.C. RECOMMENDS:

Binibon: 85 Second Avenue, on the corner of 5th Street, 475-9365. Omelettes, burgers, vegetarian dishes. Monday through Thursday: 8:00 A.M. till 10:00 P.M.; Friday and Saturday: 9:00 A.M. till 11:00 P.M.; Sunday: 9:00 A.M. till 10:00 P.M. $1.50–$3.75, a la carte. No credit cards accepted.

Phebe's Place: 361 Bowery, at 4th Street, 473-9008. American-Continental. Noon till 4:00 A.M., seven days. $1.65–$9.00, a la carte. All credit cards accepted.

WHO: LATIN AMERICAN THEATRE ENSEMBLE

Artistic Director: Mario Peña
Managing Director: Margarita Torac
Founders: Mario Peña, Margarita Torac; 1971

WHERE:

Neighborhood: Performs in various locations
Office Address:
203 West 90th Street
New York, New York 10024
(212) 362-9747

WHAT:

Artistic Profile: The Latin American Theatre Ensemble provides a unique combination of modernist, experimental theatre methods applied to material drawn from the Latin American experience and performed by multinational casts including Mexicans, Argentinians, Chileans, Cubans, and Puerto Ricans, among others. Artistic Director Mario Peña, a Cuban exile who formerly worked in Cuban television and theatre, writes most of the plays. While not overtly political, these visually, musically, and choreographically rich works allegorically do make reference to contemporary political and social realities. Performances are in Spanish and intermittently in English.

Productions 1978/79:

Popol Vuh, Mario Peña
El Milagro del Señor de las Aguas, Luis Marin
Esperando a Godot, Samuel Beckett
Dining Outside, Jesus Papoleto
Evita del Barrio, Houston Brummit
El Hijo de la Esclava, Jose Berdiales
Contra, Alejandro Acevedo
El Pez Que Fuma, Roman Chalbaud

Productions 1979/80:

Attapolis, Mario Peña; music by Karlo Jesuz
La Ramera de la Cueva, Mario Peña
Concierto de Canciones, Rony Ronnell
La Ramera de la Cueva, Mario Peña
Coronado Dance Company
Fuera del Juego, Mario Peña

Special Programs: Professional workshops in acting, dance, singing, and playwriting; workshop performances; local touring.

GETTING THERE:

Contact the office for current performing locations and directions.

RESERVING SEATS:

Box Office Telephone: (212) 362-9747
Ticket Price: $3.50–$4.00 or TDF voucher. $2.00 for students and senior citizens.
Reservations: Call theatre, tickets held until curtain.
Group Rates: Available, contact the theatre.
Performance Schedule: Year-round; plays run approximately five weeks. Evenings: Friday, Saturday; Matinees: Sunday.

WHO: LION THEATRE COMPANY

Artistic Director: Gene Nye
Producing Director: Eleanor Meglio
Founders: Gene Nye, Garland Wright; 1974

WHERE:

Neighborhood: Clinton–Theatre Row
Theatre Address:
422 West 42nd Street (between Ninth and Tenth Avenues)
New York, New York 10036
(212) 736-7930
The Space: Located on Theatre Row—that stretch of 42nd Street that once housed pornography houses and burnt-out tenements but now boasts seven brand-new theatres, an artist's housing complex and numerous off-beat restaurants—the Lion Theatre Company is housed in a modern 100-seat proscenium theatre with a raised stage and slightly raked seating. The space is fully accessible to the handicapped.

WHAT:

Artistic Profile: The Lion Theatre Company was founded in 1974 as a small repertory company that worked during off-hours in the back room of the American Shakespeare Festival at Stratford, Connecticut. Until 1976 the company presented a summer season of productions in New York City. Then the company moved permanently to New York City, established itself as a full-time, year-round, New York City–based company, and quickly expanded its nucleus of actors to include fifty theatre artists. The opportunity for this core-group of artists to come and go as necessary, and to have a home base where they can interact, evolve, and grow—a modified European idea of repertory—is central to the company's philosophy. Additional actors and directors join the core-company for individual productions. Lion operates three major programs including:

1) A Major Production Series of three or four, new and classical plays (representative productions include *The Tempest*, Jack Heifner's *Vanities*, J. Hartley Manners' Victorian comedy *Peg O' My Heart*, and the Obie award winning *K, Impressions of Kafka's "The Trial"*);

2) A Cub series of new American plays, fully rehearsed but produced with minimum production budgets; and

3) A Shakespeare Pilot Project including discussions, guest lecturers, scene study and productions.

Productions 1978/79:

Music-Hall Sidelights: A Theatrical Scrapbook, book and lyrics by Jack Heifner, from Colette's *L'envers du Music Hall*; music by John McKinney

The Three Sisters, Anton Chekov; translation by Sharon Carnicke

Duel: A Romantic Opera, book, music, and lyrics by Randal Wilson

Workshop Series:

Appointment with a High-Wire Lady, Russell Davis

Afternoon Tea, Harvey Peer

Two One-Acts, John Guare

No More Dragons, Alan Levenstein

Productions 1979/80:

Knuckle Sandwich, Howard Waxman

Star Treatment, Jack Heifner

Workshop Series:

A Romance, David Gallagher

The Seminary Murder, David Reid

Sanada Sez, John Guerrasio

Marching Song, John Whiting

Special Programs: Workshop productions; staged readings; Shakespeare Pilot Project; theatre rentals.

GETTING THERE:

Subway: IND A, AA, CC, E to 42nd Street.
Bus: Uptown: Tenth Avenue (M11, M16); Downtown: Ninth Avenue (M11); Crosstown West and East: 42nd Street (M106).
Parking: Manhattan Plaza garage across the street.

RESERVING SEATS:

Box Office Telephone: (212) 279-4200 (Ticket Central)
Ticket Price: Major Productions, $6.00; Workshops, $3.00; TDF voucher accepted.
Reservations: Call Ticket Central. Tickets held until a half hour before curtain. MC, Visa, Amex accepted.
Group Rates: Available, contact theatre for rates.
Subscription: Series provides admission to three major shows and four workshops, all at a discount. Different fee structures for weekday and weekend series.
Performance Schedule: Three major productions plus workshops presented September through June. Evenings: Wednesday through Sunday; Matinees: Saturday, Sunday.

LION THEATRE COMPANY RECOMMENDS:

La Rousse: 414 West 42nd Street, on Theatre Row, 736-4913. Reservations recommended. French Peasant. 11:30 A.M. till midnight, seven days. Lunch: $3.95–$8.95, a la carte; Dinner: $5.95–$9.95, a la carte. All credit cards except Carte Blanche accepted. La Rousse occasionally features a complete Dinner-Theatre Ticket Package for productions on Theatre Row. Call Peter Howard at the restaurant for information.
West Bank Cafe: 407 West 42nd Street, in Manhattan Plaza, 695-6909. Reservations required, 6:00 P.M.–8:00 P.M. American-Continental-Oriental. Monday through Saturday: noon till 1:00 A.M.; Sunday: noon till 11:00 P.M. Lunch: $2.50–$4.25, a la carte; Dinner: $4.25–$8.75, a la carte. MC, Visa, Amex accepted. Entertainment: Jazz, Big Bands, Comedy, Singers, Broadway Personalities: Tuesday through Saturday at 8:30 P.M. and 10:30 P.M.

Gardenia Club: 482 West 43rd Street (entrance on Tenth Avenue through Manhattan Plaza Health Club), 594-8402. Reservations recommended. Italian-French-Oriental. Tuesday through Saturday: 11:00 A.M. till midnight; Sunday: 11:00 A.M. till 11:00 P.M. Closed Monday. $5.95–$11.95, a la carte. MC, Visa, Amex accepted.

Curtain Up: 402 West 43rd Street, in Manhattan Plaza, 564-7272. Reservations accepted. Steaks, seafood, omelettes. Sunday: 11:30 A.M. till midnight; Monday: noon till midnight; Tuesday through Thursday: noon till 1:00 A.M.; Friday and Saturday: noon till 2:00 A.M. $3.00–$8.50, a la carte. All credit cards accepted. Classical Music: Wednesday, Friday, Sunday afternoons and evenings.

WHO: MABOU MINES

Artistic Directors: Collaborative—Lee Breuer, JoAnne Akalaitis, Ruth Maleczech, Frederick Neumann, Terry O'Reilly, William Raymond, Burt Dallas

Administrator: Artservices

WHERE:

Neighborhood: Noho–East Village

Theatre Address:
Public Theater
425 Lafayette Street
New York, New York 10003
(212) 598-7100

Office Address:
Artservices
463 West Street
New York, New York 10014
(212) 989-4953

The Space: For six months each year Mabou Mines is the theatre-in-residence at the New York Shakespeare Festival's Public Theater. For a more detailed description of this extensive performing arts complex see New York Shakespeare Festival (p. 125).

WHAT:

Artistic Profile: Mabou Mines has long been in the forefront of theatrical groups experimenting with "total theatre." Working as a collective, the company has developed a unique narrative technique of choral monologue which draws upon commedia, mime, melodrama, advertising, and the eastern dance theatres of Kabuki and Kathakali. Mabou Mines' mixed-media presentations include both original works and original interpretations of contemporary classics—most notably the works of Beckett and Colette. For example, the company's *Shaggy Dog Animation* combines past and present action, metaphoric and literal language, the ironic and the passionate, the use of puppetry and sophisticated stereophonic equipment, and a cast of characters that includes dogs and humans, all in an exploration of the clichés of romantic love. In their staging of Beckett's sparse radio play *Cascando*, the company develops a precisely observed, rhythmically rich tapestry of actions—tinkering with a broken clock, knitting, endlessly building a house from a deck of cards—to serve as a visual-musical accompaniment to the text. Mabou Mines traces its origins to San Francisco, where, in the early 1960s Lee Breuer, Ruth Maleczech, and JoAnne Akalaitis began working with a loose coalition of artists and performing groups. Joined by composer Phillip Glass and actor David Warrilow, the group worked in Europe from 1966 to 1969. Taking the name Mabou Mines in 1969—after a Nova Scotia mining town—Mabou Mines served as a resident company at La Mama E.T.C. from 1970 to 1973 and is currently a resident company at the New York Shakespeare Festival.

Productions 1978/79:

Shaggy Dog Animation, Lee Breuer
Southern Exposure, JoAnne Akalaitis

Productions 1979/80:

Mercier and Camier, Samuel Beckett; adapted by Frederick Newman
Prelude to Death in Venice, Lee Breuer
Vanishing Pictures, Ruth Maleczech
Dressed Like an Egg, JoAnne Akalaitis

Special Programs: Touring; theatre workshops.

GETTING THERE:

Subway: Lexington Avenue IRT 6 to Astor Place; BMT RR to 8th Street; IND B, D, F to Broadway/Lafayette.
Bus: Uptown: Whitehall Street (M1); Downtown: Broadway (M6) and Fifth Avenue (M1); Crosstown West: 9th Street (M13); Crosstown East: 8th Street (M13).
Parking: Street parking after 6:00 P.M.; nearest lot next door to the Public Theater.

RESERVING SEATS:

Box Office Telephone: (212) 598-7150
Ticket Price: $5.00–$9.00.
Reservations: Box office opens at 1:00 P.M. Phone reservations are accepted from Public Theater pass members only. Credit card sales accepted. Half price Quiktix are distributed at 6:00 P.M. (1:00 P.M. at matinees) on the day of performance.
Performance Schedule: Variable; six-month residency at the Public Theater.

WHO: MANHATTAN LAMBDA PRODUCTIONS

Artistic Director: Edmund W. Trust
Managing Director: Joe Gasper
Founder: Edmund W. Trust; 1970

WHERE:

Theatre Address: Performs in various locations.
Office Address:
1155 45th Avenue
Long Island City, New York 11101
(212) 361-0926

WHAT:

Artistic Profile: It is said that laughter is the best revenge and Manhattan Lambda Productions—lambda is the Greek symbol for equal—uses laughter as its weapon.

This gay theatre company presents revivals of well-known plays—mostly melodramas—in drag. It also presents new works—for example, a version of *Snow White* set on Fire Island in which the seven dwarfs are all interior decorators who only do bathrooms. Manhattan Lambda Productions traces its true roots to 1946 when a gay theatre group began producing plays to help finance the Mattechine Society—a social-service organization working for homosexual rights. Many individuals active with this early Off Off Broadway theatre and later with the Westside Gay Theatre now actively collaborate on Manhattan Lambda's productions.

Productions 1978/79:
Not Just Another Love, Rolf Randall
Dirty Work at the Crossroads, Bill Johnson
Phaedo, Kenneth B. Houck
Murder My Sweet Matilda, Janet Green
What Can You Buy for a Token?, Eddie Allen

Productions 1979/80:
Now Hear This, Anita!, compiled by Edmund W. Trust
Snow White, Ray Mason

Special Programs: Local touring company; acting workshops.

GETTING THERE:

Consult newspaper or call office for current performing location and directions.

RESERVING SEATS:

Box Office Telephone: (212) 361-0926
Ticket Price: $3.00 or TDF voucher; $2.00 for students and senior citizens.
Reservations: Call theatre, tickets held until fifteen minutes before curtain.
Group Rates: $2.00 for groups of ten to twenty-five; $1.50 for groups larger than twenty-five.
Performance Schedule: A new production is presented every two months, March through November. Evenings: Thursday through Sunday. Curtain at 11:00 P.M. during the summer months. Each production runs six weeks.

WHO: MANHATTAN PUNCH LINE

Artistic Director: Steve Kaplan
Executive Director: Mitch McGuire
Founders: Steve Kaplan, Mitch McGuire, Faith Catlin; 1978

WHERE:

Neighborhood: Clinton–Times Square
Theatre Address:
260 West 41st Street
New York, New York 10036
(212) 921-8288

The Space: Headquartered on the seventh floor of a once decrepit and derelict-ridden factory building, Manhattan Punch Line has speedily transformed the space into a 100-seat theatre sporting plush velvet seats once used by a porno house. In a spacious, comfortable lobby whose floor-to-ceiling windows provide a fine view of the city, one can purchase beverages, snacks, Manhattan Punch Line T-shirts, as well as moustaches and glasses with rubber noses.

WHAT:

Artistic Profile: Manhattan Punch Line is dedicated to the spirit of the comic, the gadfly, the satirist, the clown. They see laughter as a curative and cauterizing agent. "In a world that may end with neither a whimper nor a bang—just a gigantic pratfall on a banana peel—comedy, we feel, is the only rational stance." Since opening on April Fools Day in 1979 MPL has produced new comic plays, showcased improvisational groups in its late-night cabaret series, presented a monthly Fool's Night—an evening of stand-up comedy, and produced the Sunday Funnies—a film series.

Productions 1978/79:
Flagship, Donald Wollner
The Jack the Ripper Revue, Peter Mataliano
The Cat and the Canary, John Willard

Productions 1979/80:

The Vegetable, F. Scott Fitzgerald

The Duel, adapted by David Gild from a story by Anton Chekov

Room Service, John Murray, Allan Boretz

The Man Who Shot the Man Who Shot Jesse James, Thornbrake Theatre

The Incomparable Max, Jerome H. Lawrence, Robert E. Lee

Special Programs: Classes in acting, improvisation, commercial acting, career workshops, movement; stand-up comedy; summer staged-reading series; internships; post-performance lectures; film series; late-night cabarets; theatre rentals.

GETTING THERE:

Subway: IND A, E, AA, CC to 42nd Street; Seventh Avenue IRT 1, 2, 3 to 42nd Street; BMT N, RR, QB to Times Square; Flushing Line IRT 7 to Times Square.

Bus: Uptown: Eighth Avenue (M10); Downtown: Ninth Avenue (M11); Crosstown West: 42nd Street (M106) and 49th Street (M27); Crosstown East: 42nd Street (M106) and 50th Street (M27).

Parking: Street parking; nearest lot next door. Garage on 41st Street just off Seventh Avenue.

RESERVING SEATS:

Box Office Telephone: (212) 921-1455

Ticket Price: $3.50–$5.00, TDF voucher accepted.

Reservations: Call theatre, held until a half hour before curtain.

Group Rates: Available for groups of fifteen or more. Contact the theatre.

Subscription: Available, contact the theatre.

Performance Schedule: Productions presented year-round. Evenings: Thursday through Saturday; Matinees: Sunday. Late show at 10:30 P.M. Friday, Saturday.

MANHATTAN PUNCH LINE RECOMMENDS:

Hell's Kitchen: 598 Ninth Avenue, on the corner of 43rd Street, 757-5329. Reservations accepted. American. Noon till midnight, seven days; Brunch: Saturday and Sunday, 12:30 P.M.–4:30 P.M. $3.00–$9.00, a la carte. Diner's, Carte Blanche, Amex accepted.

West Bank Cafe: 407 West 42nd Street, in Manhattan Plaza, 695-6909. Reservations required 6:00 P.M.–8:00 P.M. American-Continental-Oriental. Monday through Saturday: noon–1:00 A.M.; Sunday: noon–11:00 P.M. Lunch: $2.50–$4.25, a la carte; Dinner: $4.25–$8.75, a la carte. MC, Visa, Amex accepted. Jazz, Big Bands, Comedy, Singers, Broadway Personalities: Tuesday through Saturday at 8:30 P.M. and 10:30 P.M.

Curtain Up: 402 West 43rd Street, in Manhattan Plaza, 564-7272. Reservations accepted. Steaks, seafood, omelettes. Sunday: 11:30 A.M. till midnight. Monday: noon till midnight; Tuesday through Thursday: noon till 1:00 A.M.; Friday and Saturday: noon till 2:00 A.M. $3.00–$8.50, a la carte. All credit cards accepted. Classical Music: Wednesday, Friday, Sunday afternoons and evenings.

WHO: MANHATTAN THEATRE CLUB

Artistic Director: Lynne Meadow
Managing Director: Barry Grove
Founders: A. E. Jeffcoat, Peregrine Whittlesey, Margaret Kennedy, Victor Germack, Joseph Tandet; 1970

WHERE:

Neighborhood: Upper East Side
Theatre Address:
321 East 73rd Street (between First and Second Avenues)
New York, New York 10021
(212) 288-2500

The Space: With its high-price boutiques, luxury townhouses, fine restaurants and singles bars, Manhattan

Theatre Club's Upper East Side environs cater to those on the up-and-up—and those already there. Appropriately, the theatre's large three-theatre complex evokes the comfort and sense of establishment more frequently associated with more institutionalized regional and Off Broadway theatres. Yet the century old building—formerly the Bohemian Benevolent Society—retains a sense of intimacy. While its physical space evokes stability, its atmosphere is charged with a dynamism that speaks of non-stop artistic activity—auditions, rehearsals, performances, take place on every floor, in every room, in any and every available corner. Performing spaces include a Downstage 155-seat proscenium, an Upstage 100-seat thrust, and a 75-seat Cabaret theatre, decorated with an authentically restored Ukrainian wall mural.

WHAT:

Artistic Profile: Founded by a group of private citizens as an alternative to the commercial theatre, Manhattan Theatre Club has developed into a major performing arts center offering a Downstage Series of five American and International plays, an Upstage-Cabaret Series, a Writers in Performance Series, and late-night Special Events. Seeking plays with an urgent voice rather than a flawless form—regardless of their commercial potential—MTC nevertheless has moved many productions to extended runs on and off Broadway. Highlights of recent seasons include *Ain't Misbehavin'*; the New York premier of works by Sam Shepard, David Storey, and Athol Fugard; Joanna Glass's *Artichoke*, John Hopkins's *Losing Time*, Simon Gray's *The Rear Column*, Istvan Orkeny's *Catsplay*, Gardner McKay's *Sea Marks*, and Richard Wesley's *The Last Street Play*.

Productions 1978/79:

The Rear Column, Simon Gray
Grand Magic, Eduardo de Filippo
Artichoke, Joanna M. Glass
Don Juan Comes Home from the War, Odon von Horvath
The Arbor, Brother Jonathan, O.S.F.
Nongogo, Athol Fugard

Beethoven/Karl, David Rush
Stevie, Hugh Whitemore
Losing Time, John Hopkins
Just a Little Bit Less Than Normal, Nigel Baldwin
Jim Wann/a country cabaret
A Lady Needs a Change, music: various; lyrics by Dorothy Fields; adaptation by Bill Gile
Dancing in the Dark, music by Arthur Schwartz; lyrics by Howard Dietz, et al.; adaptation by Mary O'Hagan
Give My Heart an Even Break, composed by George Quincy; lyrics by Thayer Burch
Rokko and the Hat, the musical team of Rokko Jans and Annie Hat
Jake Holmes' Street Songs

Productions 1979/80:

Losing Time, John Hopkins
The Jail Diary of Albie Sachs, David Edgar
Endgame, Samuel Beckett
Biography, S. N. Behrman
Mass Appeal, Bill C. Davis
Ice, Michael Cristofer
Nacha Guevara, a cabaret act
One-Acts by John Gwylym:
Two Rooms
One Wedding
Three Friends
Styne after Styne, conceived by Fritz Holt and Jonathan Reynolds
Dusa, Fish, Stas and Vi, Pam Gems
Sidewalkin', Jake Holmes
A Christmas Garland, conceived by Eileen Atkins
An Evening with Margery Cohen and Jonathan Hadary
My Mother, My Son, conceived by Viveca Lindfors and Kristoffer Tabori
Writers in Performance Series—a series of Monday night readings by contemporary poets and prose writers

Special Programs: Internships; post-performance lectures; newsletter; in-house readings; playwrights in residence; summer theatre rentals; Writers in Performance series.

GETTING THERE:

Subway: Lexington Avenue IRT 6 to 68th or 77th Street.
Bus: Uptown: First Avenue (M15); Downtown: Second Avenue (M15); Crosstown West and East: 72nd Street (M30) and 79th Street (M17).
Parking: Two garages on 73rd Street between First and Second Avenues.

RESERVING SEATS:

Box Office Telephone: (212) 472-0600
Ticket Price: Downstage Series: $10.00–$12.00; Upstage-Cabaret: $8.00–$10.00; Poetry Series: $4.00; Special Events: $7.00; TDF voucher not accepted.
Reservations: Call theatre, tickets held until a half hour prior to curtain. All major credit cards accepted.
Group Rates: Available, contact the theatre.
Subscription: Series A: Five-Play Downstage Series; Series B: Super Series—Five-Play Downstage Series plus six-event Upstage-Cabaret Series. Variable rates for weekday and weekend subscriptions.
Performance Schedule: Full season of Downstage productions and Upstage-Cabaret productions; Monday Writers in Performance Series; and late-night Special Events presented October through June. Evenings: Tuesday through Sunday; Matinees: Saturday, Sunday.

MANHATTAN THEATRE CLUB RECOMMENDS:

Szechuan Palace: 1329 Second Avenue, on the corner of 70th Street, 628-8652. Reservations required. Szechuan-Cantonese. Sunday through Thursday: noon till 10:15 P.M.; Friday and Saturday: noon till 11:15 P.M. $2.00–$9.00, a la carte. MC, Visa, Diner's, Amex accepted. One free drink per person with dinner for patrons of Manhattan Theatre Club.
Mon East: 1354 First Avenue, between 72nd and 73rd Streets, 249-2112. Reservations accepted. Japanese. 5:00 P.M. till midnight, closed Monday. $7.00–$12.00, a la carte. All credit cards accepted. Free bottle of wine with dinner Tuesday, Wednesday, Thursday, and Sunday.

Finnegan's Wake: 1361 First Avenue, on the corner of 73rd Street, 737-3664. American-Continental. 11:00 A.M. till 4:00 A.M., seven days. $1.00–$7.95, a la carte. No credit cards accepted. Fifteen percent off total bill for patrons of Manhattan Theatre Club.

WHO: MEDICINE SHOW THEATRE ENSEMBLE

Artistic Directors: Barbara Vann, James Barbosa
Administrative Director: Jeffrey Fuerst
Founders: Barbara Vann, James Barbosa; 1970

WHERE:

Neighborhood: Chelsea
Theatre Address:
Newfoundland Theatre
6 West 18th Street (between Fifth and Sixth Avenues)
New York, New York 10011
(212) 255-4991

The Space: The Medicine Show's Newfoundland Theatre (a converted hardware store) immediately evokes a comfortable sensibility. Beyond the deep blue walls, comfortable sofa, desks and filing cabinets of its combined lobby and office space is a 75-seat flexible theatre. Two narrow ledge balconies alternately serve as audience seating or additional playing space.

WHAT:

Artistic Profile: The Medicine Show is a collaboration of professional theatre artists choosing to create idiosyncratic comic works that define and refine human values. Libertarian in spirit, physically, vocally, and emotionally lavish, their high energy productions are informed by an experimental spirit that characterized the Open Theatre (with whom Artistic Directors Barbara Vann and James Barbosa worked for eight years). While some of the work is philosophically dark, it is imbued with, and sometimes willfully contradicted by, the prankishness and sense of joy with which it is performed.

Productions 1978/79:

Frogs, book by Carl Morse and company; music by Yenoin Guibbory; lyrics by C. Morse

Shipping Out, book by Stephen Phillip Policoff and company; music by Carol Henry; lyrics by Stephen Phillip Policoff and Chris Brandt

The Mummer's Play, company-developed from traditional texts with additional text by Stephen Phillip Policoff; music by Carol Henry

The Tragedy of Tragedies, or The Life and Death of Tom Thumb the Great, Henry Fielding; music by Carol Henry

Productions 1979/80:

Shipping Out, book by Stephen Phillip Policoff and company; music by Carol Henry; lyrics by Stephen Phillip Policoff and Chris Brandt

The Tragedy of Tragedies, or The Life and Death of Tom Thumb the Great, Henry Fielding; music by Carol Henry

Frogs, book by Carl Morse and company; music by Yenoin Guibbory; lyrics by C. Morse

The Mummer's Play, company-developed from traditional texts with additional text by Stephen Phillip Policoff; music by Carol Henry

Classic Comics, group collaboration with text by Ring Lardner, Gertrude Stein, and George S. Kaufman

The Poe Project, group-creation; writer in collaboration: Stephen Phillip Policoff; music by William Hellerman

Special Programs: Professional training in acting, vocal, and physical technique; internships; training in collaborative theatre techniques; in-schools programs; national and international touring; short- and long-term university residences; theatre rentals; seminars and lectures.

GETTING THERE:

Subway: IND B, F to 23rd Street; BMT RR to 23rd Street; Seventh Avenue IRT 1 to 18th Street.

Bus: Uptown: Sixth Avenue (M5, M6, M7); Downtown: Fifth Avenue (M2, M3, M5); Crosstown West and East: 23rd Street (M26) and 14th Street (M14).

Parking: Street parking after 6:00 P.M. and on weekends.

RESERVING SEATS:

Box Office Telephone: (212) 255-4991

Ticket Price: $3.00–$5.00, TDF voucher accepted. Discounts for students and senior citizens available.

Reservations: Call theatre, tickets held until fifteen minutes before curtain.

Group Rates: Available for groups larger than ten. Contact the theatre.

Performance Schedule: Three or four productions presented September through June. Contact theatre for evenings of performances.

MEDICINE SHOW THEATRE ENSEMBLE RECOMMENDS:

Harvey's Chelsea Restaurant: 108 West 18th Street, just off Sixth Avenue, 243-5644. Reservations recommended. German-English-Continental. Sunday through Thursday: noon till midnight; Friday and Saturday: noon till 1:00 A.M. Lunch: $3.95–$11.95, a la carte; Dinner: $4.95–$12.95, a la carte. No credit cards accepted. Personal checks accepted.

Brownies: 21 East 16th Street, just east of Fifth Avenue, 255-2838. Natural foods. Monday through Friday: 11:00 A.M. till 8:00 P.M.; Saturday: noon till 4:00 P.M. Closed Sunday. $3.50–$5.00, a la carte. No credit cards accepted.

WHO: NAT HORNE MUSICAL THEATRE

Artistic Director: Nat Horne
Executive Director: Albert Reyes
Founders: Nat Horne, Albert Reyes; 1973

WHERE:

Neighborhood: Clinton–Theatre Row
Theatre Address:
440 West 42nd Street (between Ninth and Tenth Avenues)
New York, New York 10036
(212) 736-7128

The Space: Located on Theatre Row—a revitalized neighborhood that now boasts eight Off Off Broadway playhouses, an artists' housing complex and innumerable thriving businesses and restaurants—Nat Horne Musical Theatre has two performing spaces: a ground floor, newly renovated, 119-seat proscenium theatre and a third-floor dance-studio space with minimal lighting facilities and seating for fifty. Since the company now focuses exclusively on musical productions which are too large-scale to be accommodated by the stage space, they usually perform at other theatres, renting their theatre to others or using it for workshops, classes, and recitals.

WHAT:

Artistic Profile: Founded in 1973 as a workshop to provide dancers with acting and singing instruction, and hence a better chance of winning Broadway auditions, Nat Horne Musical Theatre's multi-racial company of dancers-actors-singers, known as Dancing Plus, is trained personally by Nat Horne in jazz dance and by a staff of teacher-performers in other dance techniques, singing, and acting. Using his unique jazz dance technique (a synthesis of the styles of Jack Cole and Matt Maddox), the company develops musical theatre recitals that evoke the romance, adventure, heroism and simple truths that so often characterized theatrical productions of the 1940s. At the same time, they are dedicated to developing a unique American jazz-dance-theatre form.

Productions 1978/79:

The Phantom, adapted from *The Phantom of the Opera*, book by Al Reyes; remounted, with book by Edward Brown

Miss Truth, book and music by Dr. Glory Van Scott

The Legend of Frankie and Johnny, book by Al Reyes; choreography and concept by Nat Horne; music and lyrics by Glen Vecchione; additional music and lyrics by David Dusing

Breeders, Bob Ost

Productions 1979/80:

The Legend of Frankie and Johnny

Choreographer's Festival

Mercury, choreography by Joseph Holloway

Productions 1981:
The Odyssey, Edward Brown
The Grand Canyon Suite, Nat Horne
Joan of Arc, Al Reyes

Special Programs: Classes in jazz dance, modern dance, ballet, tap, voice basics, vocal interpretation, performer's dynamics, acting techniques, scene study, theatre management; musical theatre workshop; private voice coaching; workshop productions, lecture-demonstrations and master classes; touring to nearby colleges and community centers; internships; sponsorship of choreographers' festival; theatre rentals.

GETTING THERE:

Subway: IND A, AA, CC, E to 42nd Street.

Bus: Uptown: Tenth Avenue (M11, M16); Downtown: Ninth Avenue (M11); Crosstown West and East: 42nd Street (M106).

Parking: Manhattan Plaza garage across the street.

RESERVING SEATS:

Box Office Telephone: (212) 736-7128

Ticket Price: $3.00–$8.00, TDF voucher accepted (either theatre or dance vouchers are accepted depending on the production). Discounts for students and senior citizens.

Reservations: Call theatre, tickets held until a half hour before curtain.

Group Rates: Available for groups of ten to nineteen, additional discount for groups larger than twenty. Contact the theatre for rates.

Performance Schedule: Two to four productions plus workshops presented September through June.

NAT HORNE MUSICAL THEATRE RECOMMENDS:

Market Diner: 411 Ninth Avenue, at 33rd Street, 244-6033. American. Open twenty-four hours, seven days. $3.00–$7.00, complete meals. No credit cards accepted.

Hell's Kitchen: 598 Ninth Avenue, at the corner of 43rd Street, 757-5329. Reservations accepted. American. Noon till midnight, seven days; Brunch: Saturday and Sunday, 12:30 P.M.–4:30 P.M. $3.00–$9.00, a la carte. Diner's, Carte Blanche, Amex accepted.

Curtain Up: 402 West 43rd Street, in Manhattan Plaza, 564-7272. Reservations accepted. Steaks, seafood, omelettes. Sunday: 11:30 A.M. till midnight; Monday: noon till midnight; Tuesday through Thursday: noon till 1:00 A.M.; Friday and Saturday: noon till 2:00 A.M. $3.00–$8.50, a la carte. All credit cards accepted. Classical music: Wednesday, Friday, Sunday afternoons and evenings.

La Rousse: 414 West 42nd Street, on Theatre Row, 736-4913. Reservations recommended. French Peasant. 11:30 A.M. till midnight, seven days. Lunch: $3.95–$8.95, a la carte; Dinner: $5.95–$9.95, a la carte. All credit cards except Carte Blanche accepted. La Rousse occasionally features a complete Dinner-Theatre Ticket Package for productions on Theatre Row. Call Peter Howard at the restaurant for information.

Angelo's West Restaurant: 360 West 42nd Street, 244-8655. International-Italian. 11:30 A.M. till 11:00 P.M. Closed Sunday. $6.00–$12.00, a la carte. MC, Visa, Amex accepted.

WHO: NEW FEDERAL THEATRE

Producing Director: Woodie King, Jr.
Co-Producer: Steve Tennen
Founder: Woodie King, Jr.; 1970

WHERE:

Neighborhood: Lower East Side
Theatre Address:
Henry Street Settlement
466 Grand Street
New York, New York 10002
(212) 766-9295

The Space: The New Federal Theatre is located in the Henry Street Settlement, one of the oldest and most prestigious community organizations in America. For over eighty years the Settlement has served the Lower East Side's ethnically diverse community. Its three theatres, rehearsal studios, and modern stage equipment are all made available to New Federal Theatre. Major productions are presented in the 350-seat proscenium Playhouse theatre.

WHAT:

Artistic Profile: The New Federal Theatre was founded to serve minority audiences on the Lower East Side, a diverse cultural community that includes Blacks, Hispanics, Chinese, and Jews. While fostering the development of new talent through several ethnic acting and playwriting workshops, the theatre has brought national attention to such minority artists as J. E. Franklin (whose *Black Girl* was filmed with several original cast members from NFT's production), Ron Milner, Ed. Pomerantz, Joseph Lizardi, Ntozke Shange, and Ed Bullins. Under an arrangement with the New York Shakespeare Festival, both Bullins' *The Taking of Miss Janie* and Shange's *For Colored Girls Who Have Considered Suicide When the Rainbow Is Enuf* were first showcased at the New Federal Theatre before moving to the New York Shakespeare Festival's theatre. The theatre has also produced several plays from the library of the Federal Theatre Project.

Productions 1978/79:

Hot Dishes!, book and lyrics by Maurice Peterson; music by Grenaldo Frazier, Maurice Peterson

Black Medea, Ernest Ferlita

Take It from the Top, book and lyrics by Ruby Dee, music by Guy Davis

Flamingo, Flamongo, Lucky Cienfuega; music by Steve Tarshis

The Glorious Monster in the Bell of the Horn, Larry Neal; music by Max Roach

Retrospective of the Best Black Plays of the Forties and Fifties

Anna Lucasta, Phillip Yordan
Trouble in Mind, Alice Childress
Take a Giant Step, Louis Peterson
In Splendid Error, William Branch
A Raisin in the Sun, Lorraine Hansberry

Productions 1979/80:
Suspenders, Umar Bin Hassan
Crazy Horse, Louis Peterson
Friends, Crispin Larangeria
A Puerto Rican Obituary, Pedro Pietri
Branches from the Same Tree, Marge Eliot

Special Programs: Black, Hispanic, and Jewish playwriting and acting workshops; dance workshops; classes for non-professionals.

GETTING THERE:

Subway: IND B, D to Grand Street; IND F to East Broadway; BMT J, M to Bowery.
Bus: Downtown: Second Avenue (M15); Uptown: Vesey Street, Park Row (M22); Crosstown East and West: Grand Street (M8).
Parking: Street parking easily available.

RESERVING SEATS:

Box Office Telephone: (212) 766-9334
Ticket Price: $2.50, TDF voucher accepted. $1.50 for senior citizens.
Reservations: Tickets usually distributed on a first come, first serve basis.
Group Rates: Available, contact the theatre.
Performance Schedule: A new production is presented every month and a half throughout the year. Evenings: Thursday through Sunday.

NEW FEDERAL THEATRE RECOMMENDS:

Ratner's Dairy Restaurant: 138 Delancey Street, between Norfolk and Suffolk Streets, 677-5588. Kosher Dairy. 6:00 A.M. till midnight, seven days. $2.00–$4.95, a la carte. No credit cards accepted.

WHO: NEW YORK COLLABORATION THEATRE

Artistic Director: Eugene Pelfrey
Founder: Eugene Pelfrey; 1978

WHERE:

Theatre Address: Performs in various locations.
Office Address:
102 West 80th Street, #36
New York, New York 10024
(212) 873-4991

WHAT:

Artistic Profile: The New York Collaboration Theatre investigates problematic ideas and events affecting contemporary society through exploratory, developmental theatre methods. Their first production, *Bloodlust,* examined the public fascination with Son of Sam and was developed during a fifteen-month workshop in which actors contributed research, writing, and improvisation towards the development of the script. Continuing to pursue its interest in socially significant theatre, the company is now working on *With Men*, an all-women production exploring power relationships between the sexes.
Productions 1978/79:
Bloodlust, developed collaboratively
Productions 1979/80:
With Men, developed collaboratively

GETTING THERE:

Contact the office for current performing location and directions.

RESERVING SEATS:

Box Office Telephone: (212) 873-4991
Ticket Price: $3.50–$6.00, TDF voucher accepted. Discounts for students and senior citizens.
Reservations: Call office to make reservations.

Group Rates: Available, contact the theatre.

Performance Schedule: Performs intermittently since long developmental workshops precede the production of each play. Call the office for current schedule.

WHO: NEW YORK SHAKESPEARE FESTIVAL

Producer: Joseph Papp
General Manager: Robert Kamlot
Founder: Joseph Papp; 1954

WHERE:

Theatre Address:
Public Theater
425 Lafayette Street
New York, New York 10003
(212) 598-7100

The Space: The Public Theater—the Public Theater is a city unto itself. Formerly the Astor Library, this landmark building has been converted to a seven-theatre complex where more than twenty productions are produced each season as well as a jazz, film, and poetry series. The large lobby is always filled with people—purchasing tickets for coming productions, waiting on line for the half price Quiktix that are always distributed the day of performance (no matter how popular the production), browsing at the book counter, or buying homemade cookies, fruit, drinks, and coffee at the refreshment bar. The theatre facilities include the 299-seat proscenium Newman Theatre; the 275-seat thrust Anspacher Theatre; the flexible, 191-seat Martinson Hall; the flexible, 135-to-150-seat LuEsther Hall; the flexible, 75-to-108-seat Other Stage; the flexible, 55-to-93-seat Old Prop Shop; and the 96-seat Little Theater.

Delacorte Theater—located in Central Park (near 79th Street), a 1,936-seat open-air theatre where free productions of Shakespeare are presented each summer. Attending free Shakespeare in Central Park has become a well-established summer tradition for thousands of New

Yorkers who combine their playgoing with pre-theatre picnics in the park. It is advisable to bring a sweater, as it sometimes gets chilly after sunset.

Mobile Theater—a caravan of four trailers, complete with a stage, seating for 1,500, lighting, sound, and dressing room facilities, transforms New York's parks and playgrounds into fully equipped theatres for free performances during the summer.

WHAT:

Artistic Profile: Producing plays for over a quarter-century, the New York Shakespeare Festival is widely regarded as one of the nation's foremost theatrical institutions. Under the leadership of Joseph Papp—one of the most influential participants in the Off Off Broadway theatre movement—the Festival began in 1956 by presenting free productions of Shakespeare in city parks and established a permanent home in 1967 at the Public Theater. Each year the NYSF produces over twenty productions, both new plays and classics, as well as sponsoring jazz, film, and poetry series. These have included such notable productions as *A Chorus Line, Hair, For Colored Girls Who Have Considered Suicide When the Rainbow Is Enuf, I'm Getting My Act Together and Taking It on the Road, Runaways, That Championship Season, Short Eyes*, and *Sticks and Bones*. In addition, the Festival has produced four seasons of theatre at Lincoln Center, ten plays on Broadway, and reached a national audience with prime-time television specials and touring companies. Each summer the Festival presents free Shakespeare at the Delacorte Theater in Central Park featuring such artists as Colleen Dewhurst, George C. Scott, James Earl Jones, and Meryl Streep. Free performances are also provided by the Mobile Theater which tours New York City's parks and playgrounds.

Productions 1978/79:

All's Well That Ends Well, William Shakespeare
The Taming of the Shrew, William Shakespeare
An Evening at New Rican Village, Eduardo Figueroa
Drinks before Dinner, E. L. Doctorow

The Umbrellas of Cherbourg, book and lyrics by Jaques Demy; translation by Sheldon Harnick and Charles Burr; music by Michel Legrand
Julius Caesar, William Shakespeare
Coriolanus, William Shakespeare
Taken in Marriage, Thomas Babe
Sancocho, book by Ramiro Ramirez; music and lyrics by Jimmy Justice and R. Ramirez
Dispatches, music and lyrics by Elizabeth Swados, from Michael Herr's book
Wake Up, It's Time to Go to Bed!, Carson Kievman
The Woods, David Mamet
Happy Days, Samuel Beckett
Spell #7, Ntozake Shange
Unfinished Women, Aishah Rahman
The Master and Margarita, Mikhail Bulgakov
Fathers and Sons, Thomas Babe
Quannapowitt Quartet, Part 3, Israel Horovitz
New Jerusalem, Len Jenkin
White Sirens, Lois Elaine Griffith
Leave It to Beaver Is Dead, Des McEnuff
Nasty Rumors and Final Remarks, Susan Miller
Remembrance, Derek Walcott
Poets from the Inside, Directed by Jeremy Blahnick

Productions 1979/80:

Coriolanus, William Shakespeare
Othello, William Shakespeare
Mighty Gents, Richard Wesley
The Art of Dining, Tina Howe
The Sorrows of Stephen, Peter Parnell
Salt Lake City Skyline, Thomas Babe
Marie and Bruce, Wallace Shawn
Tongues and *Savage/Love*, Sam Shepard
The Haggadah, Elizabeth Swados
Mother Courage, Bertolt Brecht; adapted by Ntozake Shange
Hard Sell, Murray Horwitz and Roger Director
Sunday Runners in the Rain, Israel Horovitz
The Music Lessons, Wakado Yamauchi
Scenes from Everyday Life, Ned Jackson
FOB, David Hwang
Mercier and Camier, Samuel Beckett (produced with Mabou Mines)

Special Programs: Internships, workshop productions and staged readings, film series, poetry series, jazz series, newsletter, weekly events calendar, playwrights' workshop, cooperative program with other Off Off Broadway theatres.

GETTING THERE:

Subway: Lexington Avenue IRT 6 to Astor Place; BMT RR to 8th Street; IND B, D, F to Broadway/Lafayette Street.

Bus: Uptown: Whitehall Street (M1); Downtown: Broadway (M6) and Fifth Avenue (M1); Crosstown West: 9th Street (M13); Crosstown East: 8th Street (M13).

Parking: Street parking after 6:00 P.M.; nearest lot next door to the Public Theater.

RESERVING SEATS:

Box Office Telephone: (212) 598-7150 (Public Theater)
(212) 535-5630 (Delacorte Theater)

Ticket Price: Major Productions: $9.00–$10.00; Workshop Productions: $4.00–$5.00. At least 25 percent of the tickets at each theatre are sold at reduced Quiktix prices —even for shows sold out at full price. Quiktix go on sale at 6:00 P.M. (1:00 P.M. Matinees) on the day of performance only. TDF voucher accepted towards the purchase of Quiktix. Admission is free to Shakespeare in Central Park and the Mobile Theater unit.

Reservations: Phone reservations are accepted from Pass Members only. Credit card sales are accepted with a $1.00 handling charge. Box office opens at 1:00 P.M. Quiktix are distributed at 6:00 P.M. (1:00 P.M. Matinees) on the day of performance. Free tickets to Shakespeare in Central Park are distributed in the park at 6:15 P.M. on the day of the performance. (Arrive early to insure receiving a ticket.)

Subscription: A Public Theater Pass offers contributing members the privilege of purchasing reserved tickets to all Festival productions at Quiktix prices and reserving seats by phone. A First Class Pass with prepaid admission plus contribution guarantees admission to all productions.

Performance Schedule: Over twenty productions are presented throughout the year. Evenings: Tuesday through Sunday; Matinees: Saturday, Sunday.

NEW YORK SHAKESPEARE FESTIVAL RECOMMENDS:

Lady Astor's: 430 Lafayette Street, directly across from the Public Theater, 228-7888. Reservations accepted. French. Noon till 1:00 A.M., seven days. Lunch and Supper: $2.50–$7.00; Dinner: $10.00–$18.00, a la carte. No credit cards accepted.

Colonnades Restaurant: 432 Lafayette Street, directly across from the Public Theater, 473-8890. Quiche, burgers, salads. Lunch: Monday through Friday, noon till 3:00 P.M.; Dinner: 5:30 P.M. till 1:30 A.M.; Weekends: 5:00 P.M. till 2:30 A.M. only. $3.75–$14.00. No credit cards accepted.

East/West: 105 East 9th Street, between Third and Fourth Avenues, 260-1994. Reservations required on weekends between 6:00 P.M. and 8:00 P.M. Natural foods. Weekdays: 5:30 P.M. till 10:00 P.M.; Weekends: 4:30 P.M. till 11:00 P.M. $5.25–$9.00, a la carte. No credit cards accepted.

McSorley's Old Ale House: 15 East 7th Street, between Second and Third Avenues, 473-8800. Bar with sandwiches and hot lunch. 11:00 A.M. till midnight. $2.00–$4.00, a la carte.

Hisae's Place: 35 Cooper Square, between 5th and 6th Streets, 228-6886. Reservations required for parties of four or more. Oriental style. Monday through Thursday: 5:00 P.M. till Midnight; Friday and Saturday: 5:00 P.M. till 1:00 A.M.; Sunday: 5:00 P.M. till 11:00 P.M. $5.95–$10.95, a la carte. No credit cards accepted.

WHO: NEW YORK STAGEWORKS

Producing Director: Craig LaPlount
Managing Director: George Morelli
Founders: Craig LaPlount, Cecily LaPlount, Nick Roberts, Terry Alan Smith; 1977

WHERE:

Theatre Address: Performs in various locations.
Office Address:
15 West 18th Street (just off Fifth Avenue)
New York, New York 10011
(212) 242-3967

WHAT:

Artistic Profile: New York Stageworks provides a meeting ground for the writer and the director and an environment where the playwright can develop by working closely with the director and actors during the rehearsal period. In addition to new plays the company presents a yearly Directors' Festival of one-act plays. Plays are chosen by the theatre and promising young directors throughout the city are then interviewed for possible participation. A resident marionette troupe presents children's programs on the weekends and during the summer the theatre presents a revival series.

Productions 1978/79:
Him, e.e. cummings
Professor George, Marsha Sheiness
Dr. Kheal, Maria Irene Fornes
Directors' Festival
The Birthday Present, Peter Brook
Doin' It to Death, Emanuel Westbrook
Larry Parks' Day in Court, Eric Bentley
The Tiger, Murray Schisgal
Hippolytes, Euripedes
Sketches of Four, Lynn Schwartz
Monkey Monkey Bottle of Beer How Many Monkeys Have We Here, Marsha Sheiness
Serious Business, group-developed
Reunion, Andrew Foster
Marionette Shows

Productions 1979/80:
The Real Inspector Hound, Tom Stoppard
Directors' Festival
Did You See the Lone Ranger, Sean Michael Rice
When Bogart Was, Sean Michael Rice
The Pokey, Stephen Black

Kilo, Mark Berman
Cold Beer, Miguel Pinero
Tales of Another City, Yukio Mishima; adapted by Joe Broido
Landscape with Waitress, Robert Pine
Telephone Man, Dennis Kennedy
Siren Painter, Jim Shepard
Waterman, Frank Ford
Cold Beer and *Toilet Paper*, Miguel Pinero
Air Time, book, music, and lyrics by Thomas Michael
Marionette Shows

Special Programs: Playreadings, internships, children's programs, theatre rentals.

GETTING THERE:

Contact the office for current performing location and directions.

RESERVING SEATS:

Box Office Telephone: (212) 242-3967
Ticket Price: $3.50–$5.00, TDF voucher accepted. $1.50 off ticket price for students and senior citizens.
Reservations: Call the office, tickets held until fifteen minutes before curtain.
Performance Schedule: Productions presented year-round. Evenings: Thursday through Sunday; children's puppet shows presented at weekend matinees.

WHO: NEW YORK STREET THEATRE CARAVAN

Artistic Director: Marketa Kimbrell
Administrator: All administrative decisions made collectively by the company.
Founder: Marketa Kimbrell; 1968

WHERE:

Theatre Address: Performs in various locations including union halls and prisons. Contact theatre for current location.

Office Address:
87-05 Chelsea Street
Jamaica, New York 11432
(212) 242-1869

WHAT:

Artistic Profile: The New York Street Theatre Caravan is a multi-racial company that creates plays about working people everywhere. The company's work has included *Sacco and Vanzetti* (using authentic transcripts), *Molly McGuire* (a minstrel revue about the oppression of the Irish), and an adaptation of John Steinbeck's *Grapes of Wrath.* Touring nationally and internationally, the company performs in union halls, migrant camps, Indian reservations, and underprivileged neighborhoods. A topical street show, revised each year, is also presented by the company.

Productions 1978/79:
Hard Time Blues, Marketa Kimbrell and the Company
The Vietnamization of Wounded Knee, Marketa Kimbrell and the company

Productions 1979/80:
Sacco and Vanzetti, Marketa Kimbrell and the company
Molly McGuire, Marketa Kimbrell and the company

Special Programs: Extensive national and international touring; workshops in prisons and for unions; post-performance lectures; children's programs; fall company training program.

GETTING THERE:

Contact the theatre for current performing location and directions.

RESERVING SEATS:

Box Office Telephone: (212) 242-1869
Ticket Price: $5.00, TDF voucher accepted.
Reservations: Call theatre, tickets held until ten minutes before curtain.
Group Rates: $2.50 for groups of twenty or more.

Subscription: Shared season with the Labor Theatre and the Modern Times Theatre: pass for any four performances at the three theatres.

Performance Schedule: New York performances presented during the spring. Evenings: Thursday through Sunday; Matinees: Sunday. Five months of national and international touring.

WHO: NEW YORK THEATRE STRATEGY

Artistic Director: Maria Irene Fornes
Managing Director: Maria Irene Fornes
Founder: Maria Irene Fornes; 1971

WHERE:

Theatre Address: Performs in various locations.
Office Address:
One Sheridan Square
New York, New York 10014
(212) 741-0590

WHAT:

Artistic Profile: For close to a decade New York Theatre Strategy served as a playwrights' cooperative that provided member writers with the opportunity to mount their plays with absolutely no artistic interference. Sharing a commitment to the experimental spirit that characterized Cafe Cino, Cafe La Mama, Theatre Genesis, and Judson Poets' Theater during the 1960s, company members have included Kenneth Bernard, Rosalyn Drexler, Ed Bullins, Rochelle Owens, Murray Melnick, Ronald Tavel, Lanford Wilson, Julie Bovasso, Adrianne Kennedy, Charles Ludlam, Leonard Melfi, Robert Patrick, Sam Shepard, and Jean-Claude van Itallie, among others. In 1980 the organizational structure of the theatre shifted. Formerly run as a cooperative, it now works under the artistic direction of Maria Irene Fornes. A season of new work developed in an upstate New York barn is presented in Manhattan each spring.

Productions 1978/79:
Neon Woman, Tom Eyen
Kontraption, Rochelle Owens
The Ovens of Anita Orangejuice, Ronald Tavel
Suburban Tremens, Robert Heide
Too Late for Yogurt, Harry Kaoutoukas

Productions 1979/80:
Solomon's Fish, Murray Mednick
Vulgar Lines, Rosalyn Drexler
Justice, Kenneth Bernard
Evelyn Brown, Maria Irene Fornes

GETTING THERE:

Contact the office for current performing location and directions.

RESERVING SEATS:

Box Office Telephone: (212) 741-0374
Ticket Price: Variable, contact the theatre.
Reservations: Contact the office for reservation policy.
Performance Schedule: Spring season in New York City.

WHO: NEW YORK THEATRE STUDIO

Artistic Director: Richard Romagnoli
Managing Director: Cheryl Faraone
Founders: Richard Romagnoli, Cheryl Faraone; 1977

WHERE:

Theatre Address: Performs in various locations.
Office Address:
130 West 80th Street
New York, New York 10024
(212) 595-6656

WHAT:

Artistic Profile: New York Theatre Studio (NYTS) was established to present new European and American plays and infrequently produced classics. As the name studio suggests, NYTS is committed to creating an environment where actors, playwrights, and directors can collaboratively examine their craft and develop as artists. The theatre has begun to form a permanent ensemble of artists in order to facilitate the exploration of poetic and metaphorical drama. NYTS maintains a close working relationship with British playwright Snoo Wilson—one of the best-known talents of London's Fringe theatre—and has developed several improvisational works which satirically explore the trials of life in New York City.

Productions 1978/79:

Was He Anyone, N. F. Simpson
Vampire, Snoo Wilson
The Brass Ring, Brian McFadden
Kings, Michael Krawitz (staged reading)

Productions 1979/80:

It Only Laughs When I Hurt, company collaboration
Gotham Agonistes, company collaboration
The Everest Hotel, Snoo Wilson
Redback, Denis Spedaliere (staged reading)
Bark, Mary Koisch (staged reading)

Special Programs: Staged readings; acting classes.

GETTING THERE:

Contact the office for current theatre location and directions.

RESERVING SEATS:

Box Office Telephone: Contact office (212) 595-6656.
Ticket Price: $3.50 or TDF voucher.
Reservations: Contact the office for reservation policy.
Performance Schedule: Several productions and cabaret shows presented yearly. Contact the office for precise schedule and locations.

WHO: NUESTRO TEATRO

Artistic Director: Luz Castaños
Theatre Manager: James Caparelli
Founder: Luz Castaños; 1972

WHERE:

Neighborhood: Gramercy
Theatre Address:
112 East 23rd Street (between Park and Lexington Avenues)
Fourth Floor
New York, New York 10010
(212) 673-9430

The Space: The exterior of 112 East 23rd Street looks like just another small office building, giving no indication of the theatrical offerings available beyond. It's a welcome surprise to find that an intimate proscenium theatre (decorated with colorful masks used in the company's street-theatre productions) has supplanted one of the fourth-floor office spaces.

WHAT:

Artistic Profile: Nuestro Teatro was founded to awaken and further an interest in Hispanic culture. The Spanish classics, the avant-garde, contemporary works by Hispanic Americans, and popular American plays translated into Spanish comprise the company's Spanish language repertory (English synopses are provided). The company travels annually throughout the five boroughs offering a whimsical bilingual children's theatre production based on Hispanic folktales.

Productions 1978/79:
Alegria, Alegria, Alegria, Luz Castaños
Las Manos de Dios, Carlos Solórzano
Nada Como el Piso 16, Maruxa Vilalta
Prohibido Suicidarse en Primavera, Alejandro Casona
Plaza Suite, Neil Simon

Productions 1979/80:

Alegria, Alegria, Alegria, Luz Castaños
Nosotros Somos Dios, Wilberto Cantón
La Zapatera Prodigiosa, Federico García Lorca
La Mueca, Eduardo Pavlovsky
Barefoot in the Park, Neil Simon; translation by Raul Davila

Special Programs: Community outreach programs; in-schools programs, children's theatre for children; staged readings; poetry recitals; conferences; art exhibits; local touring.

GETTING THERE:

Subway: Lexington Avenue IRT 6 to 23rd Street.

Bus: Uptown: Third Avenue (M101, M102); Downtown: Lexington Avenue (M101, M102) and Fifth Avenue (M1); Crosstown West and East: 23rd Street (M26).

Parking: Street parking after 6:00 P.M. and on weekends; nearest garage on 22nd Street between Park Avenue and Broadway.

RESERVING SEATS:

Box Office Telephone: (212) 673-9430

Ticket Price: $5.00, TDF voucher accepted. $4.00 for students and senior citizens.

Reservations: Call theatre, tickets held until fifteen minutes before curtain.

Group Rates: Available for groups of twenty or more. A prepayment is required.

Performance Schedule: Three or four productions presented September through June plus outdoor summer touring program. Evenings: Fridays and Saturday; Matinees: Sunday.

NUESTRO TEATRO RECOMMENDS:

Delicias Mexicanas: 220 West 13th Street, near Seventh Avenue, 242-9389. Mexican. Noon till 11:00 P.M. Closed Sunday. $2.50–$6.00, a la carte. No credit cards accepted.

WHO: OFF CENTER THEATRE

Artistic Director: Tony McGrath
Administrative Director: Abigail Rosen
Founders: Tony McGrath, Abigail Rosen, Jerry Chase; 1968

WHERE:

Neighborhood: Chelsea
Theatre Address:
436 West 18th Street (between Ninth and Tenth Avenues)
New York, New York 10011
(212) 929-8299; 989-0764

The Space: Just a few steps from the West Side Drive between Ninth and Tenth Avenues, Off Center Theatre is certainly off center of Manhattan's midline. But the theatre derives its name from its early days when it was located on the Upper West Side, off center of the enormous dirt pit that was in the process of becoming Lincoln Center. Beyond the attractively finished lobby space—complete with a bar—is a 99-to-150-seat proscenium theatre with plush gray theatre seats (once used at Carnegie Hall).

WHAT:

Artistic Profile: One of the oldest Off Off Broadway theatres, Off Center Theatre began presenting productions as a spinoff of the Hardware Poet's Theatre in Good Shepherd Faith Church. After losing their space the company of necessity focused on street-theatre productions and children's shows—both politically oriented. The backbone of the company's repertory is comprised of comic works targeted for specific audiences. For example, *Hope of Life*, a woman's lib soap opera presented at work places throughout the city includes information on medical examinations, pregnancy tests, and employee rights; *Biting the Apple*, a street theatre piece, focuses on neighborhood improvement; and *Now's Our Time*, which tours senior centers, focuses on food stamps, rent subsidies, staying healthy and happy. Street theatre is augmented with indoor productions of new American plays, performed in what was formerly the garage space for the company's street-theatre truck.

Productions 1978/79:

Hortense Said: I Don't Give a Damn, George Feydeau
Now's Our Time, Abigail Rosen
Children's Shows (all are given unique, political reinterpretations)
Sinbad the Sailor
Hansel and Gretel
Jack and the Beanstalk
Frankenstein
Little Red Riding Hood
The Pied Piper
Three Little Pigs

Productions 1979/80:

Biting the Apple, Sidney Seidman
Just for Fun, based on the music of Jerome Kern
Now's Our Time
Children's Shows

Special Programs: Free classes in street-theatre techniques, scene study, job hunting, ballet, Alexander technique, sword fighting, playreading; touring; poetry workshops; theatre rentals.

GETTING THERE:

Subway: IND A, E, AA, CC to 14th Street; walk to 17th Street exit.

Bus: Uptown: Tenth Avenue (M11); Downtown: Ninth Avenue (M11); Crosstown West and East: 14th Street (M14).

Parking: Ample street parking at all times.

RESERVING SEATS:

Box Office Telephone: (212) 929-8299

Ticket Price: \$0–\$5.00, TDF voucher accepted. Student-rush tickets, and discounts for senior citizens.

Reservations: Accepted, tickets held until fifteen minutes before curtain.

Group Rates: Available for groups of ten or more, contact Caryl Goldsmith at 581-1264.

Subscription: Available, contact the theatre.

Performance Schedule: Variable performances year-round; outdoors and indoors in summer.

OFF CENTER THEATRE RECOMMENDS:

West Boondock Lounge: 114 Tenth Avenue, on the corner of 17th Street, 929-9645. Soul, steaks. Monday through Friday: noon till 3:00 P.M., 5:30 P.M. till 1:00 A.M. Saturday and Sunday: noon till 2:00 A.M. $4.75–$8.50, a la carte. All credit cards accepted. Jazz: nightly, no cover or minimum.

Empire Diner: 210 Tenth Avenue, at 22nd Street, 243-2736. American. Twenty-four hours. $2.00–$12.50, a la carte. No credit cards accepted. Piano: 11:00 A.M. till 3:00 P.M. and 7:00 P.M. till 11:00 P.M.

WHO: THE OPEN SPACE

Artistic Director: Lynn Michaels
Administrative Director: Harry A. Baum
Founders: Lynn Michaels, Harry A. Baum; 1970

WHERE:

Neighborhood: Noho–East Village
Theatre Address:
133 Second Avenue (at St. Mark's Place)
New York, New York 10003
(212) 254-8630

The Space: The Open Space performs in the heart of the East Village near the St. Mark's cinema. The theatre maintains two performing spaces: the mainstage, an open, thrust stage that seats 75 and the Garret, a chamber theater that seats 50.

WHAT:

Artistic Profile: The Open Space began producing plays in the East Village and moved to Soho in 1974 when artists first began colonizing the neighborhood. From 1974 to 1980 the theatre grew with the neighborhood, always maintaining a commitment to experimentation and exploration. In addition to presenting contemporary plays (two productions—James Lapine's *Photograph* and an experimental Stuart Sherman production received Obie Awards), the theatre sponsored an annual international festival of experimental plays, and produced Oriental plays performed by Asian-American companies well versed in Eastern theatrical traditions. In 1980 Open Space returned to its original home in the East Village.

Productions 1978/79:

Theatre Experiments in Soho III
Photograph, James Lapine
The Whale Show, Allan Albert
Viva Reviva, Eve Merriam
Shayna, Mordecai Siegal
Tropical Tree, Yukio Mishima
Scalp and Dreams, Alphonso Vallejo
The Mandolin Cocktail, Yokull Jakobson

Productions 1979/80:

Theatre Experiments in Soho IV
Yeats Trio:
The King of the Great Clock Tower
The Dreaming of the Bones
The Cat and the Moon
The Blind Young Man, Yukio Mishima; translated by Ted Takaya
Sotoba Komachi, Yukio Mishima; translated by Donald Keene
The Sanctuary Lamp, Thomas Murphy
Transparent Zero, Alphonso Vallejo

Special Programs: Staged readings of plays by women playwrights; summer theatre rentals.

GETTING THERE:

Subway: BMT RR to 8th Street; Lexington Avenue IRT 6 to Astor Place; BMT LL (Canarsie 14th Street Line) to First Avenue and 14th Street.

Bus: Uptown: First Avenue (M15); Downtown: Second Avenue (M15); Crosstown West: 9th Street (M13); Crosstown East: 8th Street (M13).

Parking: Street parking available; nearest lot on Third Avenue between 9th and 10th Streets.

RESERVING SEATS:

Box Office Telephone: (212) 254-8630
Ticket Price: $4.00–$6.00, TDF voucher accepted.
Reservations: Call theatre, tickets held until a half hour before curtain.
Subscription: Four plays for the price of three.
Performance Schedule: Four to seven productions presented September through June. Evenings: Thursday through Sunday; Matinees: Sunday. Fall festival of experimental works presented in repertory for five weeks.

THE OPEN SPACE RECOMMENDS:

Orchidia: 145 Second Avenue, corner of 9th Street, 473-8784. Ukrainian/Italian. Monday through Thursday: 4:00 P.M. till 1:00 A.M.; Friday through Sunday: noon till 1:00 A.M.; Sunday brunch buffet: noon till 3:00 P.M. $3.00–$10.00, a la carte. Visa, MC accepted.

WHO: PAN ASIAN REPERTORY THEATRE

Artistic Director: Tisa Chang
General Manager: Tom Madden
Founder: Tisa Chang; 1977

WHERE:

Neighborhood: Noho–East Village
Theatre Address:
La Mama E.T.C.
74A East 4th Street (between Second Avenue and the Bowery)
New York, New York 10003
Office Telephone: (212) 662-7171
The Space: Pan Asian Repertory Theatre performs in La Mama E.T.C., a theatre space with a long tradition of housing and nurturing experimental theatre groups. See La Mama E.T.C.'s profile (p. 96) for a fuller description of the space.

WHAT:

Artistic Profile: An outgrowth of the Chinese Theatre Group that began working at La Mama E.T.C. in 1973, Pan Asian Repertory Theatre was founded by Tisa Chang in 1977 to increase opportunities for Asian-Americans in mainstream American theatre, to explore Eastern traditions of music, movement, and language, and to promote new Asian-American playwrights. Both traditionalist and experimental, Pan Asian's diverse repertory includes *A Midsummer Night's Dream* set in the Ming Dynasty (allowing Asian-American actors the rare opportunity to play non-stereotypical roles); *Return of the Phoenix*, an adaptation of a traditional Peking Opera (shown as a CBS-TV special); *Sunrise*, a work by China's most renown contemporary playwright; as well as new plays by Asian-American playwrights.

Productions 1978/79:

The Servant of Two Masters, Carlo Goldoni
The Legend of Wu Chang, adapted by Tisa Chang from Hazelton & Benrimo's *Yellow Jacket*
And the Soul Shall Dance, Wakoko Yamuchi

Productions 1979/80:

Sunrise, Cao Yu
And the Soul Shall Dance, Wakoko Yamuchi
Monkey Music, Margaret Lamb

Productions 1980/81:

Flowers and Household Gods, Momoko Iko
An American Story, Ernest Abuba

Special Programs: Workshops in Eastern and Western acting and movement techniques; playwrights' workshop.

GETTING THERE:

Subway: Lexington Avenue IRT 6 to Astor Place; IND B, D, F to Broadway/Lafayette Street; BMT RR to 8th Street.

Bus: Uptown: Third Avenue (M101, M102); Downtown: Second Avenue (M15).

Parking: Lot in filling station at corner of East 4th Street and the Bowery.

RESERVING SEATS:

Box Office Telephone: (212) 474-7710
Ticket Price: $5.00–$6.00, TDF voucher accepted. Discounts for students and senior citizens.
Reservations: Call theatre, tickets held until a half hour before curtain.
Group Rates: Available, contact the company.
Performance Schedule: Year-round, variable performance schedule of approximately three productions. Check newspapers or contact the company.

PAN ASIAN REPERTORY THEATRE RECOMMENDS:

Phebe's Place: 361 Bowery at 4th Street, 473-9008. American-Continental. Noon till 4:00 A.M., seven days. $1.65–$9.00, a la carte. All credit cards accepted.
Binibon: 85 Second Avenue at corner of 5th Street, 475-9365. Omelettes, burgers, vegetarian dishes. Monday through Thursday: 8:00 A.M. till 10:00 P.M.; Friday and Saturday: 9:00 A.M. till 11:00 P.M.; Sunday: 9:00 A.M. till 10:00 P.M. $1.50–$3.75, a la carte. No credit cards accepted.

WHO: PLAYWRIGHTS HORIZONS

Producing Director: Robert Moss
Managing Director: Robin Gold
Artistic Director: André Bishop
Founder: Robert Moss; 1971

WHERE:

Neighborhood: Clinton–Theatre Row
Manhattan Theatre Address:
416 West 42nd Street (between Ninth and Tenth Avenues)
New York, New York 10036
(212) 564-1235

Queens Theatre Address:
Flushing Meadow Park
Box 1832
Flushing, New York 11352
(212) 699-0800

The Space: Playwrights Horizons moved to 42nd Street when it was an urban wasteland composed of porno movies and burlesque houses. Its pioneering efforts have helped transform this area into the bustling Theatre Row, composed of eight theatres, adjoining restaurants, interesting shops and cafes. The company has a newly renovated 100-seat proscenium theatre and a studio workshop that seats sixty-five. In addition, the company maintains a 500-seat theatre in Queens that operates much like a regional theatre for this borough.

WHAT:

Artistic Profile: For the past nine years, Playwrights Horizons has offered playwrights the chance to refine their talents in an intimate, noncommercial atmosphere. The theatre's process enables a writer's work to go through a series of developmental stages which could lead to a staged reading, a workshop production, a mainstage production, or all three. Plays launched through this process include Albert Innaurato's *Gemini* (moved to Broadway), Jack Heifner's *Vanities* (Off Broadway's longest running show), Wendy Wasserstein's *Uncommon Women and Others* (seen on PBS), Robert Patrick's internationally acclaimed *Kennedy's Children*, James Lapine's *Table Settings*, and Ralph Pape's *Say Goodnight Gracie* (moved to Off Broadway). In some cases, the process goes a step further, and the new work moves to Playwrights Horizons' 500-seat theatre —located in Queens.

Productions 1978/79 at Playwrights Horizons–Manhattan:
Say Goodnight, Gracie, Ralph Pape
Living at Home, Anthony Giardina
Vienna Notes, Richard Nelson
Breaking and Entering, Neal Bell
In Trousers, music and lyrics by William Finn
Table Settings, James Lapine

The Songs of Jonathan Tunick, music by Jonathan Tunick
The Terrorists, Dallas Murphey, Jr.
Don't Tell Me Everything and Other Musical Arrangements, music by Peter Larson, John Lewis, and Josh Rubins; lyrics by Josh Rubins
Sweet Main Street, music and lyrics by Carol Hall, et al.; adaptation: Shirley Kaplan

Productions 1978/79 at Playwrights Horizons–Queens:
Oh! What a Lovely War!, adapted by Joan Greenwood and Theatre Workshop
The Eccentricities of a Nightingale, Tennessee Williams
Hedda Gabler, Henrik Ibsen
Lady House Blues, Kevin O'Morrison
Private Lives, Noel Coward
The Show Off, George Kelly

Productions 1979/80 at Playwrights Horizons–Manhattan:
Justice, Terry Curtis Fox
Table Settings, James Lapine
Passione, Albert Innaurato
Survival Kitsch, Bill Weeden, David Finkel, and Sally Fay (workshop)
Fables for Friends, Mark O'Donnell (workshop)

Productions 1979/80 at Playwrights Horizons–Queens:
Oh! Coward!, Noel Coward; adapted by Roderick Cook
Two Small Bodies, Neal Bell
Company, book by George Furth; music and lyrics by Stephen Sondheim
Time Steps, Gus Kaikkonen
Arms and the Man, George Bernard Shaw

Special Programs: Workshop productions and staged readings; musical-theatre workshop; internships; post-performance lectures; in-schools programs; theatre rentals.

GETTING THERE:

MANHATTAN—
Subway: IND A, AA, CC, E to 42nd Street.
Bus: Uptown: Tenth Avenue (M11, M16); Downtown: Ninth Avenue (M11); Crosstown West and East: 42nd Street (M106).
Parking: Manhattan Plaza garage across the street.

QUEENS—

Subway: Flushing IRT 7 to Shea Stadium; exit park side. Pick up free limo to theatre on Roosevelt Street. Ample free parking.

RESERVING SEATS:

Box Office Telephone: Manhattan—(212) 279-4200 (Ticket Central)
Queens—(212) 699-1660

Ticket Prices: Manhattan—$5.00 on Tuesday, Wednesday, Thursday and Sunday; $6.00 on Friday and Saturday. TDF voucher plus surcharge accepted. Queens—$6.00–$9.00.

Reservations: Call theatre, reservations held until a half hour before curtain. MC, Visa, and Amex accepted.

Group Rates: Available, contact the theatre.

Subscription: Available for Queens theatre.

Performance Schedule: September through May; Evenings: Tuesday through Sunday; Matinees: Sunday.

PLAYWRIGHTS HORIZONS RECOMMENDS:

La Rousse: 414 West 42nd Street, on Theatre Row, 736-4913. Reservations recommended. French Peasant. 11:30 A.M. till midnight, seven days. Lunch: $3.95–$8.95, a la carte; Dinner: $5.95–$9.95, a la carte. All credit cards except Carte Blanche accepted. La Rousse occasionally features a complete Dinner-Theatre Ticket Package for productions on Theatre Row. Call Peter Howard at the restaurant for information.

WHO: THE PRODUCTION COMPANY

Artistic Director: Norman René

Managing Director: Caren Harder

Founders: Norman René, Sheldon Epps, Michael Haggerty, John Seeman; 1974

WHERE:

Neighborhood: Chelsea
Theatre Address:
249 West 18th Street (between Seventh and Eighth Avenues)
New York, New York 10011
(212) 691-7359

The Space: In one of the many industrial buildings that line 18th Street in Chelsea, the Production Company has thoroughly renovated a former warehouse, converting it to an intimate 68-seat flexible space.

WHAT:

Artistic Profile: The Production Company is neither an actors' theatre, nor a directors' theatre, nor a playwrights' theatre, but rather a group of theatre artists dedicated to presenting a fully diversified season of classics, revivals, and new works that explore new and richer ways of tapping the emotional life of artist and audience. In their theatre on 18th Street the company presents both fully staged productions and a cabaret program that explores the use of song within a dramatic, but not fully narrative framework.

Productions 1978/79:
A Midsummer Night's Dream, William Shakespeare
Internationally Acclaimed One-Woman Cabaret, Denise LeBrun
Mutual Benefit Life, Robert Patrick
Nocturne, Saul Zachary
Woyzeck, Georg Büchner
Casualties, Karolyn Nelke
House of Blue Leaves, John Guare
La Misanthrope, Molière
Solitaire/Double Solitaire, Robert Anderson
The Gilded Cage, conceived by James Milton
The Masked Choir, Michael McClure

Productions 1979/80:
Hosanna, Michel Tremblay
The Guardsman, Ferenc Molnar; translated by Frank Marcus
My Great Dead Sister, Arthur Bicknell

Blues in the Night, conceived by Sheldon Epps
Incandescent Tones, Rise Collins

Special Programs: Playreadings; internships; theatre rentals.

GETTING THERE:

Subway: Seventh Avenue IRT 1 to 18th Street.

Bus: Uptown: Eighth Avenue (M10); Downtown: Seventh Avenue (M10); Crosstown West and East: 23rd Street (M26).

Parking: Street parking after 6:00 P.M.; nearest lot across the street from theatre.

RESERVING SEATS:

Box Office Telephone: (212) 691-7359

Ticket Price: $6.50–$10.00.

Reservations: Call theatre, tickets held until fifteen minutes before curtain, or charge seats to credit card by calling Chargit 239-7177.

Group Rates: Available, contact the theatre.

Subscription: Significant savings available for subscription to full season of mainstage and cabaret performances.

Performance Schedule: Full season of mainstage productions and several cabaret acts presented September through May. Evenings: Wednesday through Sunday; Matinees: variable schedule.

THE PRODUCTION COMPANY RECOMMENDS:

Chelsea Place Restaurant: 147 Eighth Avenue, between 17th and 18th Streets, 924-8413. Reservations required. Northern Italian. Sunday through Wednesday: 5:30 P.M. till 11:45 P.M.; Thursday through Saturday: 5:30 P.M. till 2:00 A.M. $9.00–$13.00, a la carte. All credit cards accepted.

Harvey's Chelsea Restaurant: 108 West 18th Street, just off Sixth Avenue, 243-5644. Reservations recommended. German-English-Continental. Sunday through Thursday: noon till midnight; Friday and Saturday: noon till 1:00 A.M. Lunch: $3.95–$11.95, a la carte; Dinner: $4.95–$12.95, a la carte. No credit cards. Personal checks accepted.

WHO: PUERTO RICAN TRAVELING THEATRE

Artistic Director: Miriam Colon Edgar
Administrator: Jacklyn D. Beck
Founders: Miriam Colon Edgar, George P. Edgar, Anibal Otero, José Ocasio; 1967

WHERE:

Neighborhood: Clinton
Theatre Address:
304 West 47th Street (between Eighth and Ninth Avenues)
New York, New York 10036
(212) 749-8474

The Space: The Puerto Rican Traveling Theatre is located in the heart of the Broadway theatre district. The company recently completed a massive renovation of an old, abandoned firehouse. The new building includes a 196-seat proscenium theatre as well as extensive rehearsal and office space.

WHAT:

Artistic Profile: Begun more than a decade ago as a community-based street theatre, the Puerto Rican Traveling Theatre has significantly expanded its activities to include both a permanent theatre that presents bilingual productions by contemporary Puerto Rican, European, American, and Latin American playwrights and a touring company that presents free performances to low-income neighborhoods. Other programs include a laboratory which commissions new translations of plays and experiments with poetry as theatre; a playwrights' workshop; a training program providing free bilingual arts education; an in-schools program; and a heritage series bringing researchers and writers together to create plays about exemplary figures in Puerto Rican history. During 1980 the company presented *Spain: Avant-Garde 1980*, a bilingual collage of short works by dramatists censored by the Franco regime.

Productions 1978/79:

La Compañía, Luis Rechani Agrait
Simpson Street, Edward Gallardo; translated by Tony Diaz and Miriam Colon Edgar
El Macho, Joseph Lizardi; translated by Tony Diaz and J. Lizardi
Stories to Be Told, Osvaldo Dragon
Six Staged Readings of New Plays

Productions 1979/80:

Simpson Street, Edward Gallardo; translated by Tony Diaz and Miriam Colon Edgar
Spain: Avant-Garde 1980, a bilingual festival of short works by playwrights censored by the Franco regime
Fanlights, Rene Marques
Original Street Theatre Production
Six Staged Readings

Special Programs: Classes for nonprofessionals and children; internships; in-schools programs; workshop productions and staged readings; poetry readings; touring to colleges and universities.

GETTING THERE:

Subway: IND AA, CC, E to 50th Street.
Bus: Uptown: Tenth Avenue (M11); Downtown: Ninth Avenue (M11).
Parking: Street parking after 6:00 P.M.; nearest lot on 46th Street just west of Eighth Avenue.

RESERVING SEATS:

Box Office Telephone: (212) 354-1293
Ticket Price: $3.00–$7.00, TDF voucher accepted; $3.00 for students and senior citizens.
Reservations: Call theatre, tickets held until ten minutes before curtain.
Group Rates: Twenty percent discount for groups of ten or more.
Subscription: Available.
Performance Schedule: Year-round schedule of three productions per year plus one summer outdoor street-theatre production. Evenings: Wednesday through Sunday; Matinees: Sunday.

PUERTO RICAN TRAVELING THEATRE RECOMMENDS:

Molfeta: 307 West 47th Street, between Eighth and Ninth Avenues, 840-9537. Greek. 11:00 A.M. till 1:00 A.M., seven days. $3.75–$5.50, a la carte. No credit cards accepted.

La Milonga: 742 Ninth Avenue, on the corner of 50th Street, 541-8382. Reservations accepted on weekends. Argentinian. Monday through Thursday: 11:00 A.M. till 2:00 A.M.; Friday: 11:00 A.M. till 4:00 A.M.; Saturday: 4:00 P.M. till 4:00 A.M.; Sunday: 2:00 P.M. till 2:00 A.M. $3.95–$10.95, a la carte. All credit cards accepted.

WHO: QUAIGH THEATRE

Artistic Director: William H. Lieberson
Managing Director: Dey Gosse
Founder: William H. Lieberson; 1973

WHERE:

Neighborhood: Clinton
Theatre Address:
Hotel Diplomat
108 West 43rd Street (between Sixth and Seventh Avenues)
New York, New York 10036
(212) 221-9088

The Space: There's a unique, old-world charm to Quaigh Theatre's 100-seat three-quarter-round theatre. Tucked away on the second floor of the Hotel Diplomat in the heart of the Broadway theatre district, the theatre's location illustrates the continuing resourcefulness of Off Off Broadway theatre artists in discovering and creating performing spaces.

WHAT:

Artistic Profile: Producing over twenty productions per season, including as many as fifteen one-act plays in an afternoon lunchtime series (free to students and senior citizens) and five to seven full-length evening productions, Quaigh Theatre focuses on the development and presentation of new plays. In addition, the company is developing a living museum of dramas of the 1920s and 1930s, each year reviving a significant American work which, due to its huge cast, rarely receives a commercial or showcase production (representative productions include Elmer Rice's *Street Scene* and *Counselor at Law*; and Sidney Kingsley's *Dead End* and *Men in White*). In 1980 the company sponsored Dramathon '80, producing fifty-three hours of continual theatrical entertainment.

Productions 1978/79:

The Victim, Mario Fratti
Momma's Little Angels, Louis LaRusso III
Exorcism of Violence, Sidney Morris
Dead End, Sidney Kingsley
Light Shines in Darkness, Leo Tolstoy
Three By Three:
  At Liberty, Tennessee Williams
  The Meeting, Frederick Dürrenmatt
  Sweet Shoppe Miriam, Ivan Klima
One-Acts:
  Theatre Italian Style, Mario Fratti
  Second Chance, Elise Nass
  Lunchtime, Leonard Melfi
  Josephine Baker, Jesse Hill
  When the Sun Goes Down, Michael Shurclift
  A Love Story, George Hammer
  Ready for Teddy, Joel Ensana
  Off with the Stuff, Jesse Hill
  There's a Werewolf, E. Gardner
  Propositions, Abigail Quart

Productions 1979/80:

The Office Murders, Martin Fox
Mecca, Ted Whitehead
Uncle Vanya, Anton Chekov
The Boor, Anton Chekov
Bedtime Story, Sean O'Casey
Krapp's Last Tape, Samuel Beckett
Men in White, Sidney Kingsley

One-Acts:
The Fountain, Ann Harson
Mr. Wilson's Peace of Mind, Mark Stein
Sandcastle, Barbara Allen Hite
A Whitman Sonata—Specimen Days, Paul Hildebrand, Jr. and Thom Wagner
Jackknife, Steve Metcalf
Hopscotch, Israel Horovitz
Baseball Play, Steve Metcalf
Drums, Margot Welch
Geranium, Knox Turner
Dramathon '80

Special Programs: Lunchtime series; internships, theatre rentals.

GETTING THERE:

Subway: Seventh Avenue IRT 1, 2, 3; BMT N, QB, RR; Flushing IRT 7 to Times Square.

Bus: Uptown: Sixth Avenue (M6, M7); Downtown: Seventh Avenue (M6, M7); Crosstown West and East: 42nd Street (M106).

Parking: Lot across the street.

RESERVING SEATS:

Box Office Telephone: (212) 221-9088

Ticket Price: Evenings: $6.00; Lunchtime Series: $1.50 contribution or free to students and senior citizens. TDF voucher accepted.

Reservations: Call the theatre, tickets held until a half hour before curtain.

Performance Schedule: Year-round productions include five to seven full-length plays. Evenings: Tuesday through Saturday; Matinees: Sunday. Lunchtime Series runs ten weeks in the fall and ten weeks in the spring. Late night cabaret.

QUAIGH THEATRE RECOMMENDS:

Rosoff's: 147 West 43rd Street, just off Broadway, 582-3200. Reservations recommended. Seafood, steaks. Daily: 11:30 A.M. till 9:00 P.M. Lunch: $5.00–$9.00, a la carte; Dinner: $7.00–$14.00, a la carte. All credit cards accepted.

Une, Deux, Trois: 123 West 44th Street, 354-4148. Monday through Friday: noon till midnight; closed Saturday lunch; closed Sunday. $8.00–$15.00, a la carte. MC, Visa, Amex accepted.

Diplomat Luncheonette: 108 West 43rd Street, in the Diplomat Hotel, 279-3707. Coffee Shop. 6:00 A.M. till 4:00 A.M., seven days. $3.00–$6.00, a la carte. No credit cards accepted.

WHO: RAFT THEATRE, LTD.

Artistic Director: Martin Zurla
Managing Director: Fred Crecca
Founders: Martin Zurla, William P. Rolleri; 1975

WHERE:

Neighborhood: Clinton–Theatre Row
Theatre Address:
432 West 42nd Street
New York, New York 10036
(212) 575-9088

The Space: Raft Theatre is located on Theatre Row Phase II, a newly developed complex of theatres on 42nd Street, just west of the eight Off Off Broadway theatres known as Theatre Row. Its third floor theatre seats forty to seventy depending on the stage configuration employed.

WHAT:

Artistic Profile: A spirit of experimentation, first-hand research, and artistic collaboration has always characterized the work of Raft Theatre. The company takes its name from its first production, *Raft*, performed in the basement of a bar on Avenue B. In order to explore the themes of isolation, boredom, and survival, the actors simulated the conditions of shipwreck by sitting in an inflatable raft for three days and then distilled a 90-minute production from subsequent improvisations and a tape recording of the ordeal. Similarly, *Cagliostro*, a play concerning an eighteenth-century Catholic heretic who died in prison, was developed after Artistic Director Martin Zurla had locked himself in a small box for three consecutive days with only bread and water to eat. In addition to original company collaborations, which are comic as well as serious, the company occasionally performs revivals and new American plays. After working at Westbeth in Greenwich Village for five years, Raft Theatre moved to Theatre Row Phase II in 1981.

Productions 1978/79:
Titus Andronicus, William Shakespeare
Nightshift, William P. Rolleri

Productions 1979/80:
Returning, Martin Zurla
The Birthday Party, Harold Pinter
Mean Mabel and Roseann, Roseann Sheridan
The Traveling Lady, Morton Foote
Hers, Tsipi Keller Zurla

Special Programs: Acting workshops (by invitation only); playwrights' workshop; theatre rentals.

GETTING THERE:

Subway: IND A, AA, CC, E to 42nd Street.

Bus: Uptown: Tenth Avenue (M11, M16); Downtown: Ninth Avenue (M11); Crosstown West and East: 42nd Street (M106).

Parking: Manhattan Plaza garage across the street.

RESERVING SEATS:

Box Office Telephone: (212) 279-4200 (Ticket Central)

Ticket Price: $4.00 or TDF voucher plus $1.00.

Reservations: Call Ticket Central, tickets held until fifteen minutes before curtain.

Group Rates: Available for groups larger than ten, contact the theatre.

Performance Schedule: Year-round, variable performance schedule. Includes company productions and rentals.

RAFT THEATRE RECOMMENDS:

La Rousse: 414 West 42nd Street on Theatre Row. 736-4913. Reservations recommended. French Peasant. 11:30 A.M. till midnight, seven days. Lunch: $3.95–$8.95, a la carte; Dinner: $5.95–$9.95, a la carte. All credit cards except Carte Blanche accepted. La Rousse occasionally features a complete Dinner-Theatre Ticket Package for productions on Theatre Row. Call Peter Howard at the restaurant for information.

West Bank Cafe: 407 West 42nd Street, in Manhattan Plaza. 695-6909. Reservations required, 6:00 P.M. till 8:00 P.M. American-Continental-Oriental. Monday through Saturday: noon till 1:00 A.M.; Sunday: noon till 11:00 P.M. Lunch: $2.50–$4.25, a la carte; Dinner: $4.25–$8.75, a la carte. MC, Visa, Amex accepted. Jazz, Big Bands, Comedy, Singers, Broadway Personalities: Tuesday through Saturday at 8:30 P.M. and 10:30 P.M.

WHO: REPERTORIO ESPAÑOL

Artistic Director: Rene Buch
Managing Director: Gilberto Zaldivar
Associate Producer and Resident Designer: Robert Weber Federico
Founders: Gilberto Zaldivar, Rene Buch, Frances Drucker; 1969

WHERE:

Neighborhood: Gramercy
Theatre Address:
Gramercy Arts Theatre
138 East 27th Street (between Lexington and Third Avenues)
New York, New York 10016
(212) 889-2850

The Space: The Gramercy Arts Theatre is one of Off Off Broadway's oldest houses. Founded in 1915 as the Bramhall Playhouse in an old Armenian church, the theatre still evokes a sense of old-world charm, with its dark wood doors, lead glass windows, and three-sided balcony overlooking a proscenium stage. Even the old gas jets that were once used to illuminate the space can be seen in this beautifully restored 170-seat theatre.

WHAT:

Artistic Profile: Repertorio Español presents Hispanic plays in Spanish in rotating repertory. Dedicated to perpetuating great works of Spanish literature, the company presents works rarely seen in the United States including both Spanish classics from the Golden Age (i.e. Cervantes, Calderon) and contemporary Latin American works. A typical weekend of performances might include a Lorca tragedy, Fernando de Rojas' *La Celestina*, and a Pablo Neruda translation of *Romeo and Juliet*. Well known Latin American and Spanish actors often make guest appearances with the company, thereby further strengthening the cultural bonds between New York Hispanics, Latin Americans, and Spaniards. The company tours locally to community centers, nationally, and internationally.

Productions 1978/79:

Bodas de Sangre, Federico García Lorca
Romeo y Julieta, William Shakespeare; translated by Pablo Neruda
La Celestina, Fernando de Rojas
La Dama Duende, Calderon de la Barca
Te Juro Juana Que Tengo Ganas, Emilio Carballido
Los Japoneses No Esperan, Ricardo Talesnik
Jardin de Otoño, Diana Raznovich
La Fiaca, Ricardo Talesnik
La Revolución, Isaac Chocron
Los Soles Truncos, Rene Marques
La Moza de Ayacucho, Francisco Cuevas Cancino
Jose Marti: Un Hombre Sincero, collage of Marti's work

Productions 1979/80:

La Casa de Bernarda Alba, Federico García Lorca
Te Juro Juana Que Tengo Ganas, Emilio Carballido
Tango para Tres, Diana Raznovich
La Cucarachita Martina, puppet show for children
La Celestina, Fernando de Rojas
Toda Desnudez Sera Castigada, Nelson Rodriguez

Los Japoneses No Esperan, Ricardo Talesnik
Mundo de Cristal, Tennessee Williams; translated by Rene Buch

Special Programs: Professional training in acting; special matinees for schoolchildren; videotapes available for educational programs; post-performance lectures; touring; internships.

GETTING THERE:

Subway: Lexington Avenue IRT 6 to 28th Street.

Bus: Uptown: Third Avenue (M101, M102); Downtown: Lexington Avenue (M101, M102); Crosstown West and East: 23rd Street (M26).

Parking: Street parking after 6:00 P.M.; nearest lot on Lexington Avenue between 27th and 28th Streets.

RESERVING SEATS:

Box Office Telephone: (212) 889-2850

Ticket Price: $5.00, TDF voucher accepted. $4.00 for students and senior citizens.

Reservations: Call theatre, tickets held until ten minutes before curtain.

Group Rates: Available, contact the theatre.

Performance Schedule: Eight to twelve productions in rotating repertory presented September through July. Evenings: Friday through Sunday; Matinees: Sundays and selected weekdays.

REPERTORIO ESPAÑOL RECOMMENDS:

Patria Mia: 103 Lexington Avenue, between 27th and 28th Streets, 679-5860. Reservations accepted. Northern Italian. Monday through Friday: 11:00 A.M. till 3:00 P.M. and 5:00 P.M. till 11:00 P.M.; Saturday: 5:00 P.M. till 11:00 P.M. Closed Sunday. $4.75–$11.00, a la carte. All credit cards accepted.

La Toja: 519 Second Avenue, on the corner of 29th Street, 889-1910. Reservations suggested. Northwestern Spanish. Monday through Friday: noon till midnight; Saturday: 2:00 P.M. till 1:00 A.M.; Sunday: 2:00 P.M. till midnight. Lunch: $4.25–$14.95; Dinner: $6.25–$15.95, a la carte. All credit cards accepted.

Per Bacco: 140 East 27th Street, between Lexington and Third Avenues, 532-8699. Reservations accepted. Lunch: noon till 3:00 P.M.; Dinner: 5:30 P.M. till 10:00 P.M. Closed Sunday. $5.50–$11.00, a la carte. MC, Diner's, Amex accepted.

WHO: RICHARD ALLEN CENTER FOR CULTURE AND ART

Artistic and Producing Director: Hazel J. Bryant
Associate Artistic Director: Mical Whitaker
Managing Director: Shirley J. Radcliffe
Assistant to the Producer and Casting Director: Glenn Johnson
Founder: Hazel J. Bryant; 1968

WHERE:

Neighborhood: Upper West Side
Theatre Address:
36 West 62nd Street (between Broadway and Columbus Avenue)
New York, New York 10023
(212) 496-0120
Office Address:
171 West 85th Street
New York, New York 10024
The Space: Just a few blocks from Lincoln Center, in a fourth-floor loft (formerly an auto repair shop), the Richard Allen Center for Culture and Art makes its home. The three-sided, circular thrust stage has comfortable traditional theatre seating and is adjoined by an art gallery and a media center that documents the work of RACCA and produces original tapes for cable television.

WHAT:

Artistic Profile: The Richard Allen Center for Culture and Art (RACCA) has mounted over one hundred, new and classic musicals and dramas that reflect diverse aspects of black culture, whether historic, contemporary, American, or international. The Center has produced the plays of writers as divergent in artistic vision as Nigerian Wole Soyinka, Frenchman Jean Genet, and American James Baldwin. Through their yearly sponsorship of a major black arts festival at Lincoln Center—Black Theatre Festival U.S.A./An Arts Revival at Lincoln Center—RACCA has been instrumental in providing a forum for the interchange and expression of black culture by some of our nation's outstanding artists. Of special interest to RACCA is the development of new approaches to musical theatre that thoroughly integrate music and dramatic texts drawn from black history and folk literature.

Productions 1978/79:

Black Picture Show, Bill Gunn
Simply Heavenly, Langston Hughes
Good Ship Credit, John Scott
Second Thoughts, Lamar Alford
Johnny Moonbeam, Joe Goldin (children's play)

Productions 1979/80:

The Death of Boogie Woogie, book by Paul Carter Harrison; music by Coleridge Taylor Perkinson
God's Trombones, James Weldon Johnson
The Sign in Sidney Brustein's Window, Lorraine Hansberry
Antigone, Sophocles
The Lion and the Jewel, Wole Soyinka

Special Programs: Workshop programs; quarterly publication *Muses*; theatre rentals; staged readings.

GETTING THERE:

Subway: Seventh Avenue IRT 1 to 66th Street or Columbus Circle; IND A, AA, D to Columbus Circle.

Bus: Uptown: Eighth Avenue (M10); Downtown: Broadway (M104); Crosstown West and East: 59th Street (M103).

Parking: Street parking after 6:00 P.M.; nearest garage at Lincoln Center.

RESERVING SEATS:

Box Office Telephone: (212) 496-0120
Ticket Price: $6.00 or TDF voucher.
Reservations: Call theatre, tickets held until a half hour before curtain.
Group Rates: $5.00 for groups of ten or more. Twenty percent off regular ticket price for groups of twenty-five or more for Black arts festival.
Subscription: Five plays for 10 percent off regular ticket price.
Performance Schedule: Five productions presented November through May. Evenings: Thursday through Sunday. Black Theatre Festival U.S.A./An Arts Revival at Lincoln Center presented during May.

RICHARD ALLEN CENTER RECOMMENDS:

Loki Restaurant: 38 West 62nd Street, between Broadway and Columbus Avenue, 582-7484. Reservations accepted. American-Continental. Noon till 1:00 A.M. Closed Sundays. Lunch: $3.95–$6.95, a la carte; Dinner: $6.50–$11.95, a la carte. MC, Visa, Diner's, Amex accepted.

WHO: THE RICHARD MORSE MIME THEATRE

Artistic Director: Richard Morse
Children's Theatre Director: Rasa Allan
Administrator: Ellen Pollan
Founder: Richard Morse; 1975

WHERE:

Neighborhood: West Village
Theatre Address:
224 Waverly Place (between Seventh Avenue and 11th Street)
New York, New York 10014
(212) 242-0530

The Space: The Richard Morse Mime Theatre performs in the landmark St. John's Church nearby many of the elegant townhouses, quaint restaurants, and jazz clubs that have made the Village famous. A second-floor proscenium theatre seats ninety. Outdoor summer performances are given in the nearby courtyard.

WHAT:

Artistic Profile: Departing from the white-face practices associated with Marcel Marceau, the Richard Morse Mime Theatre is pioneering an original approach to mime theatre in America. In full-length productions that draw inspiration from contemporary life, company members not only portray people, but also objects and situations—an unfurling flag, a vengeful leaking faucet, and urban demolition. Children's programs which include active audience participation complement the repertory. The company has toured extensively in the United States and, under the auspices of the State Department, in Europe, the East, and Africa; it has appeared on television, and performed with symphony orchestras. A distinctive feature of the company is its highly developed training program.

Productions 1978/79:

Appeal of the Big Apple, Richard Morse
Tintinnabula, Richard Morse
The Play of Herod, Noah Greenberg and William Smolden
What A Devil, Richard Morse, from Igor Stravinsky's *L'Histoire du Soldat*
Inside Up, Rasa Allan
A Chip Off the Old Munk, Rasa Allan

Productions 1979/80:

Museum Alive, Richard Morse
Holiday Show, Richard Morse
The Arts and Leisure Section of the New York Times, Richard Morse
Head over Heels, Rasa Allan
Mixed Nuts!, Rasa Allan

Special Programs: Professional training in mime, dance, and acting; children's classes; special theatre birthday parties—the cast joins in a birthday salute and party space is available after the show; national and international touring; internships; post-performance discussions; midnight mime show.

GETTING THERE:

Subway: Seventh Avenue IRT 1 to Christopher Street, walk north on Seventh Avenue and west on Waverly Place.

Bus: Uptown: Eighth Avenue (Hudson Street) (M10); Downtown: Seventh Avenue (M10); Crosstown West: 9th Street (M13); Crosstown East: 8th Street (M13).

Parking: Perry Street Garage, 738 Greenwich Street, $3.00 all day with validation from box office.

RESERVING SEATS:

Box Office Telephone: (212) 242-0530

Ticket Price: Adult Show: $7.50; Midnight Mime: $5.00; Children's Show: $4.00, discounts for students and senior citizens.

Reservations: Call theatre, tickets held until fifteen minutes before curtain.

Group Rates: Available, contact the theatre.

Subscription: Admission to three adult shows plus discounts on special events including late night mime shows, children's shows, and concerts at Alice Tully Hall.

Performance Schedule: Five to six productions presented September through April. Evenings: Friday through Sunday; Matinees (children's shows): Saturday, Sunday, Christmas week. Midnight Mime: Friday, Saturday. Extensive touring outside New York City.

RICHARD MORSE MIME THEATRE RECOMMENDS:

The Wok: 173 Seventh Avenue South, between Perry and 11th Streets, 243-6046. Reservations recommended. Hunan Style Oriental. Sunday through Thursday: noon till midnight; Friday and Saturday: noon till 2:00 A.M. $3.95–$8.50, a la carte; $10.00, complete. MC, Visa, Amex accepted.

WHO: RIVERSIDE SHAKESPEARE COMPANY OF NEW YORK CITY

Artistic Director: W. Stuart McDowell
Executive Director: Gloria Skurski
Founders: W. Stuart McDowell, Gloria Skurski; 1977

WHERE:

Neighborhood: Upper West Side
Theatre Address:
West Park Presbyterian Church
165 West 86th Street (at Amsterdam Avenue)
New York, New York 10024
(212) 877-6810

The Space: In a truly resourceful adaptation of space, the Riverside Shakespeare Company of New York City has transformed the choir loft of the West Park Presbyterian Church into a theatre. The audience sits on pews that face a long, narrow playing area overlooking the church altar. On occasion, the company incorporates multi-level staging into its performance, mounting selected scenes on the altar space.

WHAT:

Artistic Profile: Respectful but not overly reverential productions of Shakespeare are the hallmark of Riverside Shakespeare Company of New York City. Whether performing indoors or outdoors, at Columbia University, Washington Square Park, or in their theatre on 86th Street, the company clearly and faithfully renders the Bard's poetry while making the plays lively, entertaining and accessible through fresh directorial approaches. These include a 1920s American version of *Much Ado about Nothing*, a torchlit, medieval production of *Hamlet*, and an art nouveau presentation of *Twelfth Night*. The link between Shakespeare and popular renaissance entertainment is explored by the company's commedia dell'arte wing and outdoor productions commence with festive greenshows of mime, juggling, fire-eating, music, and dance. RSC of NYC tours schools, community centers, and museums, presenting selected scenes that focus on the themes of love and power. Each summer they perform outdoor productions at Wave Hill in the Bronx.

Productions 1978/79:
A Midsummer Night's Dream, William Shakespeare
As You Like It, William Shakespeare
The Mandrake, Niccolo Machiavelli
Much Ado about Nothing, William Shakespeare

Productions 1979/80:
Henry IV, Part I, William Shakespeare
Shakespeare Cabaret, scenes from William Shakespeare
Love's Labor Lost
The Taming of the Shrew
The Will to Power
This Bud of Love
Twelfth Night, William Shakespeare

Special Programs: Sunday readings of the entire Shakespeare canon; touring; internships; free outdoor performances; comprehensive Shakespearean actor training program.

GETTING THERE:

Subway: Seventh Avenue IRT to 86th Street; IND CC, AA to West 86th Street

Bus: Uptown: Amsterdam Avenue (M11, M7); Broadway (M104); Downtown: Columbus Avenue (M11, M7); Broadway (M104); Crosstown East and West: 86th Street (M18).

Parking: Street parking available.

RESERVING SEATS:

Box Office Telephone: (212) 877-6810

Ticket Price: $4.50, TDF voucher accepted. Senior citizen discount, $2.50.

Reservations: Policy varies, call the office.

Group Rates: $2.50 for groups of fifteen or more.

Performance Schedule: Variable schedule of four mainstage productions plus small-scale commedia dell'arte productions.

RIVERSIDE SHAKESPEARE COMPANY OF NEW YORK CITY RECOMMENDS:

Marvin Gardens: 2274 Broadway at 82nd Street, 799-0578. Reservations recommended. Italian/French/American. 10:00 A.M. till 2:00 A.M., seven days. $4.00–$10.00, a la carte. Visa and AMEX accepted.

A Piece of Cake: 55 Amsterdam Avenue at 87th Street, 799-7682. French pastries, quiches, salads. Monday through Friday: noon till 11:00 P.M.; Saturday: noon till 12:00 P.M.; Sunday: noon till 10:00 P.M. $.75–$4.00, a la carte.

WHO: SEVEN AGES PERFORMANCE LIMITED AT PERRY STREET THEATRE

Artistic Director: Vasek Simek
Managing Director: Ingrid Nyeboe
Founder: Vasek Simek, 1977

WHERE:

Neighborhood: West Village
Theatre Address:
Perry Street Theatre
31 Perry Street (just off Seventh Avenue South)
New York, New York 10014
(212) 255-9186

The Space: Perry Street Theatre is one of the most technically sophisticated Off Off Broadway theatres. This totally flexible 99-seat theatre with a special series of risers designed by Clark Dunham is suited to any type of production.

WHAT:

Artistic Profile: Seven Ages Performance Limited operates the Perry Street Theatre as a laboratory for theatre artists. Particular emphasis is placed on new scripts and on experimentation with contemporary and classical works.

GETTING THERE:

Subway: Seventh Avenue IRT 1 to Christopher Street; and IND A, AA, E, CC, B, D, F to West 4th Street.

Bus: Uptown: Sixth Avenue (M6, M10); Downtown: Seventh Avenue (M10); Crosstown West: 9th Street (M13); Crosstown East: 8th Street (M13).

Parking: Street parking difficult; Perry Street Garage at 738 Greenwich Avenue.

RESERVING SEATS:

Box Office Telephone: (212) 255-9186

Ticket Price: Variable, TDF voucher accepted for some productions.

Reservations: Call theatre, tickets held until fifteen minutes before curtain.

Performance Schedule: Variable schedule of year-round performances. Evenings: Tuesday through Sunday; Matinees: Saturday and Sunday.

PERRY STREET THEATRE RECOMMENDS:

Arnold's Turtle Cafe: 51 Bank Street, on the corner of West 4th Street, 242-5623. American-Continental. Noon till 12:30 A.M., seven days. $4.50–$6.95, a la carte. No credit cards accepted.

Montana Eve: 140 Seventh Avenue South, between 10th and Charles Streets, 242-1200. American. Noon till 4:00 A.M., seven days. Kitchen closes at 2:00 A.M. $3.00–$8.00, a la carte. No credit cards accepted.

Charlie and Kelly: 259 West 4th Street at Perry Street, 675-5059. Reservations recommended. International. Sunday through Thursday: 5:00 P.M. till 11:00 P.M.; Friday and Saturday: 6:00 P.M. till midnight; Sunday Brunch: noon till 4:00 P.M. $4.00–$11.00, a la carte. MC, Diner's, Amex accepted.

WHO: 78TH STREET THEATRE LAB

Artistic Director: Mark Zeller

Founders: Mark Zeller, Dana Zeller-Alexis; 1979

WHERE:

Neighborhood: Upper West Side
Theatre Address:
236 West 78th Street (between Broadway and Amsterdam Avenue)
New York, New York 10024
(212) 595-0850

The Space: Just off Broadway, in an Upper West Side neighborhood that probably has a higher concentration of actors than anywhere in New York City, the 78th Street Theatre Lab makes its home. A downstairs two-sided arena seats seventy. Upstairs a large open space (which serves as classroom space during the day) is divided into two small playing areas for the presentation of one-act plays.

WHAT:

Artistic Profile: To form a bridge between actor training and performance was the founding purposc of the 78th Street Theatre Lab. It has gone on to become a year-round theatre company presenting new plays and revivals. On most weekends a full-length play is presented in the downstairs theatre and two one-acts are presented upstairs. A children's theatre program is presented Saturday afternoon. A late-night Saturday Night Party showcases improvisational groups, singers, and variety acts.

Productions 1978/79:
Winners, Brian Friel
Mrs. Dally Has a Lover, William Hanley
The Pokey, Stephen Black
Taud Show, Jerry Mayer
Serious Bizness, Original Comedy Material
Say Goodnight, Gracie, Ralph Pape

Productions 1979/80:
The Sun Always Shines for the Cool, Miguel Pinero
Mrs. Dally Has a Lover, William Hanley
The Great Nebula in Orion, Lanford Wilson
A Perfect Analysis as Given by a Parrot, Tennessee Williams
Margaret's Bed, William Inge
The Jewish Wife, Bertolt Brecht

Birdbath, Leonard Melfi
Alligator Man, Jack A. Kaplan

Special Programs: Classes in acting, scene study, auditioning, voice; Shakespeare study; children's classes and performances; theatre rentals.

GETTING THERE:

Subway: Seventh Avenue IRT 1 to 79th Street.

Bus: Uptown: Amsterdam Avenue (M7, M11); Downtown: Broadway (M104); Crosstown West and East: 79th Street (M17).

Parking: Street parking all day (metered); garage at 79th Street and Amsterdam Avenue.

RESERVING SEATS:

Box Office Telephone: (212) 595-0850

Ticket Price: Full Productions: $6.00; One-Acts: $3.00; Saturday Night Party: $5.00; Children's Shows: $3.00, TDF voucher accepted.

Reservations: Call theatre, tickets held until curtain.

Performance Schedule: Year-round productions every weekend at 8:00 P.M., 9:15 P.M., and 10:00 P.M.

78TH STREET THEATRE LAB RECOMMENDS:

Teacher's: 2249 Broadway, between 80th and 81st Streets, 787-3500. Reservations accepted. Continental. 11:00 A.M. till 1:00 A.M.; Friday and Saturday: till 2:00 A.M. $3.50–$11.00, a la carte. All major credit cards except Carte Blanche accepted.

Marvin Gardens: 2274 Broadway, at 82nd Street, 799-0578. Reservations recommended. Italian-French-American. 10:00 A.M. till 2:00 A.M., seven days. $4.00–$10.00, a la carte. Visa and Amex accepted.

Shelter: 2180 Broadway, on the corner of 77th Street, 362-4360. Continental-American. 11:30 A.M. till 4:00 A.M., seven days. Kitchen closes at 2:00 A.M. $4.00–$7.00, a la carte. MC, Visa, Diner's, Amex accepted.

WHO: SHELTER WEST COMPANY

Artistic Director: Judith Joseph
Founder: Judith Joseph; 1973

WHERE:

Neighborhood: Performs in various locations.
Office Address:
217 Second Avenue
New York, New York 10013
(212) 673-6341

WHAT:

Artistic Profile: Shelter West Company is a thirty-member repertory company committed to presenting the public with a diverse, well-rounded season of plays. Each season the company presents four plays chosen from the following categories: a new American play, an American revival, a new European or foreign play, and a European or foreign classic. As a result, a large but close-knit group of professionals work closely and non-competitively together with a full and continual awareness of the cooperative nature of theatre. The communal structure allows for and insists that actors, technical personnel, and administrators share responsibilities. Shelter West's program also includes a summer New American Playwrights' Series, an in-house actors' workshop that focuses on two-character one-acts, a directors' workshop, and a Saturday morning playreading project.

Productions 1979/80:
Adult Fiction, Brian Richard Mori
Patent Pending, Wim Vanleer
Black Forest, based on a novella by Boris Vasiliev; adaptation by Ygeny Lanskoy and Sharon Carnicke
The Carpenters, Steve Tesich
Purgatory in Ingolstadt, Marluisse Fleisser
Great God Brown, Eugene O'Neill
Free In-House Workshops:
This Property Is Condemned, Tennessee Williams
Waiting for Lefty, Clifford Odets

Birdbath, Leonard Melfi
The Straw, Eugene O'Neill

Special Programs: Workshop productions; staged readings; internships.

GETTING THERE:

Call the office for current performing location and directions.

RESERVING SEATS:

Box Office Telephone: (212) 673-6341
Ticket Price: $3.50 or TDF voucher. $2.50 for students and senior citizens.
Reservations: Call theatre, tickets held until a half hour before curtain.
Group Rates: $2.00 for groups of fifteen or larger.
Special Discount: Two-for-the-price-of-one vouchers distributed in the neighborhood.
Performance Schedule: Four mainstage productions plus workshop productions presented September through June, evenings.

WHO: SHIRTSLEEVE THEATRE

Artistic Directors: John Vaccaro, James J. Wisner
Managing Director: Sari E. Weisman
Founders: John Vaccaro, James J. Wisner; 1975

WHERE:

Neighborhood: Upper East Side
Theatre Address:
931 First Avenue (at 51st Street)
New York, New York 10022
Office Address:
c/o John Vaccaro
10 Park Avenue
New York, New York 10016

The Space: Performing in the Eastside International Community Center—on the spot where Nathan Hale uttered his famous words, "I regret I have only one life to give for my country," Shirtsleeve has converted a first-floor lobby space into a functional 100-seat theatre. The space is shared with Academy Arts Theatre Company (see p. 27).

WHAT:

Artistic Profile: Dedicated to showcasing new musical and dramatic works, Shirtsleeve Theatre presents fully mounted but simple productions. Following its premiere season at the Manhattan Theatre Club, Shirtsleeve has used the Eastside International Community Center as home base while occasionally presenting productions at other theatres such as Theatre at St. Clement's and Westside Airlines Terminal. Many Shirtsleeve productions have later achieved extended lives in the commercial arena including *Scrambled Feet, Piano Bar*, and *Children of Adam*. The company's flexible organizational structure allows it to adapt to the changing artistic concerns of its directors. For example, in 1979 Shirtsleeve focused on prison dramas, while in 1980 it explored both dramatic and comic works related to the female experience.

Productions 1978/79:
Dear Liar, Jerome Kilty
Brother Champ, Michael Kassin
Attica, Robert Allan Arthur (staged reading)

Productions 1980:
Zelda, William Luce
Twentieth Century of Jane Avril, Jane Marla Roberts
The Convertible Girl, Daniel Simon

GETTING THERE:

Subway: Lexington Avenue IRT 6 to 51st Street; IND E, F to 53rd Street (Lexington Avenue).

Bus: Uptown: First Avenue (M15); Downtown: Second Avenue (M15); Crosstown West: 49th Street (M27); Crosstown East: 50th Street (M27).

Parking: Street parking after 7:00 P.M.; nearest lot at 56th Street and First Avenue.

RESERVING SEATS:

Box Office Telephone: Call (212) 279-4200 for box office information.
Ticket Price: $3.50, TDF voucher accepted.
Performance Schedule: Variable.

SHIRTSLEEVE THEATRE RECOMMENDS:

Peartrees: 1 Mitchell Place, corner of 49th Street and First Avenue, 832-8558. Reservations accepted. American-Continental. Noon till 4:00 A.M., seven days. Kitchen closes at 1:00 A.M. Lunch: $4.00–$8.00, a la carte; Dinner: $4.50–$13.50, a la carte. Carte Blanche, Diner's, Amex accepted.
Billy's: 948 First Avenue, on the corner of 52nd Street, 355-8920. Reservations required for parties over two. American. 5:00 P.M. till midnight, seven days. $6.00–$15.00, a la carte. All credit cards except Visa accepted.
Hobeau's: 963 First Avenue, at 53rd Street, 421-2888. Reservations accepted after 4:30 P.M. Seafood. $1.95–8.95, a la carte. MC, Visa, Diner's, Amex accepted.

WHO: SIDEWALKS OF NEW YORK

Artistic Director: Gary Beck
Company Manager: Nancy Guarino
Founder: Gary Beck; 1976

WHERE:

Office Address:
44 Beaver Street
New York, New York 10004
(212) 425-3358

WHAT:

Artistic Profile: Sidewalks of New York is an ensemble company dedicated to revivifying classical comedy. Currently concentrating on the works of Molière, the company is noted for colorfully costumed, masked productions which draw upon the commedia dell'arte tradition. A Sidewalks production commences with a lively, musical parade through the audience and includes song, dance, music, improvisation, and audience interaction. The company is dedicated to community service and has performed in schools, hospitals, senior citizen centers, and children's psychiatric centers. In addition, it organized a week long festival in Bryant Park during the summer of 1977 in an attempt to revitalize this troubled area.

Productions 1978/79:
The Flying Doctor, Molière
The Jealous Husband, Molière
A Series of French Farces

Productions 1979/80:
The Doctor in Spite of Himself, Molière
Two Pretentious Maidens Ridiculed, Molière

Special Programs: Classes in clowning, theatre arts, mime, and circus arts; HEW-supported school enrichment program; workshops in hospitals, community centers, children's psychiatric centers, parks, and schools; outdoor, free performances.

GETTING THERE:

Contact the theatre for current performing location and directions.

RESERVING SEATS:

Box Office Telephone: (212) 480-9074

Ticket Price: $4.00–$5.00, discounts for students with ID card and senior citizens.

Reservations: Call theatre, tickets held until a half hour before curtain.

Group Rates: Available for ten or more. Contact theatre for rates.

Performance Schedule: Two productions that run for five to six weeks presented September through June. Evenings: Wednesday through Saturday. Outdoor performances during the summer.

WHO: SOHO REP

Artistic and Managing Directors: Marlene Swartz, Jerry Engelbach
Founders: Marlene Swartz, Jerry Engelbach; 1975

WHERE:

Neighborhood: Soho
Theatre Address:
19 Mercer Street
New York, New York 10013
(212) 925-2627
The Space: The Soho Repertory Theatre is located in an historic nineteenth-century, cast-iron loft building in Soho—Manhattan's cultural community south of Houston Street. With a thrust stage, the theatre seats 99.

WHAT:

Artistic Profile: Soho Rep produces both classic and modern plays, with an emphasis on rarely or never-performed past masterpieces. The theatre's premieres have included the New York premiere of Jean Cocteau's *The Knights of the Round Table*; Pablo Picasso's *The Four Little Girls*; Michel de Ghelderode's *Miss Jairus*; Günter Grass's *Only Ten Minutes to Buffalo*; J. P. Donleavy's *Fairytales of New York*; and the world stage premiere of Rod Serling's *Requiem for a Heavyweight*. An annual award-winning series, The One-Act Play, offers miniature masterpieces by the world's greatest writers.
Productions 1978/79:
Fallen Angels, Noel Coward
The Servant, Robin Maugham
Richard III, William Shakespeare
Miss Jairus, Michel de Ghelderode; translated by George Hauger
Amphitryon 38, Jean Giraudoux; adapted by S. N. Behrman
Overruled, George Bernard Shaw
The Love of Don Perlimplin and Belisa in the Garden, Federico García Lorca; translated by James Graham-Lujan

Guernica, Fernando Arrabal; translated by Barbara Wright
Only Ten Minutes to Buffalo, Günter Grass; adapted by Ralph Manheim
The 12-Pound Look, J. M. Barrie
If You Had Three Husbands, Gertrude Stein; adapted by Randy Knolle
Deathwatch, Jean Genet; translated by Bernard Frechtman
Action, Sam Shepard
Requiem for a Heavyweight, Rod Serling
October 12, 410 B.C., Aristophanes; adapted by David Barrett; music by Jim Ragland
Dandy Dick, Arthur Wing Pinero
Inadmissible Evidence, John Osborne
The Knights of the Round Table, Jean Cocteau; translated by W. H. Auden

Productions 1979/80:

The Insect Comedy, Karel and Josef Capek
The Cannibals, book by George Tabori; music by Lois Britten
The Barber of Seville, Beaumarchais; translated by Albert Bermel; music by Jim Ragland
We Have Always Lived in the Castle, Hugh Wheeler; adapted from the novel by Shirley Jackson
Twelfth Night, William Shakespeare
The Second Man, S. N. Behrman
The Caretaker, Harold Pinter
Tom Thumb, or the Tragedy of Tragedies, Henry Fielding
Feathertop, Nathaniel Hawthorne
The Ugly Duckling, A. A. Milne
Brewsie and Willie, Gertrude Stein
Home Fires, John Guare
Old Possum's Book of Practical Cats, T. S. Eliot; adapted by T. S. Eliot; music by Elyse Goodwin
The Gamblers, Nikolai Gogol
The Tricycle, Fernando Arrabal; translated by Barbara Wright
The Party, Slawomir Mrozek

Special Programs: Internships; theatre rentals; post-performance lectures.

GETTING THERE:

Subway: Lexington Avenue IRT 6 to Canal Street (walk west); BMT N, RR, QB to Canal Street (walk west); Seventh Avenue IRT 1 to Canal Street (walk east); IND A, AA, CC, E to Canal Street (walk east).

Bus: Uptown: Centre Street (M1); Downtown: Broadway (M6); Crosstown West and East: Grand Street (M8).

Parking: Ample street parking after 6:00 P.M.

RESERVING SEATS:

Box Office Telephone: (212) 925-2588

Ticket Price: $5.00, TDF voucher accepted.

Reservations: Call theatre, tickets held until a half hour before curtain.

Subscription: Available for full season of plays. Additional discount offered for double subscription. Master Charge accepted.

Performance Schedule: Six plays presented in rotating repertory October through May. Evenings: Thursday through Sunday; Late Show: Saturday; Matinees: Sunday.

SOHO REP RECOMMENDS:

Soho Robata: 143 Spring Street, on the corner of Wooster Street, 431-3993. Reservations required. Continental. Lunch: Tuesday through Saturday, noon till 2:30 P.M.; Dinner: Monday through Friday, 5:00 P.M. till 11:00 P.M.; Saturday: 4:00 P.M. till midnight; Sunday: 4:00 P.M. till 10:30 P.M. Lunch: $5.00–$7.50, a la carte; Dinner: $7.50–$10.00, a la carte. All credit cards except Carte Blanche accepted.

Skrambles Cafe: 402 West Broadway, on the corner of Spring Street, 966-6660. American-Greek-French. Noon till 4:00 A.M., seven days. Kitchen closes at 2:00 A.M. Saturday and Sunday Brunch: 11:30 A.M. till 4:30 P.M. Lunch: $3.50–$7.00, a la carte; Dinner: $3.50–$10.00, a la carte. Diner's and Amex accepted. Piano Bar: Wednesday through Saturday.

Broome Street Bar: 363 West Broadway, on the corner of Broome Street, 925-2086. Burgers, salads. Noon till 4:00 A.M., seven days. Kitchen closes at 2:15 A.M.

Saturday and Sunday Brunch: $2.50–$7.50, a la carte; Brunch: $3.00–$7.50. No credit cards accepted.

Smoke Stacks Lightnin': 380 Canal Street, at West Broadway, 266-0485. Reservations for large groups only. Burgers, seafood. Sunday through Thursday: 11:00 A.M. till 2:00 A.M.; Friday and Saturday: 11:00 A.M. till 3:00 A.M. Lunch: $3.00–$6.00, a la carte; Dinner: $3.00–$11.00, a la carte. Amex accepted.

WHO: SOUTH STREET THEATRE COMPANY

Artistic Directors: Michael Fischetti, Jean Sullivan
Managing Director: Jean Sullivan
Founders: Michael Fischetti, Jean Sullivan; 1973

WHERE:

Neighborhood: Clinton–Theatre Row
Theatre Address:
424 West 42nd Street (between Ninth and Tenth Avenues)
New York, New York 10036
(212) 564-0660

The Space: Located on Theatre Row—a revitalized neighborhood that now boasts eight Off Off Broadway playhouses, an artist's housing complex and innumerable thriving businesses and restaurants—South Street Theatre Company has two performing spaces: a comfortable, ground-floor, flexible 94-seat theatre and a third-floor expansive L-shaped, performance loft-space.

WHAT:

Artistic Profile: South Street Theatre began by performing on the piers and aboard the restaurant ship at the South Street Seaport Museum during the summer. Following five summer seasons at the Seaport, South Street Theatre expanded to a year-round theatre and moved to Theatre Row. Its current repertory is an eclectic mixture of dramatic and musical-theatre works including American premieres of European plays, new American plays, a free special lunchtime series of classical revivals and operas. Of special note is the theatre's dinner-theatre package which includes an evening in the theatre and a meal at nearby La Rousse restaurant.

Productions 1978/79:

The Tennis Game, George W. S. Trow (a co-production with Lenox Arts Music Theatre)
Hitting Town, Stephen Poliakoff
Funeral Games, Joe Orton
La Serva Padrona, G. B. Pergolesi
Confessions of a Reformed Romantic, Ellen Gould
Spoon River Anthology, South Street Theatre Company

Productions 1979/80:

Man and Woman, Scenes from Congreve, Chekov, Pinter, Ionesco; conceived by Jean Sullivan and Michael Fischetti
Le Serva Padrona, G. B. Pergolesi
Terrible Sunlight, Michael Brodsky
Dr. Miracle, Georges Bizet
Standard Safety/The Nothing Kid, Julie Bovasso

Special Programs: Theatre rentals; acting workshop.

GETTING THERE:

Subway: IND A, AA, CC, E to 42nd Street.
Bus: Uptown: Tenth Avenue (M11, M16); Downtown: Ninth Avenue (M11); Crosstown West and East: 42nd Street (M106).
Parking: Manhattan Plaza garage across the street.

RESERVING SEATS:

Box Office Telephone: (212) 279-4200 (Ticket Central)
Ticket Price: Specially funded series of operas and classical revivals presented free of charge; $5.00 for major productions, TDF voucher accepted (no surcharge). Student and senior citizen discounts sometimes available.
Reservations: Call Ticket Central. Credit card reservations accepted.
Group Rates: Available, contact the theatre.
Subscription: Available, contact the theatre for further information.
Performance Schedule: At least three company productions plus rentals presented year-round. Evenings: Wednesday through Saturday; Matinees: Sunday.

SOUTH STREET THEATRE COMPANY RECOMMENDS:

La Rousse: 414 West 42nd Street, on Theatre Row, 736-4913. Reservations recommended. French Peasant. 11:30 A.M. till midnight, seven days. Lunch: $3.95–$8.95, a la carte; Dinner: $5.95–$9.95, a la carte. All credit cards except Carte Blanche accepted. La Rousse occasionally features a complete Dinner-Theatre Ticket Package for productions on Theatre Row. Call Peter Howard at the restaurant for information.

Angelo's: 859 Ninth Avenue, at 56th Street, 586-0159. Reservations accepted. Italian. 11:00 A.M. till midnight, seven days. $4.00–$7.50, a la carte. No credit cards accepted.

West Bank Cafe: 407 West 42nd Street, in Manhattan Plaza, 695-6909, Reservations required, 6:00 P.M. till 8:00 P.M. American-Continental-Oriental. Monday through Saturday: noon till 1:00 A.M.; Sunday: noon till 11:00 P.M. Lunch: $2.50–$4.25, a la carte; Dinner: $4.25–$8.75, a la carte. MC, Visa, Amex accepted. Jazz, Big Bands, Comedy, Singers, Broadway Personalities: Tuesday through Saturday at 8:30 P.M. and 10:30 P.M.

WHO: SPECTRUM THEATRE

Artistic Director: Benno Haehnel
Administrative Director: Ted Baird
Associate Producer: Leda Gelles
Founder: Benno Haehnel

WHERE:

Neighborhood: Soho
Theatre Address:
Spectrum Theatre
15 Vandam Street (at Sixth Avenue)
New York, New York 10013
(212) 475-5529
Office Address:
222 East 10th Street
New York, New York 10003

The Space: After performing in the Calvary Church in Gramercy for several years, Spectrum Theatre moved to Soho, completing renovating the former Vandam Theatre into a 99-seat thrust theatre. The building, which has excellent facilities, has been used as a theatre for over a decade. It is located on a quiet residential street near many of Soho's well-known restaurants.

WHAT:

Artistic Profile: Spectrum Theatre offers its audiences a spectrum on many levels: its choice of plays ranges from the satirical wit of George Bernard Shaw to the intense psychological dramas of August Strindberg; its format of presentation—rotating repertory—allows the audience to see at least two different plays within the same week; its organizational structure—an ensemble company of diverse talents—provides the audience with the opportunity of watching a group of artists interpret different roles in each new repertory work.

Productions 1979/80:

The World of Wilder, Thornton Wilder
Diary of a Scoundrel, Alexander Ostrovski
Arms and the Man, George Bernard Shaw
The Pelican, August Strindberg
U.S.A., John Dos Passos and Paul Shyre
Waiting for Lefty, Clifford Odets
Hedda Gabler, Henrik Ibsen
Shadow of a Gunman, Sean O'Casey

Special Programs: Early 6:00 P.M. show several nights a week; seminars for student groups; open rehearsal for subscribers.

GETTING THERE:

Subway: Seventh Avenue IRT 1 to Houston; IND E, CC, AA to Spring Street.

Bus: Uptown: Hudson Street (M10); Downtown: Seventh Avenue (M10); Fifth Avenue (M5); Crosstown West and East: Houston Street (M21).

Parking: Street parking after 6:00 P.M. and on weekends; nearest lot on the corner of King and Hudson Streets.

RESERVING SEATS:

Box Office Telephone: (212) 475-5529
Ticket Price: $4.00 or TDF voucher, Visa and Master Charge accepted. Student and senior citizens, $2.00.
Reservations: Call theatre, tickets held until fifteen minutes before curtain.
Group Rates: Available, contact the theatre.
Subscription: Nine tickets for $28.00 or five tickets for $16.00. Visa, Master Charge, and Amex accepted.
Performance Schedule: Nine productions run December through June in rotating repertory (a series of plays runs on alternate nights for sixteen performances each). Evenings: Wednesday through Sunday; Matinees: Wednesday, Saturday, Sunday. 6:00 P.M. Curtain: variable schedule.

SPECTRUM THEATRE RECOMMENDS:

Da Silvano: 260 Sixth Avenue, between Bleecker and Houston Street, 982-0090. Italian. Lunch: Monday through Friday, noon till 3:00 P.M.; Dinner: Monday through Saturday, 6:00 P.M. till 11:30 P.M.; Sunday, 5:00 P.M. till 11:00 P.M. $8.00–$15.00, a la carte. No credit cards accepted.
J.S. Vandam: 150 Varick Street, at Vandam Street, 929-7466. Continental. Lunch: Monday through Friday, noon till 2:30 P.M.; Dinner: Monday through Sunday, 7:00 P.M. till 12:30 A.M., light supper till 2:00 A.M. Lunch: $3.50–$9.00, a la carte; Dinner: $8.00–$16.00, a la carte. Amex, MC, and Visa accepted.
Chez Jacqueline: 213 Avenue of the Americas, at King Street, 255-6885. French. Lunch: Monday through Friday, noon till 3:00 P.M.; Dinner: Monday through Saturday, 6:00 P.M. till 11:00 P.M. Lunch: $3.00–$6.50, a la carte; Dinner: $5.95–$12.95, a la carte. No credit cards accepted.

WHO: SPIDERWOMAN THEATRE WORKSHOP

Artistic Director: Muriel Miguel
Business Manager: Lisa Mayo
Founder: Muriel Miguel; 1975

WHERE:

Theatre Address: Performs in various locations.
Office Address:
77 Seventh Avenue, Apt. 8S
New York, New York 10011
(212) 243-6209

WHAT:

Artistic Profile: Spiderwoman Theatre Workshop—spiderwoman refers to the Hopi Indian goddess of weaving—creates theatre pieces through story weaving. Company members, who include American Indians, whites, blacks, Jews, Irish, and southern mountain women, thread together aspects of their personal life stories to create original works. Usually comic, sometimes bawdy, but always with an underlying serious intent, Spiderwoman Theatre Workshop's productions have ranged from an exploration of women and violence to cabaret entertainment culled from our most loved and hated romantic songs. Spiderwoman Theatre Workshop tours extensively, appearing at major arts festivals throughout Europe.

Productions 1979:
Women in Violence, Muriel Miguel
The Lysistrata Numbah!, Lisa Mayo
And My Sister Ate Dirt, Lisa Mayo; music by Annie Flood
Jealousy, Gloria Miguel
Friday Night, Lois Weaver, Nadja Beye, Pam Verge

Productions 1980:
Women in Violence, Muriel Miguel
The Lysistrata Numbah!, Lisa Mayo
And My Sister Ate Dirt, Lisa Mayo; music by Annie Flood
Jealousy, Gloria Miguel
Friday Night, Lois Weaver, Nadja Beye, Pam Verge
Sun, Moon and Feather, Lisa Mayo, Gloria Miguel, Muriel Miguel
The Fittin' Room, company-developed
The Pause That Refreshes, Lisa Mayo
Split Britches, Lois Weaver

Special Programs: Workshop for actors; theatre workshops for men and women; community service programs.

GETTING THERE:

Contact the office for current performing location and directions. Company often performs at Theater for the New City and La Mama E.T.C.

RESERVING SEATS:

Box Office Telephone: Contact the office, (212) 243-6209, for information.
Ticket Price: $2.50–$5.00, TDF voucher accepted. Discounts for students and senior citizens.
Reservations: Policy varies, contact the office for current information.
Group Rates: Available, contact the office.
Performance Schedule: Variable New York performing schedule. Performs year-round with extensive touring in Europe.

WHO: TEN-TEN PLAYERS

Co-Chairmen: Toy True, Byron Tinsley
Founder: Leslie Bidwell, under the direction of the Park Avenue Christian Church minister; 1955

WHERE:

Neighborhood: Upper East Side
Theatre Address:
c/o Park Avenue Christian Church
1010 Park Avenue (at 85th Street)
New York, New York 10028
(212) 288-3246
The Space: Ten-Ten Players is housed in the Park Avenue Christian Church, a 1911, Gothic-style building fashioned after St. Chapelle in Paris by Cram, Goodhue & Ferguson. When the church constructed a modern addition during the 1960s, they took the special needs of Ten-Ten Players into consideration. The company performs in a large, modern auditorium on a proscenium stage.

WHAT:

Artistic Profile: For over twenty-five years Ten-Ten Players has been servicing its Yorkville community. Begun as an activity of the Park Avenue Christian Church, the group gradually shifted its focus from the development of religious dramas to the revival of popular Broadway shows and the presentation of original musical revues. In addition, Ten-Ten Players develops an original children's production each year.

Productions 1978/79:

Boy Meets Girl, Samuel & Bella Spewack
The Fraudulent Fox, Alison McDonough
An Enemy of the People, Henrik Ibsen
Ride a Red and Yellow Horse, Diane Tomlinson

Productions 1979/80:

Too True to Be Good, George Bernard Shaw
The Butterfly Palace, book by Robert Higgins; lyrics and music by Byron Tinsley
The Gingerbread Lady, Neil Simon

Special Programs: Theatre rentals; children's shows; dramatic programs for the church centering on religious themes.

GETTING THERE:

Subway: Lexington Avenue IRT 4, 5, 6 to 86th Street.
Bus: Uptown: Madison Avenue (M1, M2, M3, M4); Downtown: Lexington Avenue (M101, M102); Crosstown West and East: 86th Street (M18).
Parking: Street parking available; nearest lot on 85th Street between Madison and Park Avenues.

RESERVING SEATS:

Box Office Telephone: (212) 288-3246
Ticket Price: $3.50 or TDF voucher. $2.00 for students and senior citizens.
Reservations: Call theatre, tickets held until curtain.
Group Rates: Available for groups larger than ten.
Performance Schedule: Four productions (including children's show) presented November through May. Evenings: Friday, Saturday; Matinees: Saturday, Sunday.

TEN-TEN PLAYERS RECOMMENDS:

Madison Restaurant and Delicatessen: 1175 Madison Avenue, at 86th Street, 369-6670. 9:30 A.M. till 11:00 P.M., seven days. $3.50–$11.95, a la carte. No credit cards accepted.

Leo's Restaurant: 128 East 86th Street, 876-9100. Coffee shop. Monday through Saturday: 6:00 A.M. till 1:00 A.M.; Sunday: 8:00 A.M. till 11:00 P.M. $2.50–$4.50, a la carte. No credit cards accepted.

WHO: THALIA SPANISH THEATRE

Artistic and Managing Director: Silvia Brito
Founders: Herbert Dume, José Corrales, Silvia Brito; 1969

WHERE:

Neighborhood: Queens
Theatre Address:
41-17 Greenpoint Avenue
Sunnyside, New York 11104
(212) 729-3880

The Space: New York's other theatre is not limited to the borough of Manhattan. Just twenty blocks from the Queensboro Bridge, Thalia Spanish Theatre found and converted a former discount store into a 101-seat proscenium theatre.

WHAT:

Artistic Profile: Thalia Spanish Theatre (formerly presenting work in Manhattan under the name Dume Spanish Theatre) presents Spanish-language plays to the Queens community. The repertory includes Spanish translations of European and American plays, as well as classic and contemporary Spanish dramas. During the summer, the company presents plays by local playwrights.

Productions 1978/79:

La Brujita Que Era Buena, Maria Clara Machado (children's play)

Memorias de un Director, Jean Anouilh
Olvida los Tambores, Ana Diosdano
Angeles Caidos, Noel Coward

Productions 1979/80:
El Globo Feliz, George Bass
El Diario de Anne Frank, Frances Goodrich and Albert Hackett
Locura de Amor, Tamayo y Baus
Mirandolina, Carlo Goldoni
Una Farfa en el Castillo, Ferenc Molnar
El Solar, Jorge Ros
Gigi, Colette
Anillos para una Dama, Antonio Gala
Arsénico para los Viejos, Joseph O. Kisselring

Special Programs: Acting classes; local touring.

GETTING THERE:

Subway: Flushing Line IRT 7 to Lowery Street.
Bus: Queens Boulevard (M32); Green Line (QM60).
Parking: Street parking available on local streets, on Greenpoint Avenue all day Sunday; nearest lot in back of theatre.

RESERVING SEATS:

Box Office Telephone: (212) 729-3880
Ticket Price: $5.00, TDF voucher accepted. $3.00 for students and senior citizens.
Reservations: Call theatre, tickets held until fifteen minutes before curtain.
Performance Schedule: Productions presented year-round. Each show runs for five to seven weeks. Evenings: Friday, Saturday; Matinees: Sunday.

THALIA SPANISH THEATRE RECOMMENDS:

Sun Luck: 45-12 Queens Boulevard, Sunnyside, 361-1328. Reservations accepted. Chinese. 11:30 A.M. till midnight, seven days. $3.00–$9.00, a la carte. All credit cards accepted.
El Sitio: 68-28 Roosevelt Avenue, Woodside, 424-2369. Reservations accepted. Cuban. Sunday through Thurs-

day: 10:00 A.M. till 1:00 A.M.; Friday and Saturday: 10:00 A.M. till 4:00 A.M. Daily Specials: $5.50.

Dazie's: 39-41 Queens Boulevard, Sunnyside, 786-7013. Reservations accepted. Italian. 11:00 A.M. till midnight, seven days. $6.75–$10.00.

WHO: THEATRE AT ST. CLEMENT'S

Artistic Director: Michael Hadge
Administrative Director: Stephen Berwind
Founder: Sidney Lanier; 1962

WHERE:

Neighborhood: Clinton
Theatre Address:
423 West 46th Street (between Ninth and Tenth Avenues)
New York, New York 10036
(212) 246-7277

The Space: St. Clement's Church, a picturesque parish church with Victorian brickwork and pointed Gothic-revival arched windows, is a true sanctuary among the old tenement buildings that line West 46th Street. That this is an institution thriving with artistic life is immediately apparent as one enters its hallway filled with flyers announcing plays, poetry readings, dance and music concerts. On the ground floor is an intimate 60-seat theatre and upstairs is Playhouse 46, a 99-seat space which Theatre at St. Clement's rents to outside groups.

WHAT:

Artistic Profile: Theatre at St. Clement's is dedicated to the development and production of principally realistic new American plays (over forty new American plays receive staged readings each year). Its physically simple productions are often acted in or directed by well-known Broadway theatre artists. The theatre has a long history of presenting important new American plays. Founded in 1962 by Vicar Sidney Lanier in order to explore the relationship between theatrical and liturgical forms, St. Clement's was the birthplace of the American Place Theatre. During the early 1970s directors Kevin O'Connor and Larry Goossen spearheaded a fruitful period of experimentation which included the New York City premieres of works by Tom Stoppard and David Mamet and the first production of *The Robber Bridegroom.*

Productions 1978/79:
The Shanty, Faizul Khan
Ty Cobb and *Warplay*, William Packard
A Barbershop in Pittsburgh, Jasper Oddo
They Were All Gardenias, Laurance Holder
Every Place Is Newark, Ira Lewis
Montezuma's Revenge, Alan Davis III

Productions 1979/80:
Chieftains, James Childs
Deer Season, Phyllis Green
Easy Money, John Kostmayer
Demeter's Lost Daughter, Bruce Serlen
The Survivor, based on the book by Jack Eisener
Two One-Acts

Special Programs: Monday and Tuesday night playreading series—open to the public; internships; theatre rentals; post-performance lectures; plays presented as part of Sunday worship services; poetry project at St. Clement's.

GETTING THERE:

Subway: IND E, A, AA, CC to 42nd or 50th Street.
Bus: Uptown: Tenth Avenue (M11); Downtown: Ninth Avenue (M11); Crosstown West and East: 42nd Street (M106).
Parking: Street parking after 6:00 P.M.; nearest lot at Tenth Avenue and 46th Street.

RESERVING SEATS:

Box Office Telephone: (212) 246-7277
Ticket Price: $4.00, TDF voucher accepted.
Reservations: Call theatre, tickets held until fifteen minutes before curtain.
Group Rates: Available, contact the theatre.
Performance Schedule: Five to six plays presented September through June.

THEATRE AT ST. CLEMENT'S RECOMMENDS:

Landmark Tavern: Corner of Eleventh Avenue and 46th Street, 757-8595. Reservations recommended. American-Irish. Weekdays: noon–midnight; Weekends: noon–1:00 A.M. Lunch: $3.00–$8.00, a la carte; Dinner: $5.00–$14.00, a la carte. No credit cards accepted.

Pantheon Restaurant: 689 Eighth Avenue, between 43rd and 44th Streets, 840-9391. Greek-American. 11:30 A.M. till 11:00 P.M., seven days. $5.75–$7.75, a la carte. MC, Visa, Diner's, Amex accepted.

El Taquito: 686 Ninth Avenue, between 47th and 48th Streets, 765-1737. Reservations accepted. Mexican. Tuesday and Wednesday: 1:00 P.M. till 11:00 P.M.; Thursday through Sunday: 2:00 P.M. till 11:00 P.M. Closed Monday. $3.00–$6.00, complete. MC accepted.

WHO: THEATER FOR THE NEW CITY

Artistic Directors: George Bartenieff, Crystal Field

Founders: George Bartenieff, Crystal Field, Lawrence Kornfeld, Theo Barnes; 1970

WHERE:

Neighborhood: Noho–East Village

Theatre Address:
162 Second Avenue (between 10th and 11th Streets)
New York, New York 10003
(212) 254-1109

The Space: The brown awning that marks the entrance to Theater for the New City is sandwiched among a remarkable spectrum of East Village ethnic restaurants—Ukrainian, Japanese, Indian, Jewish, and Chinese—in one of New York's most culturally diverse neighborhoods. The theatre complex houses three performing spaces, allowing for simultaneous presentation of diverse productions: the ground-floor, flexible, 130-seat James Waring Theatre; the downstairs 140-seat proscenium Joe Cino Theatre; and the upstairs, flexible 48-seat Chamber Space.

WHAT:

Artistic Profile: Presenting over forty productions annually, Theater for the New City (TNC) is well known as a center for the discovery, development, and nurturing of important new experimental work. The theatre has hosted such prominent avant-garde theatre groups as Mabou Mines, Richard Foreman, Stewart Sherman, The Talking Band, and Charles Ludlam and the Ridiculous Theatrical Company, as well as premiering at least ten productions by contemporary playwrights each year. Tracing its roots to the Judson Poets' Theater, TNC strives to amalgamate song, dance, live music, and poetry into a total theatre experience and has been the recipient of thirteen Obie Awards and one Pulitzer Prize. Their active community Outreach Program includes a free, summer street-theatre involving a large interracial cast of forty that brings spectacle and satire to the poorer neighborhoods of the five borough area; block party events; and a free-ticket distribution program. A special outdoor Halloween festival includes the massive participation of East and West Village residents in an elaborately costumed parade through the streets of New York City.

Productions 1978/79:

The King of the Mashed Potatoes, Crystal Field and George Bartenieff
Lovely Rita, Thomas Brasch; translated by Viola Stephan and Dennis Eichelberger
Buried Child, Sam Shepard
The Fall, Albert Camus; translated by Justin O'Brian
Homebodies, Nicholas Kazan
The Button, Michael McClure
Clara Bow Loves Gary Cooper, Robert Dahdah and Mary Boylan
Fruit of Zaloom, Paul Zaloom
Hefetz, Hanokh Levin; translated by Rina Elisha
Othello, William Shakespeare
Stewart Sherman's Eighth Spectacle, Stewart Sherman
The Writer's Opera, book and lyrics by Rosalyn Drexler; music by John Braden
After the Baal—Shem Tov, Arthur Sainer

Metaphysics of a Two-Headed Calf, Stanislaw Mitkiwicz; translated by Daniel and Eleanor Gerould
Voideville, Gordon Bressac and Ruby Lynn Reyner
Up in Seattle, Arthur Williams
Lord Tom Goldsmith, Victor Lipton

Productions 1979/80:

Apoplectic Fit, Daryl Chin
Nine to Five, a collaboration by Quena Company
Aztec Indian Dancers
The Dog That Talked Too Much, street-theatre collaboration by George Bartenieff, Crystal Field and Company
Riff Raff Revue, Mike Kellin
Politics, Sex, Death, Work and the World, Walter Corwin
Coming from a Great Distance, a traveling Jewish Theatre
Dead Fingers Walk, Red Mole Theatre Company
WNYC Story-Telling Event
One-Third of a Nation, Arthur Arent (WPA Living Newspaper)
Horizontal White, Barry Marshall
Those Darn Kids, Robert Dahdah and Mary Boylan
La Justice, Kenneth Bernard
Halloween Benefit, community parade and party
Aphrodite, Ugenia Macer-Story
Pedro Paramo, Talking Band
Bag Lady, Jean Claude van Itallie
Comic Act by Tom Murrin
Morandi's, Morton Lichter
The Consoling Virgin, Bruce Serlen
Thunderbird America, Indian Dance Concert; Pow Wow
Vanishing Pictures, based on texts of Poe and Baullier; adapted by Beverly Brown and Mabou Mines
The Derby, book by Barry Arnold; music by John Braden
Two One-Acts by Grubb Graebner:
Que Ubo?
Loney's 66
The Fittin' Room, Spiderwoman Theatre
Images of the Coming Dead, Arthur Sainer
Sunday Childhood Journeys to Nobody at Home, Arthur Sainer; with additional material by Mabou Mines and Stewart Sherman

Itchy Britches, N. Noble Barrett
Evelyn S. Brown—A Diary, Maria Irene Fornes
Graven Images, Robin Drexler
The Pope in Love, Joseph Renard
Dancers on My Ceiling, Mary Karolly
The True War Dance of Yankee Reels, Bob Jacobs
Number 14, Don Rifkin
People of the Empire, Crispin Larangeira
Billy Stars and Kid Jupiter, William Electric Black

Special Programs: Regional touring; internships; free ticket distribution.

GETTING THERE:

Subway: BMT RR to 8th Street; Lexington Avenue IRT 6 to Astor Place; BMT LL (Canarsie 14th Street Line) to First Avenue and 14th Street.

Bus: Uptown: First Avenue (M15); Downtown: Second Avenue (M15); Crosstown West: 9th Street (M13); Crosstown East: 8th Street (M13).

Parking: Street parking available; nearest lot on Third Avenue between 9th and 10th Streets.

RESERVING SEATS:

Box Office Telephone: (212) 254-1109
Ticket Price: $0–$2.50, TDF voucher accepted.
Group Rates: Available, contact the theatre.
Performance Schedule: Over forty productions presented year-round, indoors and outdoors. Evenings: Thursday through Sunday; Matinees: variable schedule.

THEATER FOR THE NEW CITY RECOMMENDS:

Mie Japanese Cooking Shop: 196 Second Avenue, on the corner of 12th Street, 674-7060. Reservations accepted for parties of three or more. Japanese. 5:00 P.M. till 12:30 A.M. Closed Monday. Complete Dinners: $5.25–$8.00. MC, Visa, Amex accepted.

Second Avenue Deli: 156 Second Avenue, on the corner of 10th Street, 677-0606. Kosher. 7:00 A.M. till midnight, seven days. $3.50–$8.00. Personal checks accepted.

WHO: THEATRE MATRIX

Producing Director: Paul Ellis
Founder: Paul Ellis; 1978

WHERE:

Neighborhood: Performs in various locations.
Office Address:
358 Broadway
New York, New York 10013
(212) 868-3330 (P. Ellis)

WHAT:

Artistic Profile: Theatre Matrix develops and produces new American plays by providing writers with a matrix—that supportive structure that serves to give shape and direction to a writer's creativity. The company's Theatre Circle Writers' Workshop meets regularly and generates many of the works ultimately produced by the theatre. An emphasis on process not only characterizes script development, but also the rehearsal process, fostering experiments and full creative involvement by actors, designers, and directors as well as playwrights.
Productions 1978/79:
Subject to Fits, Robert Montgomery
The Tempest, musical adaptation of William Shakespeare's play by Jim Petosa
Productions 1979/80:
Still Onshore, Richard Taylor
A Good Time, Ernest Thompson
The Brute, Anton Chekov
Me Too, Then, Tom Dudzick and Steven Smith
Special Programs: Playwrights' workshop; movement classes; administrative workshop.

GETTING THERE:

Call the office for current performing location and directions.

RESERVING SEATS:

Box Office Telephone: (212) 868-3330 (P. Ellis)
Ticket Price: $3.00, or TDF voucher.
Reservations: Call theatre, tickets held until fifteen minutes before curtain.
Performance Schedule: Variable performing schedule of approximately two to four productions per year.

WHO: THEATRE OFF PARK

Executive Director: Patricia Flynn Peate
Managing Director: Jay Stevens
Founder: Alan Egly of the Community Church of New York; 1975

WHERE:

Neighborhood: Gramercy
Theatre Address:
28 East 35th Street (between Park and Madison Avenues)
New York, New York 10016
(212) 679-5684
The Space: As its name indicates, Theatre Off Park is located just off Park Avenue in an easily accessible, safe neighborhood of townhouses, apartment buildings, department stores, and office buildings. Housed in the basement of a renovated brownstone, the theatre has an intimate 70-seat, narrow proscenium space.

WHAT:

Artistic Profile: Theatre Off Park focuses on the presentation of carefully honed productions that showcase the talents of playwrights, designers, and actors. Their mixed-bag repertory ranges from mysteries to musicals and includes both American and European plays.
Productions 1978/79:
Singin' My Song, lyrics and music by Johnny Brandon
The Madman and the Nun, Stanislaw Ignacy Witkiewicz; translated by Dan Gerould and C. S. Durer

The Confession Stone, Owen Dodson
Sexual Incident at the Institute of Advanced Learning, H. N. Levitt

Productions 1979/80:

Give My Regards to Leicester Square, conceived by Dean Burriss and Clif Donell
Puck and the Magic Flower, lyrics by Nick De Noia; music by Leon Odenz
Ricochet, Paul S. Nathan
Of the Fields Lately, David French

Special Programs: Theatre rentals.

GETTING THERE:

Subway: Lexington Avenue IRT 6 to 33rd Street.
Bus: Uptown: Madison Avenue (M1, M2, M3); Downtown: Fifth Avenue (M1, M2, M3); Crosstown West and East: 34th Street (M16).
Parking: Street parking after 7:00 P.M.; nearest lot at Park Avenue and 34th Street.

RESERVING SEATS:

Box Office Telephone: (212) 679-6283
Ticket Price: $3.00–$4.00, or TDF voucher.
Reservations: Reservations must be picked up twenty-four hours in advance. Seats are reserved.
Group Rates: Available for groups of fifteen or more.
Performance Schedule: Five shows presented October through June; Evenings: Wednesday through Saturday.

THEATRE OFF PARK RECOMMENDS:

Plaza Cafe: Corner of 37th Street and Third Avenue, 867-7179. Reservations accepted. American-Continental. Noon till 1:00 A.M., seven days. Lunch: $4.75–$14.00, a la carte; Dinner: $6.00–$14.00, a la carte. All credit cards accepted.
Il Hwa: 401 Fifth Avenue, between 36th and 37th Streets, 686-3546. Reservations required for private Korean dining room. International, natural foods. Monday through Saturday: noon till 8:30 P.M. Closed Sunday. Lunch: $3.25–$5.50, a la carte; Dinner: $6.00–$10.00, a la carte. MC, Visa, Diner's, Amex accepted.

Bienvenue: 21 East 36th Street, between Madison and Fifth Avenues, 684-0215. Reservations accepted for dinner only. French. Monday through Friday Lunch: 11:30 A.M. till 2:30 P.M.; Dinner: 5:30 P.M. till 10:00 P.M. Saturday: Dinner only. Closed Sunday. Lunch: $4.00–$10.00, a la carte; Dinner: $6.00–$14.00, a la carte. MC and Visa accepted.

WHO: THEATRE OF THE OPEN EYE

Artistic Director: Jean Erdman
Executive Director: Nola Hague
Founders: Jean Erdman, Joseph Campbell; 1972

WHERE:

Neighborhood: Upper East Side
Theatre Address:
316 East 88th Street (between First and Second Avenues)
New York, New York 10028
(212) 534-6363

The Space: Theatre of the Open Eye is housed in the Church of the Holy Trinity, one of the city's most magical church buildings. Set back from the street with a fully landscaped yard, this Roman brick church provides a surprising, most welcome touch of the country right in the middle of New York City. The theatre has a flexible ground-floor space that seats 100 to 300. A second, flexible 100-seat space with high, vaulted ceilings is located on the third floor and is accessible by an elegant spiraling staircase or elevator.

WHAT:

Artistic Profile: In 1972, following the world tour of her award-winning Off Broadway musical play, *The Coach with the Six Insides*, Jean Erdman, together with Joseph Campbell, author of *The Hero with a Thousand Faces,*

A Skeleton Key to Finnegans Wake, The Masks of God, and *The Mythic Image,* founded the Theatre of the Open Eye. Begun as a permanent ensemble of dancers, actors, musicians, and designers, the theatre has worked to foster the continued development of such total-theatre works as *Coach.* The Open Eye's signature piece, *Moon Mysteries,* a suite of three of W. B. Yeats' best known plays-for-dancers, toured the United States and Canada for five seasons. Besides such total-theatre works, productions have included dance festivals and the stagings of original poetic plays.

Productions 1978/79:

The Coach with the Six Insides, Jean Erdman; adapted from James Joyce's *Finnegans Wake*; music by Teiji Ito

The Masque of Dawn, book by Eric Bass; music by Bill Buchen and Richard Spendio

George and the Dragon, John Patrick Shanley; music by Tom Shelton and Susan Hunter

Festival of New Works

Productions 1979/80:

The Shining House, conceived by Jean Erdman; visual environment by Paul Jenkins; music by Michael Czajkowski; lyrics by Christopher Millis

Three Irish Noh Plays by Ulich O'Connor

Details (of the sixteenth frame), Robert Walter

Moon Mysteries: Three visionary plays by W. B. Yeats, conceived by Jean Erdman; music by Teiji Ito

Special Programs: Classes for children; internships; touring; in-schools programs; playwrights' workshops; post-performance discussions; seminars in mythology, psychology, anthropology, and the creative arts; theatre rentals.

GETTING THERE:

Subway: Lexington Avenue IRT 4, 5, 6 to 86th Street.

Bus: Uptown: First Avenue (M15); Downtown: Second Avenue (M15); Crosstown West and East: 86th Street (M18).

Parking: Street parking (alternate side); nearest lot on 88th Street between Second and Third Avenues.

RESERVING SEATS:

Box Office Telephone: (212) 534-6909
Ticket Price: $5.00–$6.00, TDF voucher accepted.
Reservations: Call theatre, tickets held until a half hour before curtain.
Performance Schedule: Four productions presented September through June. Evenings: Wednesday through Sunday; Matinees: Sunday. Very active theatre rental program throughout the year.

THEATRE OF THE OPEN EYE RECOMMENDS:

Rathbones: 1702 Second Avenue, on the corner of 88th Street, 369-7361. Reservations recommended for parties of four or more on weekends. American. Monday through Friday: 4:00 P.M. till midnight; Saturday and Sunday: noon till midnight. $7.50–$10.00, a la carte. MC, Visa, Diner's, Amex accepted.

WHO: THEATRE OF THE RIVERSIDE CHURCH

Coordinating Director: David K. Manion
Administrative Assistant: Marsha Imhoff
Founder: Gertrude Fagan; 1960

WHERE:

Neighborhood: Upper West Side
Theatre Address:
490 Riverside Drive (enter on 120th Street)
New York, New York 10027
(212) 749-7000, ext. 126, 127
The Space: Overlooking the Hudson River, the Riverside Church's towering Gothic spires and luminous stained glass windows immediately evoke a sense of awe and grandeur. The theatre makes use of numerous spaces within the church including a modern 250-seat proscenium, air-conditioned theatre; a 99-seat, tenth-floor space with pristine whitewashed walls and stained glass

windows; a 2,000-seat nave; a cafeteria with an elevated stage; and even the rooftop for Shakespearean productions.

WHAT:

Artistic Profile: TRC began by presenting religious dramas for the church community. Quickly developing into a professional theatre, TRC showcases new American dramas, musicals, and revivals. At the same time, TRC maintains a commitment to developing a theatre ministry—creating religious, community events such as a production of *Godspell* in the Church's enormous chapel; presenting devotional-evocational plays; and providing an arts-focused Lenten Action series. In addition, TRC sponsors the Riverside Dance Festival (an eight-month marathon of over sixty dance companies), houses an in-residence children's theatre—the Pumpernickel Players, and sponsors poetry readings and music concerts.

Productions 1978/79:

A Broadway Musical, book by Lee Adams; music by Charles Strouse

Romance, Tom Topor

Woyzeck, adapted by Al Asermely from Georg Büchner's text

The Frost of Renaissance, Samm Art Williams

Productions 1979/80:

Amahl and the Night Visitors, Gian-Carlo Menotti

Twelfth Night, William Shakespeare (co-production with Riverside Shakespeare Company of NYC)

Godspell, Stephen Schwartz

Lenten Action Study, includes Bach cantatas, vocal music by Seth McCoy, Mark Peters, and Ellen Harris; theatre lectures by Stuart McDowell

St. Francis of Assisi, adapted by Norman Adler from "Little Flowers of St. Francis"

Special Programs: Saturday theatre classes for children; free Friday afternoon master classes in dance by TRC Riverside Dance Festival troupe in residence; Riverside Video Theatre—scenes from plays and interviews with artists presented on Cable TV; children's arts educational programs; sponsorship of TRC Dance Festival, Pumpernickel Players and poetry readings.

GETTING THERE:

Subway: Seventh Avenue IRT 1 to 116th Street.

Bus: Uptown: Amsterdam Avenue (M11), Riverside Drive (M4, M5); Downtown: Broadway (M104), Riverside Drive (M4, M5).

Parking: Garage on 120th Street between Riverside Drive and Claremont Avenue.

RESERVING SEATS:

Box Office Telephone: (212) 864-2929

Ticket Price: $3.00–$7.00, or TDF voucher plus surcharge; discounts for students and senior citizens.

Reservations: Call theatre, tickets held until fifteen minutes before curtain.

Group Rates: Available, contact the theatre.

Performance Schedule: Theatre season: variable schedule September through June; Dance Festival: weekly performances from October through November, January through June. Holiday programming during December.

THEATRE OF THE RIVERSIDE CHURCH RECOMMENDS:

Terrace Restaurant: 400 West 119th Street, on the corner of Morningside Drive atop Butler Hall, 666-9490. Reservations recommended. French. Tuesday through Friday: noon till 2:30 P.M. and 6:00 P.M. till 10:30 P.M.; Saturday and Sunday: 6:00 P.M. till 10:30 P.M., only. Closed Monday. Lunch: $6.75–$9.75, a la carte; Dinner: $10.75–$15.75, a la carte. All credit cards accepted. Chamber music every night. Discounts often available to TRC subscribers.

The Cafeteria: Located in South Hall of the Church—one floor above the theatre, 749-7000. Monday through Friday: noon till 2:00 P.M.; Monday through Thursday: 5:00 P.M. till 6:30 P.M.; Sunday: noon till 2:00 P.M. $1.45–$2.50, a la carte. No credit cards accepted.

The Symposium: 544 West 113th Street, between Amsterdam and Broadway, 678-9470. Greek. Noon till midnight, seven days. $1.95–$7.95. No credit cards accepted.

WHO: THEATRE XII

Artistic Director: Sonia Amira
Founders: Sonia Amira, Richard Scully; 1976

WHERE:

Theatre Address: Performs in various locations.
Office Address:
c/o Sonia Amira
775 Concourse Village East #5N
Bronx, New York 10451
(212) 293-3883

WHAT:

Artistic Profile: Theatre XII is an ensemble of actors committed to the belief that the actor is the essential factor in the presentation of quality theatre. Their work focuses on the revival of realistic American plays—Inge, Shepard, Melfi, Williams—that are particularly suited to a naturalistic style of acting. Productions are physically spare, but imaginatively use the actor's special talents to evoke a sense of time and place.

Productions 1978/79:
The Disposal, William Inge
Back Bog Beast Bait, Sam Shepard
Cowboy Mouth, Sam Shepard
Two One-Acts by Lewis John Carlino:
Snow Angel
Epiphany
Nourish the Beast, Steve Tesich
The Shirt, Leonard Melfi

Productions 1979/80:
One-Act Festival:
It's Called the Sugar Plum, Israel Horovitz
Rats, Israel Horovitz
Tigers, Kendrew Lascellas
The Questioning of Nick, Arthur Kopit
The Dutchman, LeRoi Jones
Cowboy Mouth, Sam Shepard
27 Wagons Full of Cotton, Tennessee Williams
Buzzy, Mentha Marley III
The Death of a Poet, Robert Payne

Special Programs: Professional classes for company members.

GETTING THERE:

Contact the office for current performing location and directions.

RESERVING SEATS:

Box Office Telephone: Contact the office: (212) 293-3883
Ticket Price: $3.00, or TDF voucher. $1.50 for students and senior citizens.
Reservations: Call theatre, tickets held until a half hour before curtain.
Group Rates: Groups of ten or more: $1.50 per person.
Subscription: Full season (five plays) pass.
Performance Schedule: Five to eight plays presented on a year-round schedule. Evenings: Thursday through Sunday; Matinees: Sunday.

WHO: TRG REPERTORY COMPANY

Artistic Director: Marvin Kahan
Managing Director: Anita Pintozzi
Founders: Marvin Kahan, Dan Clancey, Jon Luria; 1975

WHERE:

Neighborhood: Noho–East Village
Theatre Address:
Wonderhorse Theatre
83 East Fourth Street
New York, New York 10003
Office Address:
c/o Marvin Kahan
60 East 8th Street
New York, New York 10003
(212) 757-6315

The Space: In the East Village on East Fourth Street—downtown's equivalent of Broadway—TRG Repertory Company shares the Wonderhouse Theatre with Cherubs Guild and New World Theatre. See Cherubs Guild (p. 43) for a more detailed description of this handsome 99-seat proscenium theatre.

WHAT:

Artistic Profile: Founded by three actors who worked at CSC Repertory Company, TRG Repertory (Theatre Repertory Group) produces revivals of twentieth-century British and American plays, focusing on forgotten plays that did not receive sufficient attention at the time of their first production. Tennessee Williams, Leonard Melfi, Sidney Kingsley, Sam Shepard, Thomas Babe, and Noel Coward are among the playwrights who have been revived or are under consideration for revival by the theatre.

Productions 1978/79:

Natural Affection, William Inge

You Touched Me!, Tennessee Williams and Donald Windham

Morning, Noon and Night, Israel Horovitz, Terrence McNally, Leonard Melfi

Moonchildren, Michael Weller

Productions 1979/80:

You Touched Me!, Tennessee Williams and Donald Windham

Special Programs: Post-performance lectures; theatre rentals.

GETTING THERE:

Subway: BMT LL (Canarsie 14th Street Line) to Third Avenue/14th Street; BMT RR to 8th Street; IND F to Second Avenue/Houston Street; Lexington Avenue IRT 6 to Astor Place.

Bus: Uptown: Third Avenue (M101, M102); Downtown: Broadway (M1, M6) and Second Avenue (M15).

Parking: Street Parking; lot in filling station on corner of East 14th Street and the Bowery.

RESERVING SEATS:

Box Office Telephone: (212) 533-5888
Ticket Price: $5.00, TDF voucher accepted. Students and senior citizens, $3.00.
Reservations: Call 581-2900, tickets held until fifteen minutes before curtain.
Group Rates: Available, contact the theatre.
Performance Schedule: Approximately four productions presented September through June. Evenings: Thursday through Sunday.

TRG REPERTORY COMPANY RECOMMENDS:

Phebe's Place: 361 Bowery, at 4th Street, 473-9008. American-Continental. Noon till 4:00 A.M., seven days. $1.65–$9.00, a la carte. All credit cards accepted.
Shagorika Bangladesh Restaurant: 100 Second Avenue, between 6th and 7th Streets, 982-0533. Reservations suggested. Indian Lunch: 11:30 A.M. till 3:00 P.M., Monday through Friday; Dinner: 5:00 P.M. till 11:00 P.M., seven day. $3.00–$5.25, a la carte. All credit cards accepted.

WHO: WESTSIDE COMMUNITY REPERTORY THEATRE

Artistic Director: Andres Castro
Managing Director: Timothy Hurley
Founder: Andres Castro; 1969

WHERE:

Neighborhood: Upper West Side
Theatre Address:
252 West 81st Street (between Broadway and West End Avenue)
New York, New York 10024
(212) 666-3521

The Space: With its dollhouse proportions, the Westside Community Repertory Theatre evokes the diminutive fantasy world of Alice in Wonderland. It has all the accoutrements of a traditional theatre, but on a greatly reduced scale—the lobby comfortably holds three, the small proscenium theatre has five rows of raked seating that accommodates just thirty.

WHAT:

Artistic Profile: Not only one of the smallest Off Off Broadway theatres, but also one of the oldest, the Westside Community Repertory Theatre presents classics with a contemporary approach in an effort to emphasize the eternal values of the great playwrights. Using actors of various ethnic and national backgrounds, the theatre emphasizes their diversity rather than striving for a homogeneity of accents and style. In a production of Chekov, Feydeau, Ibsen, Camus, Shaw, Strindberg, or Molière, it is not unusual to find a potpourri of accents ranging from West Indian to Irish, to Cuban, to Puerto Rican, to Brooklyn to Midwestern. The intimacy of the theatre is paralleled by the intimacy of the company which considers itself a family, having trained and performed together for many years. Many well-known ethnic actors who have gone on to achieve success in the commercial theatre, television, and films continue to regard the theatre as their home base.

Productions 1979:

Keep an Eye on Amelie, George Feydeau
Arms and the Man, George Bernard Shaw
The Lady from the Sea, Henrik Ibsen

Productions 1980:

The Philanderer, George Bernard Shaw
An Ideal Husband, Oscar Wilde
Affairs of Anatol, Arthur Schnitzler
Three One-Acts by Edward Gallardo:
 Maria
 The Mugger
 Bernie

Special Programs: Adult training workshop; Saturday teenage acting workshop.

GETTING THERE:

Subway: Seventh Avenue IRT 1 to 79th Street.
Bus: Uptown: Tenth Avenue (M7, M11); Downtown: Broadway (M104); Crosstown West and East: 79th Street (M17).
Parking: Street parking available; lot on 84th Street between Broadway and Amsterdam Avenue.

RESERVING SEATS:

Box Office Telephone: (212) 666-3521 or 874-9400
Ticket Price: $4.00, or TDF voucher.
Reservations: Call theatre, reservations held until fifteen minutes before curtain.
Performance Schedule: Year-round; each production runs for three to four months. Evenings: Friday through Sunday; Matinees: Schedule varies.

WESTSIDE COMMUNITY REPERTORY THEATRE RECOMMENDS:

Teacher's: 2249 Broadway, between 80th and 81st Streets, 787-3500. Reservations accepted. Continental. Sunday through Thursday: 11:00 A.M. till 1:00 A.M.; Friday and Saturday: 11:00 A.M. till 2:00 A.M. $3.50–$11.00, a la carte. All credit cards except Carte Blanche accepted.

WHO: THE WOOSTER GROUP

Artistic Director: Elizabeth LeCompte
Administrators: Jeffrey M. Jones, Meghan Ellenberger
Founded as the Performance Group; 1967

WHERE:

Neighborhood: Soho
Theatre Address:
The Performing Garage
33 Wooster Street
New York, New York 10013
(212) 966-9796

The Space: The Performing Garage is situated in the more rustic-commercial area of Soho, near Canal Street. It was once a flatware-finishing factory, and is now the permanent home of The Wooster Group, and the New York City house for a variety of American and foreign performance artists. With an open, adaptable space, the Garage's performance areas and seating structures are flexible and have been modeled into highly unconventional and intriguing environments for past Performance Group and Wooster Group productions. Director Richard Schechner converted the entire garage into the wagon for *Mother Courage*, and used a series of elevated ledges and complex playing areas for *The Tooth of Crime* and *The Balcony*. Director Elizabeth LeCompte created a combination academic lecture hall and subconscious surgery ampitheatre for *Nayatt School*, with three-dimensional seating and performance areas, and used a cross of traditional and multimedia techniques to create a combination offshore oil rig, summer house, and seashore convent for *Point Judith*.

WHAT:

Artistic Profile: The resident company of the Performing Garage is The Wooster Group, a collaborative of theatre artists Elizabeth LeCompte, Spalding Gray, Libby Howes, Ron Vawter, Jim Clayburgh, and Willem Dafoe. It was established in 1980 from the nucleus of the Performing Group, founded in 1967 by Richard Schechner. In 1975, while members of the Performance Group, the present ensemble began to create and perform their own group works, under the direction of director-designer-performer Elizabeth LeCompte. In works such as *Sakonnet Point, Rumstick Road, Nayatt School*, and *Point Judith*, the company pioneered the creative and performance techniques of autobiographical theatre. Company member Spalding Gray has continued the process of autobiographical theatre with a pair of three solo works he created and performed in 1979 and 1980. As the group continues to explore compositional techniques and structures for collaborative work, it is evolving new theatre forms. While members of the Performance Group, under the direction of Richard Schechner until 1980, the Group was featured in such innovative environmental productions as *Commune, Mother Courage, Tooth of Crime* and *Cops.*

Productions 1978/79:

Cops, Terry Curtis Fox
Three Places in Rhode Island, Spalding Gray, Elizabeth LeCompte, and company
Sakonnet Point
Rumstick Road
Nayatt School
Sex and Death to the Age 14, Spalding Gray
Piero Della Francesca, Ron Vawter
A Fierce Longing, Theatre X of Milwaukee
I Was Thinking & So Bored, Wilma Project of Philadelphia
Heartaches, Jim Bierman
Elephant Man, No Theatre of Northampton
Paradise Regained, Victory Theatre
Gong of Java, Barbara Benary
Video Cabaret, from Canada
Dog'd Shots in Indirection, Clarice Marshall and Interaction Dance Foundation
Free Fall, Theatre for the Forgotten
Maldoror of Lautremont, Atelier de Recherche Théâtrale from France
Come and Go and *Mercier and Camier*, Mabou Mines and N.Y.U. Beckett Festival
A Remnant and *Eh Joe*, N.Y.U. Beckett Festival
Hard Hats and Stolen Hearts, Theatre Network of Canada
Salmon Show, Bob Carroll
Double Gothic, Michael Kirby's Structuralist Workshop
Fruit of Zaloom, Paul Zaloom
Street Entertainer's Festival
Southern Exposure, Joanne Akalaitis
MacBeth, William Shakespeare (Independent Eye)
Italian Theatre Festival, N.Y.U.
The Egg Session, Joan Evans

An Evening of Dirty Religious Plays, Odyssey Theatre of Los Angeles
Martyrs, Jamie Leo
Upsidedown & Backwards, Joan Jonas
Red Riding Shawl, John Emigh
Photoanalysis, Michael Kirby and Ted Hoffman

Productions 1979/80:
Three By Spalding Gray:
India and After (America)
Sex and Death to the Age 14
Booze, Cars & College Girls
The Balcony, Jean Genet; adapted by Richard Schechner
Point Judith, Spalding Gray and Elizabeth LeCompte in in collaboration with Jim Clayburgh, Willem Dafoe, Libby Howes, and Ron Vawter
An Evening of Dirty Religious Plays
Diary of a Madman, Cambridge Ensemble
Eiko & Koma, dance program
Short Pieces, Bob Carroll
Phoebe Legere/Monad, concert
Tally Brown Live, cabaret concert
The Venus Cafe and *The Mother and the Maid,* Theodora Skipitares
Zalooming Along, Paul Zaloom
Vanishing Pictures, Mabou Mines
And That's How the Rent Gets Paid, Jeff Weiss
Calamity Ruth Foose, Jeff Weiss, Arleen Kalenich
A Theatrical Party, Charles Busch
remains, Joseph Dunn and the American Contemporary Theatre
Sheer Heaven, Eric Bogosian
Pooh Kaye and Yoshiko Chuma dance program
The Survivor and the Translator, Leeny Sack
Gilgamesh, Shared Forms Theatre
Cirkus Unikum, Theatre Drak of Czechoslovakia

Special Programs: Workshops; internships; performances and seminars in schools; workshop productions and open rehearsals; post-performance discussions; national and international touring; children's theatre workshop; theatre rentals and presentation of avant-garde American and European performing artists.

GETTING THERE:

Subway: Lexington Avenue IRT 4, 5, 6 to Canal Street (walk west); BMT RR, N to Canal Street (walk west); IND A, AA, CC, E to Canal Street (walk east).
Bus: Uptown: Whitehall Street, Centre Street, lower Manhattan (M1); Downtown: Broadway (M6); Crosstown West and East: Grand Street (M8).
Parking: Street parking after 6:00 P.M.

RESERVING SEATS:

Box Office Telephone: (212) 966-3651
Ticket Price: General admission, no reserved seats. $4.00–$6.00, TDF voucher accepted. Discounts for student and senior citizen groups.
Reservations: Call theatre, tickets held until fifteen minutes before curtain.
Group Rates: Available, contact the theatre.
Performance Schedule: Year-round performances, booked-in events, and movies presented Tuesday through Sunday.

THE WOOSTER GROUP RECOMMENDS:

Soho Robata: 143 Spring Street, on the corner of Wooster Street, 431-3993. Reservations required. Continental. Lunch: Tuesday through Saturday, noon till 2:30 P.M.; Dinner: Monday through Friday, 5:00 P.M. till 11:00 P.M.; Saturday, 4:00 P.M. till midnight; Sunday, 4:00 P.M. till 10:30 P.M. Lunch: $5.00–$7.50, a la carte; Dinner: $7.50–$10.00, a la carte. All credit cards except Carte Blanche accepted.
Skrambles Cafe: 402 West Broadway, on the corner of Spring Street, 966-6660. American-Greek-French. Noon till 4:00 A.M., seven days. Kitchen closes at 2:00 A.M. Brunch: Saturday and Sunday, 11:30 A.M. till 4:30 P.M. Lunch: $3.50–$7.00, a la carte; Dinner: $3.50–$10.00, a la carte. Diner's and Amex accepted. Piano Bar: Wednesday through Saturday.
Prince Street Bar and Restaurant: 125 Prince Street, on the corner of Wooster Street, 228-8130. American. Sunday through Thursday: noon till 2:00 A.M.; Friday and Saturday: noon till 3:00 A.M. $3.00–$7.00, a la carte. No credit cards accepted.

WHO: WPA THEATRE

Producing Director: Kyle Renick
Artistic Director: Howard Ashman
Resident Designer and Technical Director: Edward T. Gianfrancesco
Founders: Harry Orzello, Virginia Aquino; 1968

WHERE:

Neighborhood: Chelsea
Theatre Address:
138 Fifth Avenue (at 19th Street)
New York, New York 10011
(212) 691-2274

The Space: Resident in numerous theatres since its inception, WPA acquired and totally renovated a second-floor, Chelsea loft space after its artistic leadership shifted in 1976. The intimate 98-seat proscenium has comfortable raked seating.

WHAT:

Artistic Profile: WPA works to develop a characteristic style—in terms of acting technique, choice of plays, and scenic design—in an effort to celebrate and elucidate America's distinctive contribution to the theatrical tradition. The company produces only post-1920s realistic American plays specifically suited to a highly detailed, realistic acting style. Stage design likewise exploits a specificity of detail (three and one-half cubic yards of dirt covered the stage for Edward Albee's *Ballad of the Sad Cafe*, a snow-drift sculpture and a veritable replica of a New England farmhouse were created for Edith Wharton's *Ethan Frome*). In addition to presenting classic and new American realistic plays (including *Nuts* which moved to Broadway), WPA is reviewing the canon of renowned American writers—Hellman, Williams, Miller, and Albee—in an effort to revive these authors' little-known, neglected works. The company's production of *Josephine the Mouse Singer* won the Obie Award for best new American play of 1978/79.

Productions 1978/79:

Days to Come, Lillian Hellman
Josephine the Mouse Singer, Michael McClure
Ethan Frome, Edith Wharton; adapted by Owen and Donald Davis
Two One-Acts:
Motel, Donna deMatteo
Opening Night, Bury St. Edmund
The Frequency, Larry Ketron
Kurt Vonnegut's *God Bless You, Mr. Rosewater*, book and lyrics by Howard Ashman; music by Alan Menken; additional lyrics by Dennis Green

Productions 1979/80:

Character Lines, Larry Ketron
My Mother, My Father, and Me, Lillian Hellman
Nuts, Tom Topor
Jacob's Ladder, Barbara Graham
Album, David Rimmer

Special Programs: Playreading series; internships; post-performance lectures upon request; theatre rentals.

GETTING THERE:

Subway: BMT RR to 23rd Street.
Bus: Uptown: Sixth Avenue (M6, M7); Downtown: Fifth Avenue (M2, M3, M4, M32); Crosstown West and East: 23rd Street (M26).
Parking: Street parking after 7:00 P.M.

RESERVING SEATS:

Box Office Telephone: (212) 691-2274
Ticket Price: $5.00 or TDF voucher plus $2.00.
Reservations: Call theatre, tickets held until fifteen minutes before curtain.
Group Rates: Available, contact the theatre.
Subscription: Five plays for $20.00.
Performance Schedule: Five productions presented September through June. Evenings: Thursday through Saturday; Matinees: Sunday.

WPA THEATRE RECOMMENDS:

Harvey's Chelsea Restaurant: 108 West 18th Street, just off Sixth Avenue, 243-5644. Reservations recommended. German-English, Continental. Sunday through Thursday: noon till midnight; Friday and Saturday: noon till 1:00 A.M. Lunch: $3.95–$11.95, a la carte; Dinner: $4.95–$12.95, a la carte. No credit cards accepted. Personal checks accepted.

Pete's Tavern: 129 East 18th Street, on the corner of Irving Place, 473-7676. Reservations recommended. Italian-American. 8:00 A.M. till 2:00 A.M., seven days. Kitchen open 11:30 A.M. till midnight, weekdays, 11:30 A.M. till 1:00 A.M. Friday and Saturday. Saturday and Sunday brunch: noon till 5:00 P.M. $3.00–$12.00, a la carte. All credit cards accepted.

Brownies: 21 East 16th Street, just East of Fifth Avenue, 255-2838. Natural foods. Monday through Friday: 11:00 A.M. till 8:00 P.M.; Saturday: noon till 4:00 P.M. Closed Sunday. $3.50–$5.00, a la carte. No credit cards accepted.

WHO: THE YORK PLAYERS COMPANY

Artistic Director: Janet H. Walker
Company Manager: Molly Grose
Founders: Stuart Howard, John Newton, Janet H. Walker; 1969

WHERE:

Neighborhood: Upper East Side
Theatre Address:
2 East 90th Street (just off Fifth Avenue)
New York, New York 10028
(212) 289-3402

The Space: The York Players Company performs just around the corner from the Cooper Hewitt Museum in Yorkville's landmark Church of the Heavenly Rest, a 1924 Gothic edifice of towering proportions. The company performs most of its season in a flexible, 99-seat auditorium space where a thrust, proscenium, in-the-round, or gang-plank stage configuration can be constructed. The final production is mounted in the sweeping, stained glass chancel of the church.

WHAT:

Artistic Profile: Founded in 1969 by three actors, the York Players Company remains an actor's theatre, mounting well-known, tested dramas and musicals in fully staged, elaborately costumed productions that will best showcase the actor's talents. The company also has a penchant for reviving off-beat musicals—works with high quality lyrics and books that received insufficient attention when originally mounted. A second, equally important aim of the company is to provide the community of Yorkville with high quality theatre. The final production of the season, presented in the chancel of the church, is always a larger than life play which dramatically and thematically matches the Gothic grandeur and towering proportions of the church (for example, *A Man for All Seasons*, *Hadrian VI*, and *Twelfth Night*).

Productions 1978/79:

The Golden Apple, Moross La Touche
Rain, Somerset Maugham
Quadrille, Noel Coward
A Man for All Seasons, Robert Bolt

Productions 1979/80:

The Grass Harp, Kenward Elmslie and Claibe Richardson
The Subject Was Roses, Frank Gilroy
Anyone Can Whistle, Stephen Sondheim and Arthur Laurents
Hadrian VI, Peter Luke

Special Programs: Acting classes for children; internships; staged readings; post-performance lectures upon request.

GETTING THERE:

Subway: Lexington Avenue IRT 4, 5, 6 to 86th Street.

Bus: Uptown: Madison Avenue (M1, M2, M3, M4); Downtown: Fifth Avenue (M1, M2, M3, M4); Crosstown West and East: 86th Street (M18) or 96th Street (M19).

Parking: Street parking after 7:00 P.M.; nearest garage between Madison and Park Avenues.

RESERVING SEATS:

Box Office Telephone: (212) 289-3402
Ticket Price: $3.00, TDF voucher accepted. $2.00 for students and senior citizens.
Reservations: Call theatre, tickets held until ten minutes before curtain.
Group Rates: Available for groups larger than thirty, contact the theatre.
Subscription: $40.00 for eight admissions; can be used for any productions (i.e., two admissions to each of four productions or eight admissions to one production).
Performance Schedule: Four productions presented October through May. Evenings: Friday, Saturday; Matinees: Sunday.

THE YORK PLAYERS COMPANY RECOMMENDS:

Jackson Hole: 1270 Madison Avenue, 427-2820. Coffee shop, hamburgers. 7:00 A.M. till 11:00 P.M., seven days. $1.75–$3.60. No credit cards accepted.
Bailiwick: 1244 Madison Avenue, 348-1222. Reservations accepted. Continental-Italian. Monday through Saturday: 11:30 A.M. till 11:00 P.M.; Sunday: noon till 10:00 P.M. $6.50–$13.50, a la carte; $25.00–$30.00, complete dinners. All credit cards accepted.

WHO: THE YUEH LUNG SHADOW THEATRE

Artistic and Executive Director: Jo Humphrey
Founders: Shirley Roman, Evelyn Mei; 1975

WHERE:

Theatre Address: Performs in various locations.
Office Address:
34-41 74th Street
Jackson Heights, New York 11372
(212) 478-6246

WHAT:

Artistic Profile: The Yueh Lung Shadow Theatre was organized to preserve and perpetuate a 2,000-year-old tradition which has all but disappeared in Asia and is virtually unknown in the West. Following ancient practices, Yueh Lung Shadow Theatre animates colorful calf-skin figures that are approximately twelve-to-fourteen-inches tall and connected to thin rods. The figures are exact replicas of the Peking East-City figures in the permanent collection at the American Museum of Natural History. Manipulated from behind a translucent screen to the accompaniment of classical Chinese music, these animated figures convey philosophical and ethical concepts drawn from religious, folk, and epic Chinese literature.

Repertory 1980 (based on classic Chinese stories):

The Two Friends
The Crane and the Tortoise
The Chang and Melon Seeds
The Mountain of Fiery Tongues (available in English, Cantonese, or Mandarin)
The White Snake Legend
The Fisherman's Revenue (available in English or Mandarin)
Parade and Demonstration of Chinese Animal Symbolism

Special Programs: Instructional classes; lecture demonstrations; national and international touring.

GETTING THERE:

Contact the office for current performing location and directions. Company performs in museums, universities, and theatres.

RESERVING SEATS:

Box Office Telephone: Call the office for box office telephone.

Ticket Price: Varies depending on the performance location.

Performance Schedule: Year-round variable performance schedule.

WHILE YOU'RE EXPLORING: ADDITIONAL NOT-FOR-PROFIT THEATRES

Below is a brief description of non-OOBA not-for-profit theatres that have been in existence for five years or more. These theatres, along with OOBA members, represent some of the better-known theatres who are working to provide an important alternative to the commercial Broadway theatre. (Theatres that have no permanent performing spaces are designated by an asterisk.)

AMERICAN PLACE THEATRE
111 West 46th Street
New York, NY 10036
(212) 246-3730 (business)
(212) 246-0393 (box office)
Director: Wynn Handman; Associate Director: Julia Miles

Founded in 1964 as a forum for living American writers, the American Place Theatre has fostered such distinguished writers as Robert Lowell, Sam Shepard, Steve Tesich, Ed Bullins, Robert Coover, Anne Sexton, and Joyce Carol Oates. In addition to presenting four fully mounted productions, the company's season includes staged readings; the Basement Space Series (experimental plays in an intimate, informal setting); the American Humorist Series, and the Women's Project. Representative productions: *The Old Glory*, Robert Lowell; *Cold Storage*, Ronald Ribman; *Fefu and Her Friends*, Maria Irene Fornes; *Seduced*, Sam Shepard.

BAM THEATER COMPANY
Brooklyn Academy of Music
30 Lafayette Avenue
Brooklyn, NY 11217
(212) 636-4135 (business)
(212) 636-4100 (box office)
Artistic Director: David Jones; Managing Director: Charles Dillingham

To provide New York with a permanent classical repertory company is the aim of the BAM (Brooklyn Academy of Music) Theater Company. The company was founded in 1976 by Harvey Lichtenstein and Frank Dunlop. Newly organized in 1979 under the artistic direction of David Jones, BAM is evolving a core of actors who are committed to working together over an extended period of time in an effort to explore and create a specifically American approach to the presentation of classical drama. Representative productions: *A Winter's Tale*, Shakespeare; *Johnny on the Spot*, Charles MacArthur; *Barbarians*, Maxim Gorky.

***BYRD HOFFMAN FOUNDATION**
c/o Artservices
463 West Street
New York, NY 10014
(212) 989-4953
Artistic Director: Robert Wilson

Founded in 1969, the Byrd Hoffman Foundation is a not-for-profit organization supporting the work of playwright, director, designer Robert Wilson. Wilson is well known for creating large scale, slow-paced extravaganzas with casts sometimes exceeding 100 and productions often lasting several hours. His concern with the splitting and subsequent reordering of the formal elements of theatre—text, nonverbal sound, and decor has been strongly influenced by his work with deaf, brain-damaged, and physically handicapped people. His work has been seen at the Brooklyn Academy of Music, on Broadway, at the Metropolitan Opera House, and at major festivals throughout Europe. Representative productions: *Einstein on the Beach*, Robert Wilson, Phillip Glass; *Edison*, Robert Wilson; *Death, Destruction and Detroit*, Robert Wilson.

CIRCLE IN THE SQUARE
1633 Broadway (at 50th St.)
New York, NY 10019
(212) 581-3270 (business)
(212) 581-0720 (box office)
Artistic Director: Theodore Mann; Managing Director: Paul Libin

For over thirty years, Circle in the Square has presented well-known actors in new and established plays. The theatre began in Greenwich Village in 1951, first at the Provincetown Playhouse and then at the Circle in the Square Downtown on Bleecker Street, where it awakened an interest in the works of playwrights such as Eugene O'Neill, Tennessee Williams, and Dylan Thomas. The theatre now makes its home in the heart of the theatre district at Circle in the Square (Uptown). Its season of four full productions has showcased such well known talents as George C. Scott, Tammy Grimes, and Vanessa Redgrave. Representative productions: *Long Day's Journey into Night*, Eugene O'Neill; *Uncle Vanya*, Anton Chekhov; *Little Murders*, Jules Feiffer; *Loose Ends*, Michael Weller.

THE DODGER THEATER
c/o New York Shakespeare Festival
The Public Theater
425 Lafayette Street
New York, NY 10003
(212) 598-7100 (business)
(212) 598-7150 (box office)
Associate Directors: Des McAnuff, Michael David, Edward Strong, Sherman Warner

Formed in the spring of 1978 at the Brooklyn Academy of Music, The Dodger Theater spent its first two seasons there before moving to the Public Theater to share LuEsther Hall with Mabou Mines. The company looks for honest, nonescapist plays that reflect the upheavals of these unsettling times. In their search for material that confronts political, social, and spiritual issues, the Dodger does not restrict itself to new American plays, but explores the contemporary and classical literature of other cultures as well. Representative productions: *Gimme Shelter*, Barrie Keeffe; *On Mount Chimorazo*, Tankred Dorst; *Emigrés*, Slawomir Mrozek; *Holeville*, Jeff Wanshell.

FRANK SILVERA WRITERS' WORKSHOP
317 West 125th Street
New York, NY 10027
(212) 662-8463
Director: Garland Lee Thompson

Founded by Garland Lee Thompson in 1973, Frank Silvera Writers' Workshop serves as a laboratory for black and third-world playwrights, presenting more than ninety plays each year. The theatre presents a series of Monday and

Saturday night laboratory readings geared to the needs of each playwright. Other activities of the theatre include the Artistic Technical Assistance Collective and playwriting seminars conducted by leading black playwrights. Representative productions: *The Brownsville Raid,* Charles Fuller; *Let's Take It to the Top,* Ruby Dee; *Inacent Black and the Five Brothers,* A. Marcus Hemphill; *An Evening with Josephine Baker,* George Adams.

JUDSON POETS' THEATER
c/o Judson Memorial Church
55 Washington Square South
New York, NY 10012
(212) 477-0351 (business)
(212) 777-0033 (box office)
Artistic Director: Al Carmines

The Judson Poets' Theater, along with Cafe Cino and La Mama Theatre Club was among the first Off Off Broadway theatres in New York. It has produced musicals and plays for nineteen years without interruption. Initially staging only the works of poets, the theatre served as a catalyst for avant-garde dance throughout the 1960's and now focuses on smaller plays (usually directed by Lawrence Kornfeld) and large oratorios (most frequently written by Al Carmines and choreographed and directed as large musicals). Representative productions: *Dr. Faustus Lights the Lights,* Gertrude Stein and Al Carmines; *Christmas Rappings,* Al Carmines, based on the Scriptures; *Promenade,* Al Carmines and Maria Irene Fornes.

THE LABOR THEATER
336 West 20th Street
New York, NY 10011
(212) 242-4220
Artistic Director: Chuck Portz; Executive Producer: Bette Craig

Since its founding in 1973, The Labor Theater has been committed to making theatre accessible to working people by touring shows to union halls, community centers, and churches in both the United States and abroad. The theatre's focus on socially and politically significant work has been reflected in diverse productions which run the gamut from a play about a black train robber accompanied by blues music, to a one-man show about Jack London, to the Obie award-winning *Full Confessions of a Socialist*, by Ronald Muldoon. Other representative productions: *Night Shift*, Martin Goldsmith; *I Just Wanted Someone to Know*, Bette Craig and Joyce Kornbluh.

***MEREDITH MONK/THE HOUSE**
New Arts Management
c/o Arts Arcadia Associates, Inc.
853 Broadway
New York, NY 10003
(212) 477-1850
Director: Meredith Monk

Founded by Meredith Monk in 1969, Meredith Monk/The House is a group of actors, musicians, dancers, writers, and painters dedicated to creating "composite theatre" works which combine elements of speech, visual and instrumental music, dance movement, costume, objects, light, films, and most important, environment. The work resembles a plotless, nonverbal, surrealist opera and can range from solos, duets, and chamber works to large group works requiring twenty to fifty performers. The company tours extensively in the United States and abroad. Representative productions: *Recent Ruins*, Meredith Monk; *The Travelogue Series*, Meredith Monk, Ping Chong; *Education of a Girlchild*, Meredith Monk; *Quarry*, Meredith Monk.

NATIONAL BLACK THEATRE
9 East 125th Street
New York, NY 10035
(212) 427-5615
Executive Producer: Barbara Ann Teer; Managing Director: Zuri McKie

The National Black Theatre was founded in 1968 by Barbara Ann Teer. By rejecting theatrical conventions, the theatre tries to reestablish a sense of identity and self-esteem in its audiences and to help them transcend alienating cultural conditioning. Representative productions:

Ritual, Barbara Ann Teer, from Kwame Azular's poem, music and lyrics by Barbara Ann Teer and Company; *Soljourney into Truth*, Barbara Ann Teer; *Wine in the Wilderness*, Alice Childress.

NEGRO ENSEMBLE COMPANY
Office:
165 West 46th Street, Suite 1015
New York, NY 10036
Theatre:
424 West 55th Street
New York, NY 10019
(212) 575-5860 (business)
(212) 246-8545 (box office)
Artistic Director: Douglas Turner Ward; Managing Director: Gerald S. Krone

The Negro Ensemble Company is a resident theatre company of actors, directors, and designers dedicated to producing work relevant to black life. The company focuses on new work, a commitment expressed both through its selection of plays and its developmental Playwrights' Unit. Since its beginnings in 1967, NEC has been instrumental in providing a major share of the body of contemporary black theatrical literature. Representative productions: *The Offering*, Gus Edwards; *The River Niger*, Joe Walker; *Home*, Samm-Art Williams.

***ONTOLOGICAL-HYSTERIC THEATER**
c/o Artservices
463 West Street
New York, NY 10014
(212) 989-4953
Artistic Director: Richard Foreman

Since 1968, Richard Foreman and his company have been developing an original theatrical language that reflects the processes, difficulties, and "accidents" of consciousness-at-work. After initially exploring such elements as act, gesture, speech, and object, the focus of Foreman's work has shifted to the relationship between complicated production and textural elements. All works are created with the company rehearsing in fully completed sets for the entire rehearsal period. Representative productions: *Book of Splendors*; *Blvd. de Paris: I've Got the Shakes*; *Madness and Tranquility (My Head Was a Sledgehammer)*; all created by Richard Foreman.

***THE OTHER THEATER**
c/o Artservices
463 West Street
New York, NY 10014
(212) 989-4953
Artistic Director: Joseph Chaikin

Under the auspices of The Other Theater Joseph Chaikin, an actor/director recognized as a seminal force in American theatre for his work with the Open Theatre (1963–1973) continues his research in theatre. Each year the Other Theatre conducts a "Winter Project" which culminates in a group work presented at La Mama E.T.C. Other projects of Mr. Chaikin's include *The Dybbuk* which he directed at the New York Shakespeare Festival and *Tongues*, a work he collaboratively developed with Pulitzer-prize playwright Sam Shepard. Representative productions: *Re-Arrangement*, Joseph Chaiken/The Winter Project; *Tourists and Refugees*, Joseph Chaiken/The Winter Project.

PHOENIX THEATRE
Office:
1540 Broadway
New York, NY 10036
Theatre:
Marymount Manhattan Theatre
221 East 71st Street
New York, NY 10021
(212) 730-0787 (business)
(212) 730-0794 (box office)
Artistic Director: Steven Robman; Managing Director: T. Edward Hambleton

When the Phoenix Theatre was founded in 1953, it was one of the only alternatives to Broadway. Since then it has evolved into an enthusiastically supported company that is dedicated to developing new American and European plays. By collaborating with theatres outside New

York, the company has enabled plays such as Wendy Wasserstein's *Uncommon Women and Others* and Marsha Norman's *Getting Out* to flourish in New York (and, as in the case of the former, gain exposure on public television). Other representative productions: *G.R. Point*, David Berry; *Ladyhouse Blues*, Kevin O'Morrison; *City Sugar*, Stephen Poliakoff.

THE RIDICULOUS THEATRICAL COMPANY
One Sheridan Square
New York, NY 10011
(212) 260-7137
Artistic Director: Charles Ludlam; Executive Director: Christopher Scott

The Ridiculous Theatrical Company was founded by Charles Ludlam in 1967 as a vehicle for reevaluating the theatrical conventions of comic intent. Its permanent ensemble of actors creates innovative, modernist comic dramas of parody, burlesque, travesty, and farce. In addition to its repertory of over fifteen dramas—whose distinctive comic approach has been termed "Ludlamization"—the theatre operates a children's theatre program that includes numerous puppet shows. Representative productions: *The Enchanted Pig*; *Camille*; *The Ventriloquist's Wife*, and the children's theatre production, *Professor Bedlam's Educational Punch and Judy Show*.

ROUNDABOUT THEATRE COMPANY
333 West 23rd Street
New York, NY 10011
(212) 924-7160
Producing Directors: Gene Feist and Michael Fried

The Roundabout Theatre Company is committed to producing rarely seen classics by world-renowned playwrights. For fifteen years, it has presented established classics by playwrights such as Ibsen, Strindberg, Shaw, and Chekov, as well as staging the work of important contemporary writers, for example, John Osborne's *Look Back in Anger*, starring Malcolm McDowell. Representative productions: *The Father*, August Strindberg, adapted by Gene Feist;

Dark at the Top of the Stairs, William Inge; *A Month in the Country,* Ivan Turgenev; Geraldine Fitzgerald in *Streetsongs.*

***THE TALKING BAND**
c/o Artservices
463 West Street
New York, NY 10014
(212) 989-4953
Director: Paul Zimet

Founded in 1974, the Talking Band's five members work collaboratively, fusing material from various sources (oral histories, written biographies, formal songs, poems) to create aurally rich works that reinvest spoken language with meaning, energy, and musicality. Their work includes such full-length pieces as *Worksong,* a semi-documentary ode-to/critique of work and money in America. Other company productions: *Joe Breem . . . or Breen?, An Evening of Poems, Songs and Stories*; *The Kalevala, An Epic of Finland,* the Company and Elizabeth Swados.

TIME AND SPACE LIMITED
139 West 22nd Street
New York, NY 10011
(212) 741-1032 or
(212) 243-9268
Director: Linda Mussman

Time and Space Limited was created in 1973 by Linda Mussman as an alternative theatre that would bare the structure and basic polarities (time/space, light/dark, male/female, sound/silence) of modern classics (Brecht, Stein, Strindberg, Büchner) and contemporary works. Japanese concepts and training—economy of gesture, music/sound supporting action, the separation of action and dialogue—have heavily influenced this essentially American theatre company. During the 1980–81 season Time and Space was in residence at La Mama E.T.C. while continuing to operate its own space on 23rd Street. Representative productions: *Danton's Death,* Georg Büchner; *The Bandit Princess,* Kikue Tashiro; *Katana,* Kikue Tashiro.

URBAN ARTS CORPS
227 West 17th Street
New York, NY 10011
(212) 924-7820
Artistic Director: Vinnette Carroll; Administrative Director: Anita McShane

The Urban Arts Corps was founded in 1967 as an offshoot of the New York State Council on the Arts' Ghetto Arts Program, in order to train young black and Puerto Rican artists for professional involvement in the theatre. Throughout its development from a grass-roots training program to a professional company, the Corps has worked to generate strong ties with communities throughout New York City. Two Broadway shows, *Don't Bother Me, I Can't Cope*, by Vinnette Carroll and Micki Grant and *Your Arms Too Short to Box with God*, by Ms. Carroll and Alex Bradford, were originally produced at the Urban Arts Corps. Other representative productions: *But Never Jam Today*, Vinnette Carroll's adaptation of "Alice in Wonderland"; *When Hell Freezes Over, I'll Skate*, Vinnette Carroll.

FOR YOUR REFERENCE

THEATRES WITH SPECIAL PROGRAMS FOR CHILDREN

Academy Arts Theatre
  Company
AMAS Repertory Theatre
Bond Street Theatre
  Coalition
Fantasy Factory
First All Children's Theatre
Golden Fleece, Ltd.
La Mama E.T.C.
New Federal Theatre at
  Henry Street Settlement
New York Stageworks
New York Street Theatre
  Caravan
Nuestro Teatro
Off Center Theatre
Raft Theatre
Repertorio Español
Richard Morse Mime
  Theatre
Seven Ages Performance
  Limited at Perry Street
78th Street Theatre Lab
Ten-Ten Players
Thalia Spanish Theatre
Theater for the New City
Theatre of the Open Eye
Westside Community
  Repertory Theatre
The York Players Company
Yueh Lung Shadow Theatre

THEATRES THAT ACCEPT UNSOLICITED MANUSCRIPTS

Academy Arts Theatre
  Company
AMAS Repertory Theatre
The American Ensemble
  Company
American Jewish Theatre
  at the Y
American Stanislavski
  Theatre
Cherub's Guild
Circle Repertory Company
Cithaeron Theatre
Colonnades Theatre Lab
Drama Committee
  Repertory Theatre
Ensemble Studio Theatre
Force 13 Theatre Company
Frederic Douglass Creative
  Arts Center
Gene Frankel Theatre
  Workshop
The Glines
Golden Fleece, Ltd.
  (musicals only)
Hudson Guild Theatre
Impossible Ragtime Theatre
INTAR
Interart Theatre
Irish Rebel Theatre
Jewish Repertory Theatre
La Mama E.T.C.
Latin American Theatre
  Ensemble
Lion Theatre Company

Manhattan Lambda Productions
Manhattan Punch Line
Manhattan Theatre Club
Nat Horne Musical Theatre (musicals only)
New Federal Theatre at Henry Street Settlement
New York Stageworks
New York Theatre Studio
Nuestro Teatro
Off Center Theatre
The Open Space
Pan Asian Repertory Theatre
Playwrights Horizons
The Production Company
Puerto Rican Traveling Theatre
Quaigh Theatre
Repertorio Español
Richard Allen Center for Culture and Art
Seven Ages Performance Limited at Perry Street
78th Street Theatre Lab
Shelter West Company
Shirtsleeve Theatre
Soho Rep
South Street Theatre Company
Spectrum Theatre
Spiderwoman Theatre Workshop
Ten-Ten Players
Thalia Spanish Theatre
Theatre at St. Clement's
Theatre Matrix
Theater for the New City
Theatre Off Park
Theatre of the Open Eye
Theatre of the Riverside Church
Theatre XII
WPA Theatre

THEATRES THAT RENT THEIR SPACES TO OTHER PERFORMING GROUPS

American Renaissance Theatre
Cherub's Guild
Circle Repertory Company (summer only)
Colonnades Theatre Lab
Fantasy Factory
Force 13 Theatre Company
Gene Frankel Theatre Workshop
INTAR
Lion Theatre Company
Manhattan Punch Line
Manhattan Theatre Club (summer only)
Medicine Show Theatre Ensemble
Nat Horne Musical Theatre
New Federal Theatre at Henry Street Settlement
Off Center Theatre
The Open Space
Playwrights Horizons
The Production Company
Quaigh Theatre
Raft Theatre

Richard Allen Center for Culture and Art
Richard Morse Mime Theatre
Seven Ages Performance Limited at Perry Street
78th Street Theatre Lab
Soho Rep (summer only)
South Street Theatre Company
Ten-Ten Players
Theatre Off Park
Theatre of the Open Eye
Theatre of the Riverside Church (summer only)
Theatre at St. Clement's
The Wooster Group
WPA Theatre

New Avon/Discus Titles 

CATASTROPHE THEORY
Alexander Woodcock & Monte Davis **48397 $2.75**

This vanguard book explains the catastrophe theory—a revolutionary new way of predicting sudden change—to laymen, explores the controversy surrounding it, and gives fascinating examples of how it can be used to understand problems in psychology, biology, politics, economics and history that affect everyone.

PRICK UP YOUR EARS
John Lahr **48629 $3.50**

From diaries, drafts of plays, unpublished novels, and the recollections of those who knew Joe Orton—one of Britain's most promising playwrights of the 60's—John Lahr constructs a sensitive portrait of a man who was just beginning to taste the fruits of success when he was killed. 16 pages of photographs.

THE EXECUTION OF CHARLES HORMAN
Thomas Hauser **49098 $2.75**

A young American in Chile accidentally stumbles onto the evidence of covert U.S. involvement in the overthrow of the Allende government—and is afterwards murdered. This is the chilling account of Charles Horman's last days—and of his family's determination to learn the truth about his death. "Reads like the scenario of a Hitchcock thriller." *Los Angeles Times*

ECCENTRIC SPACES
Robert Harbison **49122 $2.50**

Robert Harbison examines the interplay between our imaginations and the spaces we create for ourselves: gardens, rooms, buildings, streets, museums, maps as well as fictional topographies and architectures. "He has written the ultimate guidebook, for one can not only visit real cities, but imaginary ones." *The Baltimore Sun*

COCAINE: The Mystique and The Reality
J. Phillips & R. D. Wynne, Ph.D. **48678 $3.50**

The most comprehensive work ever published on every aspect of cocaine. It examines in depth the history, pharmacology, trafficking, and socio-psychological effect of its use and abuse. It also captures the romance, excitement, and absurdity of the drug, tracing its role in the literature of Doyle, Stevenson, Sayers, and others; Hollywood movies; cultures from the Incas to the Nazis; and music from Harlem jazzmen to today's rockers. Avon Original

New Discus I 6-81 (2-A)

WILLA CATHER: A Critical Biography
E.K. Brown, Completed by Leon Edel 49676 $2.95
This biography traces Willa Cather's life as it was illuminated by her art—from her life-long fascination with Nebraska and the Southwest, where she found the beauty and raw power that inspired O PIONEERS! and MY ANTONIA, to the compelling religious experiences that influenced THE PROFESSOR'S HOUSE and DEATH COMES FOR THE ARCHBISHOP. "All readers of Willa Cather will rejoice in it." *Chicago Tribune*

ERNEST HEMINGWAY: A Life Story
Carlos Baker 50039 $4.95
A major literary sensation and a national bestseller, this is an eloquent, unflinching biography by Carlos Baker, the foremost authority on Hemingway's life and work. Illustrated with rare photographs. "This is the true Hemingway." *The Atlantic Monthly*

WOMEN AND SPORTS
Janice Kaplan 50260 $2.50
Packed with inspiration and information for the new female athlete, this comprehensive guide covers all aspects of women in sports today—nutrition, competition, psychology, physiology, the choice of sport, economics and sex. "Immensely helpful." *Publishers Weekly*

THE LIFE IN THE STUDIO
Nancy Hale 75721 $2.75
Eminent author Nancy Hale traces her childhood and growth as writer in this intimate and insightful examination of the lives of her parents, both recognized artists. "We are immersed in and captured by this private world of artists." *New York Times Book Review*

THE HUMAN USE OF HUMAN BEINGS
Norbert Wiener 50682 $2.95
A landmark in social and scientific upheaval, this is the classic study of cybernetics, the science which explores the unique set of communications existing between man and his machines.

FUTURES: The Anti-Inflation Investment
Michael Geczi 75713 $2.95
Michael Geczi, Markets and Investments Editor of *Business Week*, reveals in jargon-free language how to safely make money in the most mercurial financial arena in the world. Avon Original

Available wherever paperbacks are sold, or directly from the publisher. Include 50¢ per copy for postage and handling: allow 6–8 weeks for delivery. Avon Books, Mail Order Dept., 224 West 57th St., N.Y., N.Y. 10019.

JUN 1 2 2000
APR 1 7 2000